THE PRIVATE PAPERS OF
HORE-BELISHA

Leslie Hore-Belisha as Secretary of State for War

The
Private Papers of
Hore-Belisha

R. J. MINNEY

COLLINS
ST JAMES'S PLACE, LONDON
1960

© R. J. Minney, 1960
Printed in Great Britain
Collins Clear-Type Press, London and Glasgow

For
HILDE
who was there
at the time

CONTENTS

CONTENTS

PLATES

CARTOONS

Foreword

HORE-BELISHA kept a diary fairly consistently from an early age until the end of his life; it was usually written on the night of the events described, only occasionally, when overwhelmed by work, a day or so after. He preserved his notes and reflections. The letters he received and wrote were all filed.

Did he intend to write his autobiography? Would he have wished at least to give an account of his stewardship at the War Office, of the great effort he had made—driven by a terrible sense of urgency—to prepare the Army for the war he was certain was coming, of the prejudice and opposition he encountered, of his eventual overthrow and, as he may have seen it, his ultimate betrayal?

Soon after leaving the War Office, he suggested that I might one day undertake this for him. We had many long talks, of which I kept abundant notes. But he had no wish that these revelations should be made during the critical years of war. Then, with his brief return to office in 1945 and in the hope that he would be called to serve again, he felt that publication should be still further deferred.

After he had accepted a peerage, I suggested that he should write the book himself. In due course he decided to do this. The papers were gone through. Drafts were made and corrected again and again. His relentless striving after perfection, however, prevented him from getting more than the first chapter into a form that satisfied his standards; this he recorded on tape. Some ascribed his lack of progress to a natural laziness, but that is not a characteristic which is apparent in any record of his life and work.

After his death it was suggested by Captain B. H. Liddell Hart and others that I should resume the work I had begun. I considered whether I should write a full-length biography of Hore-Belisha and came to the conclusion that in any such biography his two and a

half years at the War Office would inevitably occupy a disproportionate part. Furthermore, I felt that by concentrating on this
climactic and most dramatic period of his career one would achieve
a deeper impression of the man and of his place in our national
story than if I had written a full-length biography covering his
whole life in detail. The documentation for this period is sufficiently
abundant to make it possible for Hore-Belisha for the most part to
tell his own story, in his own words.

I have therefore concerned myself mainly with the presentation
of his diaries, notes and letters covering the period of his life which
is of national and historical interest, and have done little more than
supply a commentary; to this I have added a brief account of his
background and earlier life, and an Epilogue to tell of his remaining
years and sudden death. The diary is drawn on equally for both
these sections. Wherever no other acknowledgment is indicated the
source of the quotations in this book is always his own diary.

He used his diary chiefly to record events. It is almost entirely
factual. He confined himself to what happened and this he set down
in vivid detail. There is an absence of any expression of strong
feeling. The diary was not used by him as an outlet or safety valve,
as so many others used theirs.

I wish to express my thanks for the great help and co-operation I
have received from those who knew him well and worked with him.
Of these I would especially mention Sir David Roseway, his Principal
Private Secretary at the War Office, Major-General Charles Haydon
and Major-General Sir Francis de Guingand, in turn his Military
Assistants, Captain B. H. Liddell Hart, who most generously placed
his own personal records at my disposal, Lord Beaverbrook, Colonel
A. C. Newman, V.C., and Brigadier S. A. Westrop.

Thanks for permission to quote from letters are due to Mrs.
Neville Chamberlain and to those others whose letters I also quote
from here: I have endeavoured to obtain permission from them
all or from their executors. For the cartoons reproduced, I must
thank the artists as well as the *Evening Standard* and *The Star*—for
the photographs, Dorothy Wilding, *House and Garden*, Fox Photos,
Keystone, Sport and General, *Wide World*, *Daily Sketch* and the
Imperial War Museum.   R.J.M.

CHAPTER I

The War Office

THE PROMISE of a brilliant summer was already apparent in the spring of 1937. The sadness over the abdication of Edward the Eighth, idolised by the nation as Prince of Wales, was being fast dispelled by the festive preparations for the coronation of his brother King George the Sixth. The days were golden with sunshine. It rained hardly at all. People poured into London from the provinces and from abroad. They stood and gazed with admiration at the gay and colourful transformation. The metropolis seemed to be continuously *en fête*. There were banquets and balls nearly every night. Representative Ministers had begun to arrive from all parts of the Empire and every important reception was resplendent with Privy Councillors and Ambassadors in their magnificent uniforms.

These carefree weeks, so jubilant and so brilliant, were to mark the end of an epoch, for the months that followed were haunted by anxiety and darkened by the shadow of a war that the world was striving to avert and still hoped it could avert. When the war came a new era of austerity dawned and not even peace, dissipating the rigours at a pace that was painful, was able to restore the glamour and the glory of the years that had gone. Values changed. Wealth vanished. Privy Councillors put away their striking uniforms. Much of the colour was drained from the every-day scene.

Stanley Baldwin, the architect of the abdication and the new reign, had already announced his intention of retiring from the Premiership. Behind the scenes his successor, Neville Chamberlain, who had been Chancellor of the Exchequer for six consecutive years, pondered at his desk at the Treasury over the selection of the men who were to serve under him when he took over after the coronation.

13

The Press was busy crystal-gazing about those most likely to be chosen for high office.

On Monday the 4th May 1937 a forecast appeared in the *News Chronicle* under the name of its political correspondent, David Keir. It was displayed in large type and with bold headlines on the main news page: " DUFF COOPER LEAVING THE WAR OFFICE. NEW POSITION FOR HORE-BELISHA."

" MR. NEVILLE CHAMBERLAIN WILL MAKE A NUMBER OF IMPORTANT CABINET CHANGES WHEN HE BECOMES PRIME MINISTER AT THE END OF THE MONTH. . . . MR. HORE-BELISHA, TRANSPORT MINISTER, IS LIKELY TO BE SECRETARY OF STATE FOR WAR IN SUCCESSION TO MR. DUFF COOPER."

Press opinions following on this first forecast are revealing. *Time and Tide*[1] in an editorial commented:

" If Mr. Hore-Belisha replaces Mr. Duff Cooper, that reduces definitely the chances of Mr. Winston Churchill. The Belisha record at the Ministry of Transport shows that he can supply the drive and the ideas which have been urged as Mr. Churchill's special contribution. The Churchillians ' forgot Belisha.' Disappointed die-hards are saying that ' Winston called off his opposition too soon.' But they have not quite given up hope."

The *Star*,[2] referring to Hore-Belisha's " spectacular career " at the Ministry of Transport, added: " This would not be an altogether popular appointment for Conservatives. but Mr. Belisha's attractive methods and public popularity would stand him in good stead in recruiting campaigns and publicity for the delights of Army life. It is doubtful if he will enjoy himself so much. He will not have so free a hand for his own ideas." The *Manchester Guardian*[3]: " Mr. Chamberlain recognises the ability beneath the flamboyance; Mr. Hore-Belisha is a man who ' gets things done,' and that appeals strongly to the new Premier."

Of the anticipated change Hore-Belisha was as yet unaware. He had entered Parliament as Liberal member for Devonport in 1923. He had sat with the 157 other Liberals who, fighting the election as a reunited Party under the banner of Free Trade, were still an

[1] 8th May 1937.　　[2] 22nd May 1937.　　[3] 24th May 1937.

important and influential group. They exercised their power by supporting the 191 Labour members in the House of Commons against the depleted ranks of the Conservatives who numbered 258. The election of 1923 brought the Socialists into office for the first time in the history of the country and introduced a change, destined to endure, from the old swing between the two established parties. Hore-Belisha, never at ease with the Socialists despite his own reforming zeal, was to see them return again in 1929. It was his vigorous opposition to them and his adroit manœuvring of a section of the Liberals into the National Government that brought him office in the autumn of 1931. He was made Parliamentary Secretary to the Board of Trade. His competent handling of business and his debating skill on the Front Bench earned for him rapid promotion and a year later he was transferred to the Treasury as Financial Secretary. During his two years there Neville Chamberlain was able to appraise the ability and worth of his young assistant and it was doubtless on his commendation that Hore-Belisha was raised to higher office in June 1934 and was made Minister of Transport. That marked the turning point in his career. He at once started a campaign to reduce road accidents which had reached alarming figures. " Mass murder on the roads " he called it. By every means of publicity he strove to make the people traffic-conscious. During 1935, in spite of the increase of motor traffic, the number of deaths fell by 822 and the number of injured by 12,805, as compared with 1934, when both totals had reached a record figure.

He gave the country a new Highway Code, the pedestrian crossing and the Belisha beacon. He introduced silent zones. The sounding of motor horns was prohibited between the hours of 11.30 p.m. and 7 a.m. The innovation, he said, was made " for the benefit of those who live along the roads and whose tranquillity is so much disturbed by mechanical noises at night." He imposed on every new motorist a driving test. Everywhere they talked of him and his beacons. They jested about them on the stage and the radio. Beacons were sold in miniature as cigarette holders and pencils. He became a national figure. His organising skill and above all his unflagging energy and drive singled him out as a man who was determined to get things done. He was made a Privy Councillor in 1935 and given a seat in the Cabinet in October 1936.

No official intimation of his appointment as Secretary of State for War was made to Hore-Belisha until three weeks after the forecast. He writes in his diary on the 25th May 1937:

After Question time Neville's Private Secretary saw me behind the Chair and said the Chancellor would like to see me. Neville was most friendly and complimentary of the work I had done at the Ministry of Transport. He said he had for some time been turning over the question of my position in his mind. He had thought of several alternatives, but had decided that my qualities of ' industry, enthusiasm and courage ' could best be used at the War Office. He did not minimise the difficulties I would have to face as he considered much reorganisation at the War Office needed to be done. On my saying that I would not wish to be a party to anything that might injure Duff Cooper's career he informed me that Duff was to be First Lord of the Admiralty. I was very happy to hear this.

Neville went on to say that he himself possessed some of the qualities S.B.[1] had, but he had also qualities which S.B. had not. He intended to take a new line. He wished all his Ministers to be in the closest touch with him, to tell him their difficulties, to inform him not only about their immediate plans in their departments, but what they were planning for the future.

I told him I welcomed this and I added that nothing could detract from the affection in which we held S.B., but I had sometimes wondered why, during the whole time I had been Minister of Transport, he had never given me the opportunity of discussing things with him.

Hore-Belisha had especially in mind the occasion when he had asked to see Baldwin to tell him of his plans for the Trunk Roads of Britain. As a young Minister, he was full of enthusiasm for what he hoped would be an entirely new highway system in the country. But he had come away from the interview rather damped. Baldwin showed no particular interest and had intimated that it was really a matter for experts.

Neville continued that he himself had got on by industry and that

[1] Stanley Baldwin.

16

Hore-Belisha in the First World War, in his early twenties

Hore-Belisha with his mother, Lady Hore, in the garden
of her cottage near Eastbourne

in his own political career he had always worked as one of a team. He urged this spirit on me, as he was going to do on all his Ministers. I thanked him and said that whatever the difficulties with which I might be faced, I would do my best to serve the country and to serve him.

That same night Hore-Belisha dined with Lady Cunard at her house in Grosvenor Square.

It was a large party and I had a long talk with Duff. He was very nice about my promotion and I told him of my conversation about him with Neville. Although perhaps he might not remember, I never forget a good turn, and I would have hated to hurt him. He said he would have liked to stay at the War Office and that he had told Neville so. He mentioned that the military element might be very unyielding and they might try to make it hard for me as a Jew.

In both those talks, with the Prime Minister to be and with his immediate predecessor as Secretary of State for War, he was warned of the difficulties he would encounter. They proved far greater than either Duff Cooper or Hore-Belisha himself could have envisaged.

On the afternoon of Friday, the 28th May, Hore-Belisha was sworn in and received the seals of office from the King. The evening newspapers announced the list of Cabinet ministers.

Despite the expectations of some of the Press forecasters, the name of Winston Churchill was not included among these new appointments. He had been out of office for eight years, but this did not appear to disturb the Conservative Members of Parliament, for not many of them were well disposed towards him. Indeed, a great many had been distinctly hostile ever since he had begun his constant and often bitter criticism of Baldwin. What they were concerned about—in fact they were greatly agitated over it—was the inclusion of so many Liberal Nationals in high positions in the Cabinet. Four places in all had gone to them in a Cabinet of only twenty-one. Sir John Simon, leader of the Liberal Nationals, became the new Chancellor of the Exchequer, Hore-Belisha was promoted to the War Office, Ernest Brown was made Minister of Labour, and Leslie Burgin succeeded Hore-Belisha as Minister of Transport.

This was no more than the number they had in the previous Government, but, although it was done to maintain its national character, it was undeniably out of proportion to the strength of the Liberal National Party in the House of Commons. At the General Election of November 1935, barely eighteen months before, only 32 Liberal Nationals had been elected. Conservative Members numbered 385, more than twelve times as many. On an exact reckoning the Liberal Nationals should have received at most no more than two places in the Cabinet.

But the appointment which roused the criticism of some Conservative die-hards was that of Hore-Belisha. The War Office was becoming one of the key positions. Many felt that, with the wave of anti-Semitism lapping ominously against our shores, this was not an office for which a Jew should have been selected. The Army would not like it. The Army, at that time, was very different from what it was to become as a result of the reforms introduced by Hore-Belisha. Despite the changes the last war had wrought, it had reverted to its earlier standards as soon as the war was over. Even in 1937 the general outlook was not far removed from that of the officers of whom Kipling wrote. Many of them had served in India. Proud and lofty in their bearing, bound by tradition, they were conscious of their right to be leaders and, although commissions were no longer bought, private means was still regarded as a requisite in all the crack regiments; even in regiments of lesser importance, which did not always insist on birth and background, it was desirable for an officer to have some private income. Patriotism was high, as was also devotion to duty. But anti-Semitism was not unknown even before the rise of Hitler. Little more than a generation separated them from the days of Dreyfus and their attitude was much closer in 1937 to that of the French military caste than it is to-day. Their privilege and their air of superiority had come to be regarded as part of the Army's way of life and it was felt that there should be no monkeying about with it.

According to the *News Chronicle*[1] Hore-Belisha's appointment "aroused most comment, but the general impression was that his talents of drive and courage would assist recruiting as they have assisted the cause of road safety." The *Manchester Guardian*[2] was

[1] 29th May 1937. [2] 29th May 1937.

even more specific: " The Minister who is to handle such problems"
—should there be another European war—" will need to be fertile
in ideas, since ultimately wars are won by ideas, and exceptionally
tenacious in purpose, since the sower may find that the ground is
pretty stony.   But Mr. Hore-Belisha, at the Ministry of Transport,
has had ideas and has defended them tenaciously against a most
varied opposition; his experience should serve him well in a field
that asks both for clear thinking and for large and generous views."
Both those newspapers, supporters of the Liberals who had remained
with Sir Herbert Samuel[1], had been critical of those who had broken
away and become Liberal Nationals, and had no predisposition
to praise one who had, as it appeared to them, left the true Liberal
fold six years before. That they stressed Hore-Belisha's suitability
for the task was indicative of the impartiality that animated their
outlook.

There was a further criticism, much more widely raised and not
restricted to any one party. It was against what many believed to
be Hore-Belisha's love of personal publicity. That it assisted the
work he was doing none attempted to deny, but since it brought
him personally a prominent place in the limelight, many regarded
him as flamboyant. " He certainly did not scorn publicity," wrote
Harry Boardman, Parliamentary correspondent of the *Manchester
Guardian*,[2] " and, having dabbled in journalism in earlier years, knew
how to get it. The Beacons began to be planted in London during
the summer holiday of 1934. He knew Fleet Street's needs in the
' silly season.' His Beacons became front page news at once. . . .
Hore-Belisha had been guilty of great vulgarity, as was to be
expected of a Liberal. So his Tory Ministerial colleagues thought
as they fished, or shot grouse, or disburdened their minds of
public affairi and lazed at Antibes. He had violated the close
season for politics. . . . They had the further mortification of
seeing the author of this mischief later being made Secretary for
War."

But if there was criticism, there was also encouragement and
goodwill. Lord Birdwood, writing on the 29th May, " as the senior
Field-Marshal in the Army, next to the old Duke of Connaught,"
warned the new Secretary of State: " You, of course, know well

---

[1] Later Viscount Samuel.   [2] 21st February 1957.

19

the great and many difficulties you will have to face, but I know you will face them as you always have done."

Stanley Baldwin wrote on the 8th June:

" I am glad to think that you joined the Cabinet when I was Prime Minister and the country may look to you for many years of great service. I shall follow you all in your wild careers with unfailing and affectionate sympathy—and I hope understanding! "

Baldwin, as Prime Minister, had made a habit of sitting on the Front Bench for long stretches, listening to debates, even when they were unimportant. Hore-Belisha's speeches as a back-bencher were largely a maturer rendering of the lighthearted, witty yet castigating, speeches which helped him as an undergraduate at Oxford to rise to be President of the Union. Baldwin enjoyed his thrusts at Ramsay MacDonald and other Socialists, and as far back as 1931 he had written to Hore-Belisha[1] urging him to "give us more of your speeches, those brief but pellucid surveys of Government action and policy, which belong neither to Victoriana nor to the Sitwells,[2] but are in true and glorious succession to Aristophanes."

Leo Amery, the Conservative statesman who had served for a time at the War Office on the personal staff of Lord Derby, added to his good wishes some wise counsel: " My hearty congratulations on a great opportunity. Some day soon I should like to have a good talk to you about Army reorganisation. Meanwhile I'll only say that you are not likely to do much good unless you can secure an increase of pay and a complete reorganisation of the terms of service. The former will mean a battle royal with the Treasury; the latter with the senior soldiers."

Hore-Belisha was to find the advice sound and the prognostication only too true.

[1] 13th July 1931.
[2] A reference to a book by Sir Osbert Sitwell called *Victoriana* which Hore-Belisha had sent him.

CHAPTER II

The Man

HORE-BELISHA was forty-three years old when he became Secretary of State for War. He was not small in stature as the caricaturists represented him—he was in fact just an inch short of six foot. That he had considerable charm was apparent. His gaiety of spirit broke through in an ever recurrent smile, prompted by an appreciation of the humour latent in a situation, which he generally embellished by his own ready wit. He did not belong to one of the great families, nor had he been educated at Eton. His father's antecedents were Spanish in origin, but the Belisha family had resided in England for a hundred and fifty years. Of his father he has left a memory given to him by his mother.[1]

" He could not resist the call of the trumpet and the roll of the drum. Whenever, as a boy, he heard the tramp, tramp, tramp of soldiers marching he had to join in. Twice in his boyhood he had run away from home and enlisted. Twice my grandfather had bought him out. But the Army continued to wield its spell over him and what he was not allowed to make his full-time profession became his hobby. There was a call in the eighties and nineties for the reinforcement of the regular formations by volunteer battalions. My father, after serving in one of the Lancashire regiments, moved to London and was given his commission in the Royal Fusiliers. My mother first set eyes on him in Hanover, where he had come to fetch home his sister, her friend and fellow-pupil in a finishing school. I suppose the Army must have set its stamp on him, for she was much struck by his military bearing and

[1] Recorded on tape in the summer of 1956.

21

described him as a knight-errant. He offered to elope with her. Nothing came of his proposal at the time, but a few years later they married.

"My father became more and more enthusiastic about his regimental duties. He felt no end could be more honourable for a man than to die in uniform. On a spring morning in June 1894 my mother was watching him with admiration as he was preparing to go on parade. He had buttoned up his red tunic and was adjusting his busby before the mirror. Suddenly and without any warning sign he fell. In so seemingly perverse and untimely a way was his wish for an ideal death granted. He left behind his widow, who was in her twenty-first year, and me, his son of nine months old."

A recollection of his childhood, 20th September, 1930 :[1]

Reading Maurois' *Byron* I recalled here and there my own childhood: the fear at night—Byron ran along the passage to look out of the window for lights, I used to hold my eyes open with my fingers so that I should not fall asleep in the dark; the sensitiveness, the mixture of defiance and gentleness, the sudden angers. He was conscious of an importance attaching to him by reason of his forbears. I dreamed of the great things I was going to do.

The young widow and her infant son were to remain closely dependent on each other throughout his childhood and even in maturity, until in fact the end of her life. She indulged his every whim. Nothing was denied him. He came first in all her thoughts. When he was in his teens she married a distinguished Civil servant, Adair Hore,[2] and the boy added his mother's new name to his own. His stepfather, far from finding the relationship irksome, took a keen personal interest in the boy, guided his education, and advised on the furtherance of his early career. His mother, Hore-Belisha has recorded,[3] " wanted to help me, her only child, to lead a full and useful life. She had held that one of the most direct ways in which a man could aid his fellow-men was to become a doctor, but, despite

---

[1] In his diary.
[2] Later Sir Adair Hore, Permanent Secretary, Ministry of Pensions.
[3] *New Westminster Review*, January 1947.

her wish, I was too sensitive to the sight of suffering to adopt this profession." It was while passing the Law Courts with his mother when he was twelve that his first sight of barristers in their wigs and gowns stirred him to take up law. Lady Hore was a woman of great charm, spoke French and German, had read widely and wrote fairy stories, which were published after her death. Her gentleness, her invariable understanding of the problems of others, her wise counselling were ever an example to him. She died on the 9th December 1936, the eve of the abdication, when he was Minister of Transport.

An impression by his housemaster at Clifton:

" He had a passion for oratory, and in his early 'teens he had learnt many of Burke's speeches by heart, which he used to declaim with becoming gestures up and down the corridors of his House. His Head Fag's speech at a House supper is still remembered by those who were present as a *tour de force* worthy of a skilled orator of mature years. He was an ambitious boy, not without that touch of romance which caused him to identify his own career with the future greatness of his country. . . . C. H. Spence, who was Head of the old Modern Side, recognised his talent and, although he was rather a lazy boy and undistinguished academically, he insisted on his being pushed into the sixth form in spite of the remonstrances of his colleagues. . . .

" His interest in Clifton and in his old House remained with him to the end of his life. . . . When he was War Minister he had on one occasion to lay the foundation stone of a new building at Cheltenham. As he hit the stone with his hammer he turned to the bystanders and said with a chuckle: ' At last Clifton has made its mark on Cheltenham.' Finally it was to a Clifton friend that he turned when he wanted a classical quotation for a poem he had written and this he subsequently had inscribed on the walls of his office at the War Ministry. It was a Homeric one and epitomised his whole life and outlook. τελέσαι δέ με θυμὸς ἀνώγει. ' My heart bids me achieve.' "[1]

From Clifton he went to the Sorbonne and then to Heidelberg before going on to St. John's College, Oxford. His studies were

[1] *The Cliftonian*, March 1957.

interrupted by the outbreak of war in 1914. He was actually on holiday in Germany on the 4th August. Hurrying home, he enlisted in the University and Public Schools Battalion, and, after three months' drilling on Salisbury Plain, he was on his way back to the Continent with a commission in the R.A.S.C. His division was engaged in heavy fighting at Neuve Chapelle. The air duels had a particular fascination for him. " What a great career flying under war conditions is! " he wrote in his diary. " The airmen are the only fellows who get a perspective of the battle."

He tried to join the Royal Flying Corps, but was told by his commanding officer that he would forward his application, but would not recommend it.

In the autumn of 1915 he received his captaincy and was attached to the Third Army. During his two further years in France he saw what he described as "the death of the old Army, which went into battle in the early months of war as though it were still fighting the South African war." He observed the new armies, "drawn from the more intelligent ranks of the community, as Cromwell's army had been, and they were all the more effective and powerful for that." He noted the acute, the tragic shortage of arms and equipment. Associated with the elaborate and complex mechanism of supply, amid the whirring wheels, he became aware that now, more than ever in the time of Cæsar or Napoleon, supplies played a vital part in the winning of a war.

Early in 1917, he was sent to Greece, where he was attached to General Milne's headquarters. He went on a mission to Cyprus and visited Egypt. He was mentioned in despatches and promoted to the rank of Major. In March 1918 he was invalided home with malaria. During the journey he acted as King's Messenger and travelled through Macedonia, across the wild, bleak mountains of Albania, by way of Koritza and Santi Quaranto to Corfu, thence across the Ionian Sea to Taranto and Rome, where the official bag was delivered to our Ambassador. Shortly after the Armistice he was invalided out of the Army with a disability pension, but, finding the recurrent attendance before military boards too irksome, he gave up the pension and returned to Oxford to pick up the fallen ends of the strand that had been snapped.

The town was unscarred by war. The buildings stood in their

familiar grandeur and grace. The clocks chimed their clanging symphony at intervals. There were a thousand new faces. Many of his contemporaries were four years his junior, but a large number, like himself, had come back from the war, some with glory, all with a maturity far beyond their years. They turned to their books again with eyes that had grown grave. Among them were many destined to win fame. Anthony Eden was there, always immaculate, swinging his arms as he walked. Malcolm MacDonald was at Queen's. There was Edward Marjoribanks too, enormously tall, raven-haired with a forward-falling lock, whose brilliant promise as a politician, fostered by his stepfather, the first Lord Hailsham, was cut short by his early death. Of the writers there were the two poets, Robert Graves and Robert Nichols; L. P. Hartley, one of our most discerning and sensitive novelists; Richard Hughes, who wrote his first play while an undergraduate, a play that Shaw praised. Edmund Blunden was there, Charles Morgan and James Laver, C. E. M. Joad and Louis Golding. And among the women Dorothy Sayers, Vera Brittain and Winifred Holtby. Living in or near Oxford were Robert Bridges and W. B. Yeats, John Masefield, John Buchan (later Lord Tweeds-muir) and A. E. Coppard, and, also fresh from the war, Lawrence of Arabia. They formed little groups and coteries and met to provide each other with literary, artistic or political stimulus.

For Hore-Belisha, returning from the cataclysm that took such a heavy toll of his companions at school and at the university, the scene was tinged with wistfulness. He wrote in the *Oxford Outlook* in May 1919:

" It was our sad amusement, during our years of exile, to think of Oxford as we knew her, and as we should know her again. The children of Oxford in the fields of Flanders would surely inspire another one hundred and thirty-seventh psalm. The routine, the river, even the priggish discipline of the place were a pleasant memory. By comparison with our present state they were a golden vision of the future.

" We came back. But it was by the waters of Isis that we sat down and wept when we remembered Oxford. In truth we were ill at ease in the Zion of our longing. A new generation had sprung up in the land—a generation puny in numbers, and, perhaps for that very reason, more sedulous of dons and ritual, more pharisaic than the Pharisees—and we had come as ghosts to trouble joy. And so we hardly recognised Oxford. But we, too, were unrecognisable."

Before long his youthful ideals took on a reforming fervour. He felt that all human problems were soluble. If the orthodox cures failed—and they had failed—then the unorthodox must be tried. Flabby moralising would not achieve a solution. So he began to equip himself for the tasks that lay ahead. He observed with care and with a quick, sympathetic eye. At the debates of the Union, his dazzling epigrams, his flashing phrases made even the supercilious young men of that disillusioned age listen with appreciation and applaud tumultuously.

Louis Golding recalled: " He was respected and envied. He was witty, devastatingly witty, with an irony no one wished to provoke. He could hold his audience spellbound. I remember one evening at the Union. We were all listening enraptured to Hore-Belisha. He had worked up to a tremendous peroration, but, with his arm upheld to deliver it, he seemed to remember something, for he walked down from the platform and out of the room. The house sat in absolute silence during the minute or two he was away. Then he returned and finished his speech to applause one has rarely heard."

Here was a glittering, delectable world that stimulated and developed many sides of his personality. He revelled in the life. In his rooms he had an abundance of purple cushions. His guests stood in the pale light of lamps mounted upon brackets of carved Venetian bronze. He entertained with magnificence, mortgaging the income from his patrimony for months ahead. He opened magnums of champagne and handed round Turkish coffee made in pots that he had brought home from Salonika.

The passing of examinations imposed some obligations: he had begun to read for the Bar and used to go up to London to eat his dinners at the Inner Temple. He joined every club he could. He was elected to that ancient and select society the Archery Club, and wore its green blazer. He used to punt on the river. He played rugger. He kept up his running, which had brought him distinction at Clifton, and was beaten only by Tabor, who later became an international. He plunged into every activity and gaiety with abandon. Years later the realisation that his academic opportunities had not been used to the best advantage wrung from him this public admission: " In the course of my Oxford career I accumulated a liability which was subsequently discharged by great industry on my part." But his zest for reading, always intense, enabled him to acquire a wide historical knowledge. His mind was stored with diversified facts, current and ancient, which he brought into effective play.

He became the first post-war President of the Union. At the debates he spoke with an undergraduate exuberance. But there breathed through all this amateurity an earnestness, an impatience, a reforming zeal that, shared though it was by many undergraduates, was voiced by him with a rousing vigour.

Parliament attracted him and from time to time he visited the House of Commons to listen to a debate.

Of his youthful ambitions he says :[1] " It was there (at school), while reading history, that I first turned my eyes to Westminster. Ambitions in one's early years are apt to be personal, but in the unfolding of time they become more and more detached. Egoism is replaced—or should be—by widening ideas of service. At school one sees oneself bestriding Alexander's horse, wearing Cicero's toga, outshining Byron, or breaking records on land, sea or in the air. The years between apprenticeship and achievement are completely eliminated. In one's dreams one is already 'there.' In my own case, I stood with Fox and Pitt, Disraeli and Gladstone at the Despatch Box."

He was called to the Bar in October 1922. Shortly afterwards a telephone call at his Adelphi flat set him on the road to a Parliamentary career.

" I can still remember,[2] after the Writ had been issued for the General Election of 1922, the youthful excitement with which I received the summons of Lord Gladstone, then Chairman of the Liberal Party, to go to Abingdon Street, the Liberal headquarters.

[1] In an article in the *New Westminster Review*, January 1947.
[2] In an article in the *Devonian Year Book*, 1947.

I can remember verbatim the conversation with that son of the Grand Old Man. Would I go and fight Devonport? There wasn't a chance, of course. The Liberal had lost his deposit at the previous General Election. What, I would go? Excellent. When? The next train? Oh, there wasn't as much urgency as all that. ' Oh, yes, there is,' I said, and I did catch the next train. Then I can see that train arriving at North Road, Plymouth. No one to meet me. Not a single acquaintance in that town, so lonely and impersonal as it then seemed. The walk with my bag across to the Duke of Cornwall Hotel. The top back room. My adoption as a candidate and the beginning of an uncharted career."

Aware that he must make an impression on the electors, he hired an old stage coach he found in a backyard, harnessed four bay horses to it and drove through the constituency, seated beside the driver. To his lips he raised a coaching horn and blared out his call to the electors. At every street corner he stopped and addressed them.

His opponent was Sir Clement Kinloch-Cooke, a Conservative. He had represented Devonport for more than twelve years. His majority at the last General Election was 9,125, in a three-cornered fight, with the Liberal at the bottom of the poll. He was contemptuous of the challenge from still another Liberal and dismissed Hore-Belisha as that " little chit of a fellow." The jibe was promptly seized by Hore-Belisha.

" I am proud to be called ' a little chit of a fellow ' because I am rather older than Napoleon was when he led to victory the greatest armies that the world has ever seen ; because I am older than Alexander was when he conquered the then known world; because I am rather older than Hannibal, probably the greatest general the world has ever seen. . . ."

After citing scientists, poets like Keats and Shelley, politicians including Pitt, who was Prime Minister at the age of twenty-three, he finished with these words:

" There was one more little chit of a fellow that we must never forget ; one of the greatest generals in English history—Wolfe. When the heights of Abraham had to be stormed they went up

to the old general and he had ' the wind up.' They went to a
younger general and he said ' I would not care to undertake the
job.' They went to Wolfe, a young chit of a fellow. He said
'I'll do it or I'll die.' He did it and he died. There were three
million ' little chits of fellows ' who protected my opponent and
his home in the War. If you want a monument to the achievement
of the older politician you may find it across the Channel. It is
three hundred miles long and half a mile deep, and it is studded
with the tombstones of ' little chits of fellows.' "

It was a rousing rebuttal and it evoked a resounding response.
Soon Kinloch-Cooke was, as they said, " fighting for dear life."
Hore-Belisha polled 8,538 votes and, though this did not bring
success, it was a considerable achievement. He missed victory by a
mere 1,921 votes. He defeated Kinloch-Cooke the following year,
in the General Election of October 1923, when Labour was returned
as a minority Government.

His feet were now upon the road he was to tread with some
distinction. His career at the Bar had been brief. A telegram from
Lord Beaverbrook, offering congratulations on his success, invited
Hore-Belisha to come and see him. It was the beginning of an
association that kept Hore-Belisha busy writing for the *Evening
Standard* (The Londoner's Diary) and presently for Beaverbrook's
other two newspapers, the *Daily Express* and the *Sunday Express*.
R. D. Blumenfeld, editor-in-chief of the two latter newspapers, has
written of their first meeting: " I found a smiling, charmingly
mannered young man, walking up and down and dictating to a
secretary. I hustled him in the manner usually employed by editors
and he smiled back as if to say: ' Don't worry. I'll be ready shortly.'
And he was. . . .

" We used to say in the *Express* offices that if Hore-Belisha liked
he could reach any height in any calling that he chose to make his
own. . . . I found later on closer acquaintance that he was a depend-
able friend and a staunch defender of ideas which he held to be
right; and I for one regretted the step he took when he cut loose
from Fleet Street."[1]

He remained with the Beaverbrook press for six years, but his

[1] R.D.B.'s private papers.

29

journalism was not confined to this one group. He was " The Man with the Lamp " in the *Saturday Review* and regularly contributed to the *Spectator*. He wrote for magazines and journals both in Britain and America. His income was substantial. But he found that Beaverbrook was an exacting task master. Often, at the end of a long day in Parliament, there would be a telephone call asking him to a late supper at Beaverbrook's home, The Vineyard, at Putney. Talks on politicians and the Press would go on half-way through the night. There was a struggle between these two strong temperaments whenever they happened by conviction to pull in different directions. Beaverbrook's attitude was that his view and his view alone should be expressed in his papers, whereas Hore-Belisha felt that nothing but his own opinion should appear under his signature.

Fortunately the clash was not frequent, but it was recurrent, and the strain was exhausting. So Hore-Belisha left to find his feet and his voice in the House of Commons.

CHAPTER III

The Inheritance

DISARMAMENT HAD been the keynote of the policy of successive Governments for more than a decade after the war. Britain took the lead in setting an example to the world. The mood of the people was for peace. The combined force of moral persuasion, political agitation and the almost religious fervour which dominated meetings of the League of Nations Union in support of their crusade for disarmament, was too compelling for any Government to overlook or withstand. The after-war slogans of a " Land fit for Heroes to live in " and " No more Passchendaeles " had their repercussions. There was a persistent call for the strictest economy in defence expenditure. " Axe the Services " was the popular and political cry, and Conservative and Labour ministries vied with each other in axeing them to the bone.

Between the years 1925, when the Treaty of Locarno was signed, and 1932, Service Estimates were cut annually. The Regular and the Territorial Armies were drastically reduced. Regiments and batteries were recklessly disbanded. Naval construction was restricted, and personnel dropped lower than it had been for nearly half a century. Unemployment stalked through the Royal Dockyards and Hore-Belisha, the Member for Devonport, " the little cherub sitting up aloft,"[1] made repeated appeals from the Opposition back benches during the years 1924 to 1931 to both Conservative and Labour Governments for more naval construction. Closure of at least one Royal Dockyard was threatened. Work upon the fortifications of Singapore was stopped.[2] The Royal Air Force was relegated to fifth place in Europe.

Shortly after the war, in 1919, during Mr. Lloyd George's

---

[1] As Mr. J. C. C. Davidson, Parliamentary Secretary to the Admiralty (later Viscount Davidson) called him in the Navy Estimates debate.
[2] By the Labour Government of 1929-31.

administration, a rule was laid down that Service Departments should base their Estimates on the assumption that "the British Empire will not be engaged in any great war during the next ten years and that no Expeditionary Force will be required." In July 1928, when Winston Churchill was Chancellor of the Exchequer, the ten-year rule was put virtually on a permanent basis. His proposal, which was accepted by the Cabinet, was "that the basis of the Estimates for the Service Departments should rest upon the statement that there would be no major war for a period of ten years and that this basis should advance from day to day, but that the assumption should be reviewed every year by the Committee of Imperial Defence."

In Lord Chatfield's opinion[1] this "vicious" rule injured the very roots of the three Services. Its effect on the productive capacity of the ordnance and other armament factories was most serious. Practically the whole of the armament industry was closed down in the years following the war. By 1932, when the rule was cancelled, plants had been scrapped and considerable deterioration in Royal Ordnance factories had set in. The Army's industrial organisation of supply, its teams of technicians, its entire productive potential disintegrated through the lack of orders. It had to be built up again from scratch and new Royal Ordnance factories had to be constructed. Mass production methods were almost unknown in the thirties in Britain's highly specialised private industries. When the rearmament programme was initiated in 1935 machine tools had to be imported, re-modelled or re-made. Without a definite ruling that rearmament must take precedence over normal trade, a manufacturer naturally favoured his regular, rather than his intermittent customers.[2]

The final design of the 3.7 inch anti-aircraft gun was only approved in midsummer 1937 and the 4.5 inch was then still on the drawing board. These were the two main anti-aircraft weapons.

Experience has shown that it takes the better part of two years

[1] *It Might Happen Again* by Admiral of the Fleet, Lord Chatfield (Heineman 1947): Lord Chatfield succeeded Inskip as Minister for Co-ordination of Defence in February 1939.
[2] "What hope was there of persuading manufacturers to accept sporadic Army orders if their civilian contracts would be prejudiced?" Hore-Belisha noted in his diary on the 26th October 1938.

before a new project comes into production and it is only in the third year that a substantial flow can be assured.

It was not until the spring of 1936, after the return of the National Government in the preceding November, that a significant beginning was made to re-arm. Public opinion, however, was in the main still wedded to the illusion of peace by disarmament and anyone who thought otherwise was branded a warmonger.

In Parliament the Labour Opposition, supported by the Liberals, rejected the Government's policy as a whole. They insisted that competition in armaments would not lead to safety, and any rearmament policy should be correlated with the system of collective security under the League of Nations. Motions of censure were put down and White Papers on Defence and increased Service Estimates were consistently challenged. Until 1935 a Parliamentary candidate who advocated increased defence expenditure ran the risk of finishing at the bottom of the poll, if he did not actually lose his deposit. In the East Fulham bye-election of 1933 George Lansbury, leader of the Parliamentary Labour Party, in a message to the constituents, proclaimed: " I would close every recruiting station, disband the Army, dismiss the Air Force."[1] A Conservative majority of 14,521 was turned into a minority of 4,840. The notorious Peace Ballot[2] in 1935 was yet another illustration of the temper of the people.

It needed the shock of Munich in September 1938 to rouse the nation to the danger to the country's security. But even then, only twelve months before the war, neither Parliament nor people was prepared to abandon peacetime methods and to gear the industrial machine of the country to war production, as in Germany.

France was well aware of the influence of this anti-war feeling in Britain on Government policy. Albert Sarraut, Prime Minister in 1936, giving evidence before a Commission of Enquiry,[3] after the Second World War, stated:

" Politically it is well known how preponderant has always been

---

[1] Lansbury's pronounced pacifism led to his replacement as Leader of the Labour Party by Attlee in the following year.

[2] Organised by the League of Nations Union with Labour and Liberal assistance. Out of eleven and a half million votes cast, the overwhelming majority was for disarmament.

[3] *Les Evénements Survenus en France de 1933 à 1945*, vol. iii.

the influence of British public opinion on the British Government. In 1936 public opinion in Britain was clearly and explicitly unfavourable to any use of force against the Reich. Blinded, moreover, by the sophistry of the principle of nationalism, which Hitler so adroitly always used until Munich in his dealing with Britain, public opinion in Britain held that after all the Rhineland was German territory and it was normal that it should return to Germany."

Twice in a little over a generation France had been invaded and overrun by the German Army. Britain's policy of trying to reconcile at Geneva the conflicting claims of French security and German demands for equality in arms seemed to the French as illogical as it was impracticable.

During the twilight period between disarmament and rearmament, the Navy maintained its pride of place in the Service Estimates and the Army lagged well behind. The full significance of air power was not yet realised, nor was it appreciated how seriously the insular position of Britain had inevitably been altered to her disadvantage.

As late as 1936 the total Defence Estimates of £188 millions, were only £50 millions more than in the previous year. The Navy, with the largest share, was able to lay the foundation of a three-years' construction programme, which stood it in good stead at the outbreak of war. The Air Estimates were nearly doubled, but expenditure on the Army was still poor. In the following February Chamberlain, then Chancellor of the Exchequer, introduced a Defence Budget of £1,500 millions, to be spent over five years, 1937-42. A single policy was to govern the programmes of the Navy, Army and Air Force and it would take three years for the first stage to be completed. An unusual feature of the Defence Budget was that £400 millions was to be raised by a Defence Loan.

In March 1936 Sir Thomas Inskip had been made Minister for the Co-ordination of Defence. The terms of reference of his appointment were somewhat vague. His chief task, as originally intended, was to co-ordinate policy, but in actual practice supply and the strict rationing of the three Service Departments within the figure of £1,500 millions over the five-year period was his main responsibility. Each Service Department had to draw up a programme which could be effectively completed within that time, setting out the essential items and those of lower priority. Particular attention had to be paid to the cost of each item. A Treasury Inter-Service Committee scrutinised the separate programmes, taking into account the demands of all the Services and the aggregate cost. A pull-devil, pull-baker struggle often ensued, resulting in review after review of a programme. A proposal, for instance, by the War Office, even though essential, was referred back if it involved an outlay in excess of the ration allotted, and the Secretary of State was advised to do his best within the provision made and to get his department to produce a new scheme that would fit into the ration.

There was objection to even the smallest increase in expenditure. Hore-Belisha was to write in his diary on the 13th July 1937, soon after he became Secretary of State for War :

My proposal for the provision of war equipment, war reserves and maintenance for four Territorial divisions was turned down to-day. I regarded it not from the point of view of what should be achieved as an ideal, but from the practical point of view. At some time a decision will have to be made that some of the T.A. divisions will have to be fully equipped, and there are many reasons why it would be advantageous to make a decision now.

It would not involve the immediate spending of money, but, if authority were given, it would place those at the War Office responsible for organising munitions production in a more confident position when dealing with contractors, and enable contractors to make their plans, so that they could go ahead with the equipment of the extra divisions when the opportunity offered.

I argued with Simon, but he was quite firm that at present there should be no increase in the cost of the Army's programme. I pointed out that the Army's programme was behind that of the Navy and Air Force—authority had been given to the Army later —and that the Army's programme was still largely undefined and the organisation of industrial production to meet its needs was in difficulties. It was a disheartening business for the War Office.

In the end, I asked if it were found that economies could be made in the approved programme, whether the four Territorial divisions I had proposed could be added to it. Simon seemed to think the Treasury might agree to this.

In those days Britain was dependent on her own financial resources for her rearmament. The maintenance of financial stability, so disastrously shaken in the crisis of 1931, was regarded as the fourth arm of Defence, without which purely military effort would be stultified. Chamberlain felt we must balance our budgets and avoid interference with the export trade as long as possible.[1] " If we were now to follow Winston's advice and sacrifice our commerce to the manufacture of arms, we would inflict a certain injury on our trade from which it would take generations to recover, we should destroy the confidence which now happily exists, and we should cripple the revenue." Thus economy remained the watchword and Government spending was regulated by it.

In spite of his cautious attitude towards expenditure on the Armed Forces, Chamberlain was always concerned about the Army while he was Chancellor of the Exchequer. In his diary of 25th October 1936 he wrote: " I must really have some decision as to the future function of the Regular and Territorial armies." When he became Prime Minister, he was fully aware that the Army was "the Cinderella " of the three defence services and had, as he expressed it, " sat too long by a cold hearth, and suffered longest from the financial inhibitions to which, part unconsciously," the experts deferred.[2]

Another aspect of Hore-Belisha's inheritance as Secretary of State for War had also not escaped Chamberlain's notice. " The obstinacy of some of the Army heads in sticking to obsolete methods is incredible," he noted. This prejudice against modernising the Army could be traced back through the years. In 1927, six years before Hitler came to power, a small mechanised force, with aircraft in support of tanks, was tried out in a series of exercises on Salisbury Plain. It was the world's first Panzer force in embryo. Men of vision had urged that it should speedily be built up into a division,

---

[1] Keith Feiling's *Life of Neville Chamberlain* (Macmillan, 1946).
[2] *Life of Neville Chamberlain.*

and then multiplied until the entire British Army was reconstituted on this pattern. But the wraith of traditionalism wailed through the corridors of the War Office and this wise counsel was disregarded. The older, the long-established formations were regarded as sacrosanct. The tank was viewed with distrust and, since money could not be found for both the traditional formations and these new-fangled experiments, with tragic blindness it was decided in the following year, 1928, that our first Experimental Armoured Force should be disbanded.

And although mechanisation did begin in the early 1930's[1] we did not possess a single armoured division until 1937, by which time the Germans already had four fully equipped ones.

In the face of all these difficulties, Chamberlain recognised that a dynamic personality would be needed as Secretary of State for War, to make the Army into an efficient fighting unit. Hore-Belisha seemed to him to be the obvious choice and he expressly told him that he wished to see " drastic changes."[2]

---

[1] An armoured Mobile force was in the course of formation which was to comprise two mechanised cavalry brigades, one tank brigade, one armoured car regiment, one R.H.A. mechanised brigade of three battalions and one field squadron of Royal Engineers. The tank brigade was to consist of four battalions.
[2] *Life of Neville Chamberlain.*

CHAPTER IV

The First Task

THE FAREWELLS were said at the Ministry of Transport. Hore-Belisha went round the department and thanked all who had worked for him. Sir Cyril Hurcomb,[1] Permanent Secretary at the Ministry of Transport, wrote :

" I feel far more strongly than I can express your great kindness to me in all our dealings. I have greatly enjoyed working with you and appreciate your constant and successful efforts to uphold and raise the status of the Ministry[2] more than anyone else is in a position to do. I know also the many difficulties and anxieties you have had during your term of office here and am all the more grateful for your invariable pleasantness and the way in which you have made it easy to co-operate. You have a great future before you and I hope that we may be officially associated again in some way and meanwhile meet as friends."

Arriving at the War Office, he undertook the preliminary courtesies of meeting those who were to work with him. A clear indication of his approach to all problems was given at the outset. When Lieut.-General Sir Charles Deedes, his Military Secretary, came into his room and introduced himself, Hore-Belisha asked what his duties were. Deedes explained that it was his job to advise the Secretary of State on the appointments and promotions recommended by the Selection Board. He thereupon handed Hore-Belisha the new list for his approval.

Hore-Belisha, after examining it, inquired by what process certain

[1] Later Lord Hurcomb.
[2] Hore-Belisha was given Cabinet rank as Minister of Transport in October 1936.

names were selected and others set aside. He said that in future he wished to know the reason for each recommendation, as well as the reason why others who were eligible had not been considered suitable.

He added that he knew nothing about the Army but intended to learn. So, repeatedly, he asked the question " Why? " He asked it of the Chief of the Imperial General Staff, Field-Marshal Sir Cyril Deverell, and of each of the members of the Army Council. He wished to understand the problems, he said, and he supplemented these inquiries by going out to the Commands to see for himself how things were done and why. One could not learn by sitting at a desk. That he was going to do things in his own way was quite clearly apparent.

The immediate need, he saw, was for more men. The Regular Army in June 1937 was short by 20,000 of its establishment and the Territorial Army by 40,000. In July Hore-Belisha noted in his diary :

> I am informed that so serious is the prospect five years hence that we may not be able to supply any drafts for our overseas garrisons. I am looking into the Cardwell system.

That further considerable problems lay ahead he was well aware, but recruiting was the foremost task. He concentrated on its solution all the thought and effort he could command. Why were men not being attracted to the Army? Why were so many who were already in the service leaving it? Were they dissatisfied with the pay or with the conditions? What were the quarters like in which they had to live? To obtain the answers he talked not only to members of the Army Council, to the generals and senior officers at the Staff College and at Aldershot, but to the men as well. Reports were not enough for him. He inspected the barracks. He looked into the kitchens. He sampled the food. He visited troopships about to sail for Palestine, Egypt, or India. He wanted to visualise the sort of life the men would have to endure on their long voyage. He brought to these investigations all his human understanding. He weighed the advantages of those who had jobs in civilian life with the opportunities that could be offered to the men he sought to attract into the Army, for such comparisons were undoubtedly being made by the men themselves. How could the Army be made a worthwhile career, not merely for officers but also for the other ranks?

He was told by his advisers that the pay of the soldier should be raised. He did not agree that this was the only solution. He thought there were other drawbacks than the pay they were receiving. " We ought to try to discover, in the first place, what has led the men we already have to join the Army. Then we should develop and extend these advantages. Higher pay for higher qualifications—yes: that is another matter. We should make the Army a career, a career which would provide a pension relatively early in life." That was the way his mind was working.

His day to day work at the War Office and his round of inspections continued. He attended the Aldershot Tattoo, went to the reunion of the Staff College Club at Sandhurst, was with the King in Hyde Park when His Majesty reviewed 80,000 ex-servicemen and women, the biggest parade of the kind ever held. A further hint of his line of thought was given when he went to the first performance of the Northern Command Tattoo in Roundhay Park, Leeds, on the 1st July. In expressing his appreciation, he said: " The soldier is part of the community, and people should know more about him and his life." Later he used the telling phrase: " The Army is a part of the nation and not apart from the nation." Progressively his plans were beginning to take shape.

He received each of the foreign military attachés in turn and had long talks with them about the armies of their countries. At the end of the Parliamentary Session he went down to a small furnished house he had rented in the village of Eastdean on the Sussex Downs in order to study in seclusion and detachment the numerous problems that had to be disentangled and solved. Here he spent a month of the summer, for the most part alone. He kept in constant touch with the War Office, came up to town for discussions, and sought the advice of military experts, such as Liddell Hart and others.

On Saturday the 7th August, Hore-Belisha went to Devonport and, in the course of a speech to his constituents, foreshadowed his immediate plans to stimulate recruiting.

" Men join the Navy, serve for over twenty years and then get a pension. . . . One of the reasons why men hesitate to join the Army is because, unlike the Navy, it does not offer a career. . . . The soldier generally enlists for seven years with the colours and five years with the reserve. It is quite exceptional for a private to be allowed to stay on in the Army, and this however anxious he may be to follow the profession he has mastered.

" If the Army offered to more soldiers of good character and efficiency the opportunity of making a career and of earning a pension, those who preferred to leave the active list after a short time of service could still do so if they considered that they had better prospects in civil life. Next week I hope to introduce a scheme which will give them an option in that regard."

" It is only an experiment that I am going to announce," he added, " but I am going to test the opinion of the soldier himself." He was going to let the soldier supply the answer to the Adjutant-General, Sir Harry Knox, who, he noted in his diary, " kept on predicting that I would not get a single man to rejoin."

And the scheme? " With his unfailing adroitness," said the *Manchester Guardian*,[1] " he has got the country in a state of lively expectation about the change, days before it is officially disclosed." In August again, it recalled, in the " close " political season, just as when " he turned London upside down with his Belisha beacons and crossings. . . . It is August again and Mr. Belisha's colleagues are dispersed, and this time he has the Army, not the roads, at his mercy. . . . He has got going pretty quickly. He has been at the War Office only two months."

[1] 10th August 1937.

CHAPTER V

Early Reforms

ON THE 10th August, a few days after Hore-Belisha's speech in Devonport foreshadowing his plans for improving recruiting, he returned from his cottage at Eastdean in Sussex to the War Office. A Press Conference had been arranged. This unusual step set tongues wagging. David Roseway,[1] his Principal Private Secretary, who gave unstinted and devoted service, recalls : " I must confess I did not like it. We none of us did, neither the Army nor the Civil Service. We feared that H.B. might bring with him the methods he had introduced at the Ministry of Transport, and we were shocked to find that sort of thing going on at the War Office—the Press, cameras, publicity in all its forms. H.B. had been in Fleet Street, he knew the proprietors and the editors, he had all the contacts and he brought them fully into operation. It was his resolve to tell the public what the Army was doing and why. It was not long before many Whitehall departments began to appreciate the advantages of a good Public Relations organisation ; to-day even the Prime Minister has one. The advantage of what H.B. had introduced was soon apparent to most of us. He was not out to get publicity for himself, as we had imagined, though that inevitably came ; but it was the Army that was to be put across to the people, and even the Commanders. The spotlight was on them all."

10th August 1937
My first reform. We tried to put it over in a big way.

The Press was assembled in the large panelled room where the Army Council normally met. At a long table against the handsome

[1] Later Sir David Roseway.

marble mantelpiece sat the Secretary of State with War Office officials on either side. As it was August, the senior members of the Army Council were away, with the exception of the Adjutant-General, Sir Harry Knox, who had all along been gloomy about the scheme bringing in even " a single recruit." The Quartermaster-General, Sir Reginald May, wrote[1] from Scotland: " I know the Army appreciate what you are doing and believe you will 'deliver the goods' in the end. All power to your elbow. I can only assure you that your weekly Army Council meetings are splendid and do a great deal of good which perhaps you do not realise."

The Secretary of State himself unfolded the details of his plan:

" 1. Serving soldiers, on completion of their first term of service with the colours, were to be allowed to extend their service.

2. Reservists, old soldiers on the reserve for five years following their seven years of service, were to be allowed to rejoin the colours.

3. Both classes of men, on completing twelve years' service, were eligible to serve for a total of twenty-one years and thus qualify for a pension."

It was a simple scheme. It had the added merit of not needing the sanction of Parliament, but could be introduced quickly as an administrative measure.

The same night after the News, Hore-Belisha in a broadcast explained his scheme:

" A serving soldier or reservist accepting this offer will, after twenty-one years' total service, generally at about forty years of age, become eligible for a pension for life. . . . Where is the trade that will guarantee a man a pension while he is still in the prime of life and is still able to supplement it? "

The pessimists were perplexed. Within nine days of the scheme being launched, over 2000 reservists had accepted the offer. By the 25th of the month the number was over 3000.

A few days later he made his next change. He raised the recruitment age for all combatant ranks from twenty-five to twenty-eight, soon he made it thirty. With the mechanisation of the Army it

[1] 11th August 1937.

LOW'S TOPICAL BUDGET

Evening Standard, 23 October 1937

was obvious to Hore-Belisha that experienced mechanics, machine-minders and motor transport drivers were needed and that the net of recruitment should be spread to catch them. " Obvious, however, as this may be," said the *Saturday Review*, " it is to Mr. Hore-Belisha's credit that he was the first to act upon the idea."

His letter to Sir Elmsley Carr, Editor of the *News of the World*, throws a light on his views at this time :

" I never dreamt a job could be so hard. But then the W.O. is an old place. . . . What in my judgment does an overwhelming harm to recruiting is the constant representation of the Army as an ill-paid, unenlightened career in intolerable conditions. How can men be attracted to it when these things are repeatedly printed? A general bias is created. What is remarkable is that we have got so many men despite this difficulty; despite better employment, despite Peace propaganda, despite grants for physical fitness and playgrounds for civilians at public expense. I wish the other side of the picture could be painted.

" Our most recent recruiting figures are the best for five years. Moreover, 3,000 Reservists to date have rejoined in response to my offer—that is at a rate of well over 100 a day since it was open. . . . In our wildest dreams we never imagined we should get this total in a time when these men are mostly in good employment."[1]

To those who did not wish to stay the full term of twenty-one years, he extended facilities for training in some craft or profession during their last six months in the Army. While undergoing this instruction, they received their full pay, as well as board and lodging, and they left the Army better equipped to earn their living.

Progressively he relaxed the petty restrictions and restraints which had been imposed many years before for the control of an ignorant and drunken soldiery and were irksome to the better-educated and better behaved men of the present Army. He permitted soldiers to sleep out of barracks if they married below the age at which accommodation was provided in the married quarters. This change sprang from an actual case of hardship which had come to his notice. A recruit who happened to be married but was under twenty-five, the age at which marriage was officially recognised by the Army, was compelled to sleep in barracks and not live with his wife. Hore-Belisha's view was that the man was entitled to a home life just as much as a civilian. In reply to a criticism that this was mollycoddling and would lead to a deplorable decline in discipline, he said : " You must not degrade the Army to a status below that of the civilian. The Army should be regarded as an important and high calling. This man should be allowed to sleep out if he chooses. So long as he is efficient at his work and a good soldier we have no right to regulate his private life, any more than an employer has in a commercial office."

The concession to sleep out was in time extended to every soldier at Home stations who was above the age of twenty-one. His aim was to remove impediments to recruiting. He realised the disadvantages suffered by a soldier who, spending an evening with

[1] 29th August 1937.

friends, had to say good-bye to his girl and hurry back to barracks, while his civilian companions could enjoy extended hours of freedom and gaiety. Soldiers under the age of twenty-one were allowed to sleep out if they lived with their parents or guardians. He was insistent that the soldier should at no time be made to feel that his status was in any way inferior. Provided discipline was maintained, the new Army needed men with more individual responsibility and free from the shackles of outmoded regulations.

He opened still other doors for service in the Army by adjusting the out-of-date standards with regard to teeth and eyesight. Hitherto it had been the rule that no recruit should have less than " eleven sound points," by which was meant at least eleven of his own teeth. This seemed to Hore-Belisha absurd. He reminded his advisers that men with full sets of false teeth had been conscripted during the 1914-18 war and that dentures had not been found a disadvantage even in the mastication of bully beef. He was told that the rule had been introduced so that a soldier should not throw his teeth away " in the face of the enemy " and have to be sent back to the base. The old rule, he insisted, should be waived, and it was.

A letter from a young man who had been champion boxer in his school complained that he had failed to get into the Army because of some slight defect in his sight. Hore-Belisha, after undergoing the Army's standard eyesight test himself, had the regulation modified. In future every soldier, if his eyes needed correction, must be provided, he said, with two pairs of glasses in stout cases. " We want recruits, and not excuses for not having them."

Everything was done to build up the physique of sub-standard recruits. A daily ration of milk was issued. Hore-Belisha, touring the barracks constantly, and developing the reforms initiated by his predecessor Duff Cooper, evolved a whole series of improvements to better the conditions under which the men worked and lived. He envisaged barracks of an entirely new type, centrally heated, equipped with shower baths and supplied with well-sprung beds, recreation rooms with wireless sets in them ; in the married quarters stainless-steel and tiled kitchens, garden plots and space in which the children could play. The barracks at Warminster, Bordon, Shrivenham, Tidworth, Shorncliffe, Pinehurst and elsewhere (they make a long list) constructed during his régime, are still often spoken of as " Belisha Barracks."

He established schools of cookery for the special training of Army cooks so that the men should have better cooked food and a greater variety. Uniforms were brought up to date. The puttee, the soldiers' curse for half a century, was discarded. It was replaced by the more easily manipulated anklet, which was far less likely to encumber men engaged in driving tanks and lorries. The battledress was adopted. It was subsequently copied by the armies of other nations, and was not unlike the simple ski-ing suit Hore-Belisha had used in Switzerland and the boiler suit worn by Winston Churchill during the Second World War.

These changes and concessions—not all initiated by him, but he carried them through—had the enthusiastic support of progressively-minded soldiers. But a great many others, more traditionally conditioned, raised strong objections, described the improvements as " demoralising," and voiced their resentment of a civilian's interference with their hallowed institutions. Records were brought out. Precedents were cited. Time had to be spent in persuasion and argument.

" Ideas of ' Peace at any price ' and that ' the profession of arms is unworthy ' are passing away. There was a feeling that the safety of Britain is now a matter of prime concern, and we saw an improvement in recruiting for which the present War Secretary deserves great credit," said Winston Churchill at a dinner of the 42nd East Lancashire Territorial Division in Manchester.[1]

But Hore-Belisha himself was far from contented with the results so far obtained. He expressed in the House his dissatisfaction on a heroic scale—a " Shelleyan unrest " it was called. " I am not satisfied with anything or anybody," he said, "but the position has improved."

Constantly in his mind was the need to increase the strength of the Territorial Army. In midsummer 1937 there were 8,756 officers and 146,344 other ranks. At the anniversary banquet of the Honourable Artillery Company in London on the 12th July, Hore-Belisha described the Territorials, the citizen army, as not only a form of military insurance, but as the cheapest kind of national defence.

[1] *Manchester Despatch* 12th March 1938.

" The highest civilisation that the world has seen, the Greeks, relied for its defence on the citizen soldier. The greatest Empire of the ancient world, the Roman, was built by the citizen soldier. The finest soldiers of the medieval world were by general recognition the Swiss. They originally made their reputation as a citizen force.

" To-day the voluntary system in Great Britain undergoes its supreme trial. To give up holidays, to give up leisure, to give up the society of wives and families, in order to discharge a military duty are deprivations which in this land are not exacted but are willingly assumed."

To revivify the force and to raise the status of the Territorial Army Hore-Belisha decided to remove any feeling of inequality that might exist. There should be no distinction, no differentiation, between officers and men in the Regular and Territorial divisions. The familiar brass T, which Territorials hitherto had been required to wear on the shoulder, was discarded.

At a dinner at the Mansion House given by the City Lieutenants Club on the 20th October, he announced his plans for the Territorial Army. Henceforth, he said, it was to have a voice, not only in the direction of its own affairs, but in that of the Army as a whole.

The Director-General of the Territorial Army, General Sir Walter Kirke,[1] was to be made a member of the Army Council.

A new post of Deputy Director-General of the Territorial Army, with the rank of Major-General, was to be created. Colonel Sir John Brown, an architect by profession, was selected for this unique distinction. He had been an outstanding and highly efficient Territorial for 36 years. In his zeal and enthusiasm he had travelled all over the country rousing young men to enrol, and had persuaded their employers to give them time off for training during a period when public interest in the Territorial Army was at a low ebb. It was a signal indication of his popularity in Northampton where he lived that, whenever the local " Terriers " set off for camp, the people used to turn out to cheer them as they marched through the streets.

Another Territorial officer, Lieut.-Col. J. K. Dunlop, was

[1] A Regular Army officer.

48

appointed Assistant Adjutant-General of the Territorial Army, with the temporary rank of Colonel.

The monthly Army List of the following January contained, for the first time in its 128 years of publication, a section headed " Major-General Territorial Army." A promise that Territorials should be given command of divisions was specifically made by Haldane when he created the Territorial Force. But this was never fulfilled. It had been side-tracked because, it was argued, it would deprive a Regular Army officer of a command.

When Hore-Belisha expressed his intention to raise to the rank of Major-General yet another Territorial, Colonel C. F. Liardet, an insurance broker at Lloyds, and to give him command of a Territorial Division, he encountered the fiercest opposition from the C.I.G.S. He was told a day or so later that Liardet had refused the appointment as it would interfere with his normal work. It emerged that Liardet had been informed that he was to be given a division in the North. He had in fact been selected for the London Territorial Division. He readily accepted this and the appointment was listed on the 15th November 1937.

A sharp rise in the recruiting figures for the Territorials followed these reforms. By the early spring of 1938 the numbers of officers and men had increased at the rate of nearly 2,000 a month.

CHAPTER VI

The Men Around Him

UNLIKE CARDWELL and Haldane, his great predecessors at the War Office, each of whom had many untroubled years of peace in which to carry out his reforms, Hore-Belisha had only twenty-seven months before war came. He realised that if he was to accomplish what was required, indeed what was in fact essential for the security of the country, he must have around him men who would be prepared not only to accept, but would be capable of initiating, progressive reforms in the modernisation of the Army, men who would be able to assess the full value of new weapons, the influence of air power, and profit by the lessons of modern war as it was being waged at that time in Spain. The Army had to be developed along entirely new lines. Were the military members who sat with him on the Army Council prepared to agree to the fundamental adjustments that would be necessary? Or did tradition have too firm, too unyielding a grip on their outlook? That was what he strove to discover during his early months in office.

That there was a reverent regard for the way things had always been done was of course natural and not peculiar to the War Office alone. But there was a tendency that there should be no other way. Many senior officers, not only inside the War Office, but in the Commands, were slow to accept that a change was needed: a change in training, in equipment, in tactics—sweeping changes in fact. Hore-Belisha found these deeply-embedded prejudices difficult to shake, let alone eradicate. With the darkening clouds that overhung Europe, he was certain that there was not much time for a leisurely evolution. Energetic action would have to be taken. Irresolution would lead to disastrous consequences. His stand was accordingly firm. Behind the restiveness he displayed lay an unshakable determination to get things done.

General Deedes was, by virtue of his position as Military Secretary, in the slip-stream. He had already been made aware that Hore-Belisha would give no approval to the selections for the Higher Commands without adequate and convincing reasons and that the principal consideration for all key appointments should be the fitness of the officers selected to carry out their duties in time of war.

Deedes, like his predecessors, had for the most part acted as a mouthpiece for the Chief of the Imperial General Staff. That was the normal procedure. Hore-Belisha made his intention clear: " I am not going to be just a rubber stamp."

The pace was getting a bit too brisk. Deedes, in his fifty-ninth year and not in very good health, did not feel equal to the more energetic methods that were being introduced. He asked for leave to resign. This was granted.

The selection of his successor, Hore-Belisha found, was ruled by precedent. Should this be the overriding factor? Hore-Belisha studied the Army lists, asked for detailed reports on all the possible candidates, went to Aldershot and Camberley, and had talks with the senior officers. In forming his impressions he particularly took into account an officer's attitude towards the reform and reorganisation of the Army.

It was a meeting at a luncheon in London and a subsequent long interview at the War Office, that led to the choice of Major-General Lord Gort, as his Military Secretary. They had in fact met for the first time the previous winter. A collision on the ski-ing slopes at St. Moritz had resulted in a heavy fall for both of them and in some furious swearing. At the luncheon they laughed as they recalled it and the talk that followed led Hore-Belisha to feel that Gort was eager for the reform and modernisation of the Army. He felt that they would be able to co-operate in the task that lay ahead.

Gort was fifty-one, eight years older than Hore-Belisha. He had joined the Grenadier Guards in 1905, had served in France and Belgium during the First World War and had won the V.C. at Cambrai. He was Commandant of the Staff College at Camberley. After discussing the matter with Deverell, Hore-Belisha wrote to

Gort on the 17th August, offering him the appointment of Military Secretary " with C.I.G.S.'s complete approval " and added : " I feel the desire to appoint one of the younger Major-Generals as an indication to the Army that we wish to encourage promotion at as early a stage as ability and efficiency justify."

Deverell was, in fact, opposed to the choice of Gort and lost no time in getting in touch with him : his arguments caused Gort to hesitate about accepting the offer. On the 26th August Deverell wrote a long letter to Hore-Belisha. While agreeing that Gort would do well as Military Secretary and that his appointment might certainly have the desired effect on the Army, he expressed strongly the view that it would not be helpful to Gort's future use in the Army and that the casting out of many senior officers in Gort's favour would cause considerable comment and would not be well received by many.

Hore-Belisha replied the following day: " The considerations which you mention were before us when we agreed that Gort was the man who best fulfilled the necessary qualifications for the post of M.S. . . ." The appointment, he added, must therefore stand.

" All our promotions and appointments," Hore-Belisha went on, " must be guided by the urgent sense that we are preparing for a war, not only by having the material, but the men ready. I realise that in the Pensions Scheme, as it exists, we may fall short of the Admiralty code. I took the matter up at once and I was assured it would be dealt with sympathetically and without much delay. As time presses, however, we must subject purely sentimental considerations to the overriding national and military interests."

Gort, interviewed again, accepted the appointment, which carried the local rank of Lieut.-General, and it was announced on the 23rd September. The Times described it " as another indication of the progressive policy instituted by Mr. Hore-Belisha" and "an earnest of his intention to carry out reforms in spheres wider than that of recruiting."

At the end of September a Directorate of Public Relations was created at the War Office. The function of this new organisation which, it was announced, " would serve directly under the Secretary of State, was to promote a closer mutual understanding between the

Army and all sections of the civil life of the country." It was essential, Hore-Belisha said, "because the Army has had bad publicity since the days of Cromwell." Brigadier Alan Dawnay, Army Instructor at the Imperial Defence College and a close friend of Lawrence of Arabia, was appointed Director with the local rank of Major-General.

Fundamental differences in outlook between some of the older members of the Army Council and the Secretary of State, who was their junior by a generation, became increasingly apparent.

His revolutionary suggestion that there should be a greater promotion of officers from the ranks was received with disfavour. The scheme he was turning over in his mind was to send promising young men, after a year's service in the ranks, to Sandhurst or Woolwich on an Officer Cadet course. It would not only be a stimulus to recruiting, but it should attract more men from the middle-classes to adopt the Army as their profession. Even more important was the consideration that officers, having served in the ranks, would have a far better understanding of the men's point of view.

Earlier, in July, a serious clash had occurred with the C.I.G.S. over the question of reducing the large garrisons that were being maintained in India. This vital matter had been under review for some months. Cardwell, as Secretary of State for War nearly three-quarters of a century before, had established the linked battalion system, one battalion being kept overseas with its replacement at home. Since the Indian Mutiny lines of communication had altered greatly. With the opening of the Suez Canal in 1869 troops, instead of having to go round the Cape, could make the journey to India in less than half the time. In India improved railway communications, in addition to motor transport, had increased the mobility of the troops, enabling reinforcements to reach any scene of trouble with far greater speed. On the other side of the picture the Army's commitments all over the world had been widely extended. Garrisons had to be maintained in Egypt, the Sudan, Somaliland and Kenya, as well as in Palestine, Iraq and Aden. Provision had also to be made for the defence of Malta, Gibraltar, the West Indies and other Atlantic stations; Mauritius, Ceylon, Singapore and Malaya, Hong Kong and ports in China. These far-

THE PRIVATE PAPERS OF HORE-BELISHA

flung responsibilities called for an urgent redistribution of our forces, and India was the main source on which we could draw. The C.I.G.S. had served for twelve years in India. His view, based on his own personal experience, was that there could be no radical reduction of the forces there.

"Would you," Hore-Belisha asked him, " prepare a note for me giving a scientific analysis of the position in India as it is now ? "

Some days later, Hore-Belisha's diary notes, the Field-Marshal sent him " an old paper in favour of maintaining the present size of the garrison in India. It was accompanied by a note saying that he could not better what was set out there."

A further discussion took place at a meeting of the Army Council. Hore-Belisha records : " They assembled with their minds already made up, instead of examining the problem *de novo* scientifically."

The Prime Minister in a letter to Hore-Belisha on the 29th October, wrote :

"I have been reading *Europe in Arms* by Liddell Hart. If you have not already done so, you might find it interesting to glance at this, especially the chapter on the ' Role of the British Army.' "

Hore-Belisha replied two days later :

" I immediately read the ' Role of the British Army ' in L. H.'s book. I am impressed by his general theories."

Liddell Hart, " the theoretical originator of mechanized warfare,"[1] had been called in by Inskip earlier in the year for advice on defence questions. He had also often been consulted by Duff Cooper, who had in fact introduced him to Hore-Belisha. It was not without precedent for a Minister to draw on expert knowledge outside his department. Asquith, while Prime Minister, often consulted J. A. Spender, the Editor of the *Westminster Gazette*. Two unofficial military advisers of the previous generation were George Clarke, later Lord Sydenham, and Lord Esher, both of whom exercised a considerable influence at the War Office. Winston Churchill relied on Professor Lindemann[2] for guidance on scientific aspects of modern war and also on Sir Desmond Morton, who was one of his

[1] As General Guderian described him in the German encyclopedia " Der Grosse Brockhaus."
[2] Later Lord Cherwell.

54

most intimate advisers throughout the Second World War. These outside experts helped to shed additional light on vexed questions and enabled a Minister to examine a problem with greater objectivity. Liddell Hart had made a comprehensive study of military history and was well-equipped, Hore-Belisha felt, to provide him with reports that might help forward some of his schemes. Already they had gone into the advantages of setting up a directorate for Operational Research which would make a systematic analysis of past experiences as a guide in framing doctrine and policy, examine what was being done abroad, and advance suggestions suited to our own military needs—a tactical section to work in close co-operation with the scientific branch. This was something quite new and was set up by Hore-Belisha.

After Hore-Belisha's first conversation on new appointments with Deedes, he invited Liddell Hart to make an analysis of the Army list " such as you made for Duff Cooper, but bring it up to date and draw up a list of outstanding officers right down to junior ranks." He had noticed that the names of tank officers did not appear on the official list of recommendations for promotion.

" He wanted to go further than some of the suggestions I made," says Liddell Hart.[1] " For example, to my suggestion that sixty might be made the retiring age, he said : ' Why not fifty-five—save in exceptional cases ? ' I had proposed that the new appointments might be made for three years instead of four. ' Why not two years, renewable—or better still, no definite term ? ' "

The advice of one regarded as an outside authority was not liked by the War Office. An illustration of this attitude, described by Liddell Hart, occurred during the Army exercises in East Anglia. On the 9th September Hore-Belisha went to Cambridge, accompanied by the C.I.G.S., to see the exercises. Liddell Hart, who was present as military correspondent of *The Times*, recalls that he found it impossible to have a word with Hore-Belisha without somebody coming up and interrupting. " It was quite palpable that he was being watched. Deverell naturally knew that Hore-Belisha had asked me for independent reports and every time he saw me, Deverell would murmur rather balefully : ' There must be no radical changes.' Once he came up to me and half-jokingly pulled out some

---

[1] In a statement to the author; also in Liddell Hart's records.

papers from under my arm, imagining they were some of the reports
I had drawn up for the Secretary of State. But when he took them
from their envelope he found they were merely the Aldershot
Command exercise papers."

The French Military Attaché in London, General Lelong, who
was present at the Army exercises, in a talk with Hore-Belisha, asked
if he could make some comments.

He criticised in a most candid way our methods of training—
" too many tattoos, rather like the Russian ballet." He said there
was an excessive amount of drill in the British Army and not
enough practice for war. . . . The French keep the men interested
by various exercises and rehearsals for actual contingencies they
may have to meet. He asked me to compare their manœuvres
with ours and see for myself.

Accordingly on the 13th September, immediately after the
exercises in East Anglia, Hore-Belisha flew to Deauville to see the
French Army manœuvres in Normandy. He was accompanied
by the C.I.G.S. A car took them to Alençon where General
Gamelin, Vice-President of the Conseil Supérieur de la Guerre,
met them.

General Hering, Military Governor of Strasbourg, directed the
operations. Military missions had come from Poland, Czechoslovakia, Switzerland and Norway. The Russian General Staff had
asked to be allowed to send a mission too, but their request was
refused.

Daladier, the French Secretary for War, attended personally on
Hore-Belisha, while Gamelin was with the C.I.G.S. The weather
throughout was deplorable. Morale, nevertheless, was high. The
troops engaged numbered 45,000, about forty per cent of them
reservists ; there were also 6,000 horses and 3,500 motor vehicles.
In all little new material was to be seen. There was one battalion
of the new infantry light tank (R. 35), a large number of motor
cycles adapted for the carriage of light and heavy machine-guns,
some *chenillettes* for drawing anti-tank guns or for conveying mortars
and machine-guns. There was one mechanical vehicle for the use
of artillery observation officers so that they could follow up an attack
and remain throughout in touch by wireless with their headquarters

56

or batteries. This vehicle was on a tracked chassis, was lightly armoured and carried a crew of six. With the divisional headquarters of the motorised division were lorries fitted as offices, together with a series of tents for more permanent quarters. Hore-Belisha paid a warm tribute to the French Army : " Being with M. Daladier," he wrote in his diary, " I was able to talk freely with soldiers, N.C.O.s and officers and was most impressed by their intelligence, endurance and patriotism. The French generals regard their profession as a business."

During the following week Hore-Belisha visited the fortifications of the Maginot Line in the Strasbourg area. He was the first British Secretary of State for War to inspect them. M. Maginot, whilst serving as a sergeant in the French Army in 1914, had been greatly impressed by the impregnability of the steel and concrete defences at Verdun, which withstood assault after assault by the German Army and artillery. When he was War Minister in 1930 work on the Maginot Line was begun.

Gamelin, writing after the war, stated :[1] " I have always thought that the system thus planned was well adapted to the end in view. France, resolutely peaceful, had to insure herself against an offensive launched by her powerful neighbour. She therefore needed a system which could be held permanently by a minimum of forces so as to cover her mobilisation and her concentration."

But, he added " the Line had, in my personal view, two serious defects. Built, more often than not, fairly far from the frontier on ' purely defensive ' plans, it did not guarantee the protection of the whole national territory, or even, at times, of regions important from the industrial point of view. . . . Moreover, important fortifications, built four or five kilometres apart, sometimes more, with crossed artillery fire, offered serious disadvantages. Costing a great deal— some of them as much as 200 million francs—they swallowed up credits which would have been better used in extending the front that could be effectively held. Again they took a long time to complete, some as long as five or six years. . . . Finally since they consisted of real underground towns, from which rose towers and turrets, and since, besides these, they possessed no other lookout

[1] *Servir*, by General Gamelin. Vol. I, section 4. Published in 1946. Vols. II and III in 1947.

posts than the casemates that flanked them, they had every appearance of ' blind monsters.' "

Nevertheless, Gamelin, as well as Weygand, would have preferred to see the Line extended and obtained credits from the Government in 1932 for part of the extension, but Pétain successfully opposed it. Three years later, when Gamelin became Vice-President of the Conseil Supérieur de la Guerre, he considered again an extension of the Line at least to the Scheldt, but finally abandoned the idea because of its great cost, the fear that war might break out before it was completed, and principally because he considered that the money available could be better spent on tanks rather than on permanent fortifications. " It was therefore decided," he wrote in *Servir*, " that the non-fortified parts of the front would be given a skeleton outline of field-of-battle defence, consisting of anti-tank obstacles, barbed wire entanglements, and a certain number of casemates or block-houses."

Paul Reynaud, Prime Minister when France fell in 1940, was a stern critic of leaving the Line unextended. " Of the whole front of 760 kilometres stretching from Switzerland to the North Sea, only 120 kilometres had been fortified. . . . As I said in the Chamber one day : ' Your frontier with Belgium is nothing but a sketch. There is no permanent fortification there.' But that Franco-Belgian frontier is the classic road for invasions of France, and that for a very simple reason—it is the shortest and the flattest road—that of the ' Berlin-Paris Express.' "[1]

In February 1937, three months before Hore-Belisha went to the War Office, the French Chamber of Deputies had announced that, as part of a £181 million programme for speeding up armaments, the Maginot Line would be extended from the Alps to the Channel.[2] France's failure to accomplish this, as Hore-Belisha was to discover in his subsequent visits to the Maginot Line, for it ended many miles short of Givet, led to dramatic developments that affected his career.

In Hore-Belisha's notes on his visit to the Maginot Line in September 1937 he recorded :

[1] *Les Evénements Survenus en France de 1933 à 1945.* Vol. I.
[2] *Evening News*, 24th September 1937.

"I was informed that the Maginot Line only required 100,000 men to hold it, which left a large reserve for the French Field Army. When the French realise that we cannot commit ourselves to send an Expeditionary Force, they should be all the more induced to accelerate the extension of the Maginot Line to the sea."

CHAPTER VII

Army Council Changes

DURING HORE-BELISHA's absence in France, a War Office Exercise without troops had been held at Bedford, to test commanders, staffs and signals communications. Liddell Hart, describing it in *The Times*[1] as " a great continental war raging in the southern half of England," went on to explain that the reason for the unobtrusiveness of the war " was that it took the form of a skeleton exercise in which only the higher commanders and staffs and the signal communications with their personnel were actually present."

Although the new mobile division (later known as the First Armoured Division) had not been formed by September, its headquarters staff had by then been appointed and they were thus available for this exercise. Liddell Hart, as an expert witness, was very critical of the handling of this new division. In a letter to Hore-Belisha he wrote :

" The worst thing of all was the mishandling of the Mobile Division, brought up belatedly and thrust into a cul-de-sac which anyone ought to have foreseen from a study of the ground. It was certainly a striking confirmation of one's recent remarks, both to you and in *The Times*, on the need of giving command of such new-style formations to men who have had experience in mechanised movement, and the folly of entrusting them to those who have not. . . .

" And this has a bearing on a wider aspect of the War Office Exercise. The scheme of that Exercise shows unmistakably how the ruling minds in the W.O. are still running on 1914 tram lines.

[1] 22nd September 1937.

The Anglian force here represented was their idea of our future field force, and this is practically identical with the 1914 pattern except in its detailed equipment. The picture which they had in mind in framing the scheme was the use of our Army to force the Aachen Gap. It seems a somewhat fantastic conception, in view of the delay that must elapse at the earliest before our Army reaches the Continent. While I hardly imagine that they would actually contemplate such an operation if war broke out, there is significance in the fact that their thoughts run along such lines—and that they run the biggest Exercise the Army has had since the War along such lines, instead of basing it on a more probable kind of action."

Hore-Belisha, uneasy about Liddell Hart's comments, was determined that the right man should be chosen to command the new Division. He discussed the matter with the C.I.G.S. who recommended Major-General Blakiston-Houston, the commander of the Mobile Division in the War Office exercise. Hore-Belisha asked for his record and carefully scrutinised it. Blakiston-Houston was fifty-nine. He was Commandant of the Equitation School at Weedon and Inspector of Cavalry. This hardly seemed to Hore-Belisha the ideal appointment for the command of the Mobile Division. Surely there must be a number of younger officers, with actual experience of tanks and mechanised formations, who would be much more fitted.

Deverell felt that cavalry officers, now to be part of the new Mobile Division which was replacing the old Cavalry Division, could not be asked to serve under an officer brought in from the new mechanised branch. The view expressed by the C.I.G.S. was part of a controversy which had been raging since Hore-Belisha became Secretary of State for War—as to whether the Tank Brigade should be included in the Division or not.

Hore-Belisha insisted that the names of suitable officers with mechanised experience should be considered. Eventually a short list of three senior R.T.C. officers was brought him. One of these was P. C. S. Hobart. He was fifty-two, had served in the Royal Tank Corps since its formation in 1923, and had been in command of the first Tank Brigade since 1934. Deverell said that Hobart was well qualified for command of the division, but remarked that he was still only a brigadier, and he went on to assert that he would not be acceptable because of his divorce ten years before.

Appointments, Hore-Belisha had already decided, should not be made on the basis of "Buggins' turn." He indicated that the arguments Deverell had advanced were unacceptable. Eventually as a compromise an artilleryman, Major-General A. F. Brooke,[1] was selected to command the Mobile Division. He was a soldier of outstanding ability who was at the time Director of Military Training. Hore-Belisha insisted that, if Brooke was appointed, his successor as D.M.T. must be a Tank Corps officer, able to direct training with knowledge and experience of mechanised operations. The man in his mind was Hobart. He was unyielding when further doubts were expressed and Hobart accordingly replaced Brooke as Director of Military Training at the War Office.

By far the most serious of his clashes with the Army Council was over anti-aircraft defence. Although a vital part of the Army's modern role, it had but lately been introduced as an added responsibility of the War Office and appeared to the older generation of soldiers to be outside the soldier's accustomed sphere. Early in 1935 only two Territorial air defence brigades were available for the defence of Great Britain, with a total of barely one hundred guns, not all of which were in serviceable condition. Later that year one of the fourteen Territorial Infantry divisions was formed into the 1st Anti-Aircraft Division for the defence of London and the South of England, but it was not until a year later, at the end of 1936, that the 2nd Anti-Aircraft Division was formed for the defence of the North and the Midlands. The guns were all of the old 3-inch pattern, and when Hore-Belisha came to the War Office the 1st A.A. Division had no more than sixty of these guns. The new and greatly improved 3.7 inch gun was not yet in production.

Hore-Belisha, after studying carefully a paper prepared by Liddell Hart earlier in the year for Sir Thomas Inskip, the Minister for the Co-ordination of Defence, accepted his recommendation that the two A.A. divisions should be doubled to four and that they should have a total of at least twelve hundred guns. That was the minimum

[1] Later Viscount Alanbrooke.

need. But the C.I.G.S. and others regarded this and Hore-Belisha's insistence on the mechanisation of the Army as too revolutionary. As it was impossible to get more money out of the Treasury it meant diverting money from the Army's normal and established needs for developments that might be ideal but were far too costly to be supported on that extensive scale. Thus the "minimum" scheme became the " Ideal " scheme. Weeks passed without much being achieved. The conflict over this was so intense that Hore-Belisha realised changes would have to be made in the Army Council. Yet he was not unmindful, as his notes show, of the genuine distress his new plans were causing to those schooled in time-honoured traditions and practices. But reforms there had to be, for subservience to outworn ideas was having a paralysing effect.

The Army Council exercises control over the entire British Army.[1] Head of the Council is the Secretary of State for War, who as its President is responsible to the Sovereign and Parliament. At that time there were two other ministers,[2] the Parliamentary Under-Secretary of State for War, Lord Strathcona, and the Financial Secretary to the War Office, Sir Victor Warrender, both of whom had been there for some years. The only other civilian member is the Permanent Under-Secretary. All the remaining members are military. At the time of Hore-Belisha's appointment these numbered four : the Chief of the Imperial General Staff (Field-Marshal Sir Cyril Deverell), the Adjutant-General (Lieut.-General Sir Harry Knox), the Quartermaster-General (Lieut.-General Sir Reginald May) and the Master-General of the Ordnance (Lieut.-General Sir Hugh Elles). Hore-Belisha added the Director-General of the Territorial Army (Lieut.-General Sir Walter Kirke). He also arranged for Major-General Sir John Brown, Deputy Director-General of the Territorial Army, to attend the meetings. A standing committee was set up, responsible for the conduct of all matters of day to day Army administration and for advising the Secretary of State on them. The C.I.G.S. was thereby relieved from detailed work in order that he might be free to advise the Secretary of State on broad questions of high policy.

[1] British troops serving in India came under the control of the Indian Government.
[2] After the war these two offices were merged.

THE PRIVATE PAPERS OF HORE-BELISHA

It had not been customary for the Army Council to meet regularly, but Hore-Belisha instituted weekly meetings. This was not regarded with approval.

Major-General Sir John Brown has recorded :[1]

" I was never a full member of the Army Council, but, being present, I was able to express my views on any matters that arose when I considered they might be of value. These Army Council meetings were held each week and all items that were settled were noted down and items that had to be settled were also noted down, with the name of the officer who was to deal with the problem, such as the C.I.G.S., the A.G., etc. The following week those items not settled were first brought forward and the officer designated to deal with them was asked what the situation was."

One day, the record adds, " the A.G. of the time (General Knox) came up to me and said, ' These Army Council meetings are all nonsense. Before Hore-Belisha came to the War Office they occasionally had them. If two members of the Army Council initialled a resolution it was inserted in the minutes without further questions.' . . . It did seem to me that it was part of the attitude of the War Office that everything that could be should be kept away from the Secretary of State."

In 1927 the responsibility for the development of mechanised transport had been transferred from the Quartermaster-General's department to that of the Master-General of the Ordnance. " But it was a long time," Liddell Hart records,[2] " before the production of new forms of mechanised transport fulfilled its pre-1927 promise. . . . Instead of progress quickening when the rearmament programme was launched early in 1935, the first years were a more stagnant period of mechanical development than those preceding it, when disarmament was the dominant idea." It was Hore-Belisha's task to remedy this as speedily as possible. The Army was critically short of military equipment of all kinds, particularly of tanks. Blueprints would be drawn up for each new and improved type of tank as it was evolved, but the order to go ahead would be withheld in the

[1] In a memorandum on his association with Hore-Belisha at the War Office.
[2] In *The Defence of Britain* p. 340.

hope that to-morrow might bring a still better type, possibly the " ideal "[1] type. He records in his diary:

In the past the Army had time, but very little money. Now a little more money is available, but there is no time. Events won't wait until a long term programme is complete. We must have a more practical attitude and be content to go into production with a machine that will meet reasonably probable conditions. The programme should be made adaptable to the possibility of an emergency arising prematurely.

A few weeks later, following a series of talks Hore-Belisha had with Lord Weir, the eminent engineer who had been Secretary of State for the Royal Air Force in the First World War and was now adviser on air rearmament, the M.G.O.'s department was merged with that of the Director-General of Munitions Production.

To three of the Home Commands new G.O.C.-in-C.'s had been appointed in the months preceding Hore-Belisha's arrival at the War Office. Later he was to add Major-General A. P. Wavell,[2] who was in command of the British forces in Palestine, and had flown home recently to interview him. Wavell was to become G.O.C.-in-C. Southern Command, to succeed Burnett-Stuart, who was eight years his senior. In the further promotions made towards the end of the year all but one of the officers appointed to Major-Generals' posts were picked out from the Colonels' list. This brought down the average age considerably—the youngest of all, the recently promoted Major-General H. R. L. G. Alexander,[3] became a divisional commander at the early age of forty-six.

[1] Rearmament programmes in peacetime tend to follow the same pattern. On 29th July 1953 *The Times* in its editorial " Delays in Defence " commented:
" The rearmament programme is proceeding with surprising slowness. . . . Five or six years ago the expert planners pointed privately to 1953 as the year by which the armed forces must be steeled to meet the shock of war. . . . The Army still anxiously awaits bulk deliveries of many of the new weapons which it badly needs. The automatic rifle has become a political jest. The heavy gun tank, which Mr. Head praised last March, has not been heard of since. . . ."
Six years later, on the 25th February 1959, in a debate in the House of Commons, the criticism was levelled against the Government that "despite a total defence expenditure of more than £11,000 millions since 1951, there continued to be grave inadequacies in the armament and equipment of Her Majesty's forces."
[2] Later Field-Marshal Earl Wavell.
[3] Later Field-Marshal Earl Alexander of Tunis.

On the 12th October the Prime Minister wrote to Hore-Belisha in his own hand :

" I have been turning over in my mind the suggestion[1] we discussed last night. For my confidential consideration do you think you could put down on a half sheet of notepaper the main reforms which you feel to be necessary, but which require a personality outside the service to cope with."

On the 1st November Hore-Belisha wrote to the Prime Minister :

" I am going to send you the minutes of the last Army Council meeting which Lord Weir attended, as I think they will really impress you. After I have got certain organisation questions here settled, which will take me still a little time, and the man-power question on the way, I hope to give you something coherent on the role of the Army.

" In reply to your last letter there are so many subjects to tackle, mainly psychological. I here put down the attached points and hope to speak to you about them :

" 1. The elimination of the 1914-18 mentality, which consists in regarding the whole role for which the Army is being prepared as a repetition of its task in the last war.

2. The elimination of the attitude towards any new development, such as mechanisation and Anti-Aircraft defence, as taking away money needed for the new ' 1914-1918 ' Army.

3. The elimination of the India obsession, which refuses to allow objective examination of the proper disposition and organisation of our Imperial Forces, and assumes that the India commitment is fixed for all time on unchanging traditions and that it must govern the pace and capacity of development of the rest of the Army.

4. The elimination of the sentimentality which regards appointments and promotions as governed by the comradely principle of ' Buggins' Turn.'

5. The elimination of the insuperable reluctance to take a

---

[1] That Lord Weir should attend Army Council meetings and make his independent observations.

decision on any subject (e.g. the extended use of the man-power of the Empire or the refusal to accept recruits with dentures) and the incurable tradition of writing minutes which can subsequently be used as protective cover.

6. The elimination of the inclination to seek such perfection in material that no ' go ahead ' order can be given on any existing design.

7. The elimination of the complacent assumption that events will wait until a staged programme can be completed.

8. The vitalisation of a stagnant atmosphere."

On the 4th November Lord Weir wrote to Hore-Belisha :

" My dear H.B.—Let me be 100 per cent frank in regard to attendance at Army Council meetings. For over two years I have acted as Adviser to the Air Ministry, and, to-day, the calls in this direction are heavier than ever. At least three days a week I have to be available. Next, I have been a member of Defence Policy Requirements Committee since it was constituted twenty months ago, and I really do much more than attend the meetings. I try to help at any point on Defence as a whole, and this again means a considerable claim on my time. I have had to sacrifice practi-cally all my own affairs and for a very long period.

" At the War Office, you are faced with a wide field of essential reform, and if I attended your meetings, my nature is such that I would find myself definitely involved in much work arising out of the meetings. At the moment, for example, I have so much in front of me that, with all the goodwill in the world and my real desire to help you, I cannot conscientiously take on anything more. I do hope you will understand that when I say I cannot come, it is not because of any lack of desire to help, but because of sheer physical inability.

" Now, let me add this. You can and will succeed at the War Office in spite of the difficulties and the atmosphere, but you need willing and enthusiastic colleagues on your Council. You will run less risk in promoting carefully selected younger men than in attempting to carry on with the existing team.

" Next, you need someone to talk openly to and to help you

unofficially. Try and make Trenchard your unofficial adviser, not as a member of the Army Council, but in a measure use him as Swinton[1] uses me.

"Finally, although I cannot attend your meetings, come along here regularly and have a meal and perhaps I may be able to help you a little. Yours ever, WEIR.

Trenchard was also unfortunately not able to spare the time. Hore-Belisha saw the Prime Minister and stated that he was now left with no alternative but to replace Deverell and possibly also the Adjutant-General. There followed several crucial discussions spread over many days. Eventually on the 22nd November, Neville Chamberlain commented : " That means I have to choose between the Secretary of State and the C.I.G.S. There isn't much doubt which I prefer."

Hore-Belisha had interviewed a number of possible candidates for the office of C.I.G.S. First he saw Lieut.-General Sir John Dill, G.O.C.-in-C., Aldershot Command. He seemed suitable, but following a recent riding accident, he lacked, for the time being, the energy to undertake the very exacting work the appointment would involve. General Sir Edmund Ironside, G.O.C.-in-C. Eastern Command was another candidate, but, following the recent War Office Exercise at Bedford, when Ironside's performance was severely criticised by the Director (Deverell, the C.I.G.S.) in the presence of a large number of officers, his appointment would not have inspired confidence in the Army. Wavell was also considered, but Hore-Belisha felt he would be better in his new appointment of G.O.C-in-C. Southern Command. His choice thereafter fell on Gort.

23rd November 1937

Saw the Prime Minister. We continued discussion about the changes in the Army Council and senior personnel. In the afternoon I sent a letter to him by hand and a copy to Warren Fisher,[2] with whom I have been in touch for some time about the whole matter and who has been most helpful :

[1] Lord Swinton was Secretary of State for Air.
[2] Sir Warren Fisher, Permanent Under-Secretary at the Treasury, and head of the Civil Service.

" Further to our conversation to-day, I have reached the conclusion, which Lord Weir emphatically put in writing to me, that there is less risk in making a change in our senior personnel than in trying to inspire that personnel to the necessary action.

" The risk of changing the senior personnel is that there may be—although I do not fear this—some public questioning. The risk of not changing the senior personnel, is that the War Office will never be ready to meet its responsibilities.

" My view, after the fullest survey, including a visit to France, is that our Army should be organised to defend this country and the Empire, that to organise it with a military prepossession in favour of a Continental commitment is wrong. The C.I.G.S., although he may overtly accept this view, does not accept it in fact or in practice, and he has told me that he is unable to advise any modification in our organisation.

" Further, I have no doubt whatever that he has not the mental or personal equipment to keep pace with, still less to stimulate, modern developments. A cardinal feature of any readaptation of the Army is an impartial examination of whether India's share of our personnel is not disproportionate. Such an examination he is unwilling to undertake, having the *ex cathedra* view that what was good enough at the time of the Indian Mutiny is not suitable for reinvestigation to-day.

" He has opposed every one of my major appointments, having a greater regard for sentimentality than efficiency. For such reasons as these, and because the mental attitude which he represents and encourages has placed the War Office well behind the other Service Departments in purpose and in practice, I am prepared to take the consequences of inviting the C.I.G.S. and subsequently the Adjutant-General to make room for more alert, adaptable and resolute successors.

" Who should be the next C.I.G.S. ? I am satisfied that in these times the duties of the post should be divided, as was the case after the War. I propose for C.I.G.S. Gort, who is the most dynamic personality I have met in the Army, and who is bred in an independent school. He could devote most of his time to executive reorganisation of the Army.

" I would propose Major-General Sir Ronald Adam, now Commandant at the Staff College, as Deputy C.I.G.S., to concentrate on the strategic side. He has a good and objective mind. He strikes me as being of better metal than most of those who fall in the academic category.

" Dill is too conventional, and Wavell, though he has more brain than Gort, is, I fancy, not without calculation as to the effect of showing courage on his personal position.

" Jumping down the ladder to men in their early fifties to take on heavy responsibilities may cause head-shakings and heart-burnings.

" The trouble is that under recent régimes here promotion has been made a reward for past services rather than a rank given to discharge present tasks, with the result that we have accumulated a large number of Generals for whom there is not any employment.

" This policy I have altered so that promotions are only made to fill posts, but the fact that there are numbers of Generals on the list may add to the reluctance to take the promotion of junior Generals, like Gort and Adam, gracefully. Is it not better to endure criticism now rather than to have it later in a different kind and in a more serious form ?

" I would propose, if you agree, to speak to the King on this matter."

Two days later the Prime Minister replied :

" I have received your letter of the 23rd November and I agree with your view that it is necessary to make some changes in the personnel of the Army Council in the case of the C.I.G.S. and the Adjutant-General.

" I had some points to raise about the successor to the appointment of C.I.G.S. and consequential appointments, but in view of what you said to me this afternoon, I now agree with what you propose and that you should now approach the King in the matter."

Warren Fisher's reply was brief :

"Quite admirable, and because it is right and courageous, it can only *come right.*

"The blend of Gort as No. 1 and Adam as No. 2 is excellent.

"If there is at any time in any way anything you think I can do, you can count on me. Bless you, Warren."

On Tuesday morning, the 30th November, Hore-Belisha had an audience with the King, who gave his assent to the recommendations.

1st December 1937

I informed the Cabinet this morning of the proposed changes. Duff congratulated me on my courage. Malcolm MacDonald,[1] passed me a note across the table: "Superbly spoken and done." Hailsham[2] was the only one who was a bit frightened.

Hore-Belisha was now faced with the far from pleasant task of having to inform the C.I.G.S. and the Adjutant-General. The blow he had to administer would be a painful one, but it was not a task he could shirk. Should he see each of them personally? But the decision reached was final and not open to discussion or argument. He therefore decided to write to them. In drafting the letters he had the assistance of Sir Herbert Creedy, the Permanent Under-Secretary, and they were shown to the Prime Minister. Creedy and Hore-Belisha's two secretaries were the only ones in the War Office cognisant of these developments. The Secretary of State's visits to Sandhurst and Aldershot had to be cancelled, but the Press, despite their alertness, were quite unaware that such important changes were imminent.

During the afternoon of the 1st December the following letter was delivered to the C.I.G.S.:

"My dear Field-Marshal—You will not have been unaware that in various quarters doubts have been expressed whether the War Office was making as rapid progress in rearmament as the other Defence Departments, and this has been a source of concern to the Government in these anxious times when action brooks no delay.

"There may be faults in our organisation and some of these

[1] Secretary of State for the Dominions.
[2] The first Lord Hailsham, Lord Chancellor and former Secretary of State for War.

71

are in process of readjustment ; it may also be the case that there is a certain lack of harmonious co-operation on the part of those responsible for giving effect to declared policy.

" The Government have regretfully come to the conclusion that it would be in the national interest that the important office of C.I.G.S., now held by you, should be placed in the hands of a younger man, who would be more in accord with recent developments.

" Should you prefer to tender your resignation in order to facilitate the promotion of younger men, as is often done in the Navy, I should be pleased to cause an announcement to be made in these terms.

" I need not say how sorry I am personally that I should have to convey this decision to you, and I should like to take the opportunity of assuring you that the Government fully appreciate the value of the great services which you have rendered to the State during your long and distinguished career.

" If you should wish to speak to me about this letter, I should be happy to see you.—Yours sincerely, Leslie Hore-Belisha."

Deverell replied the following day :

" Dear Secretary of State—I have received your letter of December 1st and I note the decision contained therein.

" My conscience is clear as to my duty to the Army, and as to its rearmament. Time will show that your criticisms as far as I am concerned are as unjust as they are cruel.

" I am in agreement as to the desirability of younger men, and had you asked me to make way as a gesture of that policy, I should have done so without demur. I had in fact told my personal staff officer that when the above principle was promulgated to the Army I should myself set the example. I understood from you that a Committee was to be set up under Sir Warren Fisher to consider the whole question of retirement and pensions in the higher ranks of the services.

" My only anxiety regarding the method of announcement is that a course be taken in the best interests of the Army. Believing that it is in the best interests I, therefore, tender my resignation

72

of my appointment as C.I.G.S. to make way for a younger man."

Hore-Belisha replied at once :

" I am most glad to learn that you have put your resignation on the ground of making way for younger men. This, I feel, will be best for the Army and puts you in a most gracious light. It is particularly appropriate for, as you say, you are in agreement with the policy of having younger men.

" Believe me that I have never in my life had so unpleasant a duty to perform, and nothing but what I felt from the most impersonal motives, gave me the strength to do it. We cannot perhaps agree about this, but I would like to feel that in the discharge by both of what we conceive to be our public duty, there is no rancour or personal feeling.

" I would not like you to do anything which you might feel it difficult to do, but if ever you want to see me, I shall be glad. In any event, we shall meet in the natural course of things."

To this there was no reply.

He wrote in similar terms to the Adjutant-General, Sir Harry Knox, on the same afternoon, the 1st December. Knox, replying the following day, said :

" The Adjutant-General's main responsibility to meet a possible emergency is the provision of personnel. That the Army is below establishment is not due to any shortcoming of mine or of those under me.

" You informed me that the Government consider it to be in the national interest to appoint another officer Adjutant-General to the Forces, and I have the honour to acknowledge the receipt of this decision.

" My only anxiety regarding the method of announcement is that the course be taken which is in the best interests of the Army. If my resignation meets this condition I tender it accordingly.

" I would ask that my resignation take effect from the 20–1–38, at about which date I will have completed 42 years' service for pension.

" I thank you for the concluding paragraphs of your letter and

73

acknowledge with thanks the Government's appreciation of my long service."

His request with regard to the date of his resignation was readily agreed to, and Knox wrote and expressed his gratitude, adding : " I will certainly come and see you before I leave the W.O." Two months later, on a vacancy occurring for the Governorship of the Royal Hospital in Chelsea, Hore-Belisha offered it to Knox.

" I feel I must send you a line," Knox replied,[1] " to thank you for your kindness this morning. I have been feeling things more than I should, and the prospect of Chelsea has done much to cheer me up. I'll love the place and the work with those old men."

2nd December 1937
After lunch saw Dill and Ironside and explained the reasons for the changes. I told them that it was important to have in the Commands some of our fighting soldiers, ready if required to take command of troops in the field. Also saw Chetwode.[2]

Hore-Belisha kept in constant touch with Hardinge,[3] the King's private secretary, before the changes were publicly announced and informed him of the interviews he had had with the senior officers. In the course of his letter to Hardinge on the 2nd December he wrote :

" The G.O.C.s are pleased at the idea of being more closely associated with policy and at the consequent improvement in their influence and status."

On the same day Hardinge replied :

" His Majesty congratulates you on the courageous way in which you have tackled this very unpleasant business, and has every hope that you will now be able to go right ahead, with a younger team, and get the Army on to a sound footing."

Before the communiqué was sent to the Press Hore-Belisha saw

[1] 1st February 1938.
[2] Field-Marshal Sir Philip Chetwode, who had been Commander-in-Chief of the Army in India. Later Lord Chetwode.
[3] Later Lord Hardinge of Penshurst.

the heads of the newspapers personally, or talked to them on the telephone where a meeting was not possible. His diary entry for the 1st December states : " I asked Walter Layton,[1] Southwood[2] and Kemsley[3] to come to the War Office so that I could explain to them, and in confidence, the reasons for the impending changes. Spoke to Camrose[4] (he was unwell) on the telephone. Saw Harmsworth[5] at Warwick House on my way home. Spoke to Garvin[6] on the telephone at night. He expressed great approval in real Garvin manner. He made a historical survey of the great men of the past who, when young, had led armies and conquered worlds."

The next morning at a meeting of the Cabinet, Malcolm MacDonald passed the following note to Hore-Belisha : " Dear Stalin, Have you shot any more generals this morning ? " To which Hore-Belisha replied : " To shoot any more would exhaust the depleted stocks of ammunition."

After lunch he saw Christiansen, Editor of the *Daily Express*, and Herbert Sidebotham, Atticus of the *Sunday Times*.

The communiqué to the Press was sent out at 6 p.m.—

Lieut.-General Viscount Gort to be C.I.G.S.—his age was 51 as against Deverell's 63.

Major-General C. G. Liddell, who was 54, to succeed Knox, aged 64, as Adjutant-General.

Major-General Sir Ronald Adam, aged 52, who had succeeded Gort as Commandant of the Staff College at Camberley, to be Deputy C.I.G.S.

Major-General A. P. Wavell to be G.O.C.-in-C. Southern Command.

Major-General R. H. Haining to succeed Wavell as G.O.C., the British Forces in Palestine and Trans-Jordan.

Engineer Vice-Admiral Sir Harold A. Brown, Director-General of Munitions Production, to take over the duties of the Master-General of the Ordnance from Lieut.-General Sir Hugh Elles, " who is relinquishing his present post to facilitate a reorganisation under

[1] Later Lord Layton (*News Chronicle*).
[2] The late Viscount Southwood (Odhams and *Daily Herald*).
[3] Viscount Kemsley (*Sunday Times* and at that time also the *Daily Sketch*).
[4] The first Viscount Camrose (*Daily Telegraph*).
[5] Esmond Harmsworth, later Viscount Rothermere (*Daily Mail*, the *Evening News*, and the *Sunday Dispatch*).
[6] J. L. Garvin (*Observer*).

which the two departments are to be merged." Brown was to retain the title of Director-General of Munitions Production.

Lieut.-General M. C. Taylor to be Deputy Master-General of the Ordnance to assist Brown.

The diary adds :

> Went home about 8 p.m. but returned to the House of Commons at urgent request of Lobby journalists re Army changes.
> *3rd December 1937*
> Changes announced in the Press. Went over far better than we anticipated.

NEW BROOM AT THE WAR OFFICE

Evening Standard, 8 December 1937

The newspapers featured the changes under heavy headlines— " Purge," " Sweeping Changes in Army Control," " New Broom at the War Office." The editorials welcomed the appointment of younger men. Hore-Belisha's " courage " was the keynote of them all.

The Times: " They refute the assumption that in the dictatorships alone there are the vision and courage to give the rising generation its chance." Referring to Gort's appointment it added : " The question, which must always remain in such a case, is whether his proved courage and popularity, which would recommend his promotion even if it were a mere piece of window-dressing, are reinforced by the intellectual grasp required in the great position which he is to fill."

The Daily Telegraph: " Such a transformation in the Army Council is without precedent since it was constituted in its present form. It signifies, of course, that the Minister for War and many of his leading military advisers have found themselves in serious disagreement on important matters of policy relating to the organisation of the Army Council."

The Manchester Guardian praised Hore-Belisha's courage in making such a clean sweep.

The News Chronicle: " It is not too much to say that Mr. Hore-Belisha has taken his political life in his hands. But the country at large will applaud Mr. Hore-Belisha's courage."

On the 3rd December Hore-Belisha wrote to the Prime Minister :

" Now that the cold plunge is over, may I thank you deeply for the support and succour you gave me when I am sure most other men would have quailed. Your confidence has been justified in the sense that the changes have been received much better than anyone could have expected. I send you a copy of a letter I have received from the Palace, as it may interest you.

" I took a lot of trouble seeing senior officers. Dill was most encouraging. Chetwode was surprisingly approving. What the senior officers like is the idea of being more closely associated with the War Office. They feel that an added status is given to the Commands. It was never the idea that the War Office should live in the impressive seclusion in which it has enveloped itself. I want fighting Generals to be more anxious to be outside than in.

" I hope that the Treasury and T. Inskip will realise, as you do, that it is another piece of bad luck for the War Office that the review of expenditure should be taking place at a time when it has been impossible to lay our plans properly. I hope that the conclusion of that review will not close the opportunity."

77

A P.S. added : " The kindest thing that has been said to me this morning was by Garvin. ' Such action would have delighted Joe Chamberlain's heart.' "

In a personal letter to Geoffrey Dawson, the Editor of *The Times*, he wrote :

" I am particularly grateful that *The Times* in its splendid leader dealt so courteously and kindly with Sir Cyril Deverell. I did not want to leave any sting. It was hard to do this, Heaven knows, but there was no other course in the general interest."

To this Dawson replied :

" Thank you so much for your note. It is particularly consoling to me because in one respect the leader, through haste in revision, did not say quite what I intended. I was determined to give full credit to the retiring C.I.G.S.; but I was afraid, when I came to read it this morning, that one sentence may have seemed to be a reflection on his successor ! What I *meant* to say was that gallantry and popularity are not the only qualities required in this high position, and that there must always remain a doubt about a youngish man promoted to it until he has proved himself.

" I have no doubt at all that he will do this, and I should like to congratulate you on your courage in making these wholesale changes. I know very well how difficult that sort of action is."

Lord Trenchard wrote on the 14th December 1937 :

" I hope things are going well with you. I have done my best privately to support what you are doing and when I went down to inspect my Regiment at Aldershot the other day, I took the opportunity of saying a good many things."

He followed this up a few weeks later with a further letter :[1]

" It may be that the best service I can do you is to stand outside and help by ordinary talk with people I meet.

" I have written to Gort and wished him good luck and given him a few points that I think are worth considering.

" I hope when I come back in April to find all your great

[1] 13th January 1938.

78

schemes cut and dried and that you have made your speech on Army Estimates.

" All good luck. I am off to-morrow for three months in Rhodesia, Belgian Congo and West Africa."

Early in the week following the Army Council changes, Major-General Sir Fabian Ware, a distinguished educationist who had received rapid advancement in the Army during his years of service in the 1914 war, came at Hore-Belisha's request to discuss the work of the Imperial War Graves Commission, of which Ware was the permanent Vice-Chairman. In the course of the interview, Ware, who was in his 69th year, mentioned the Army Council changes.

7th December 1937
" Fabian Ware said he could speak from his own first-hand knowledge. ' Nothing will happen at once,' he said, ' but you will find in the months ahead attacks on you from various quarters. There will be whispering in drawing-rooms and words will be dropped in influential ears. They will get you out.'

" ' How long will it be before they do get me out ? ' I asked him.

" ' Eighteen months to two years,' was the reply.

" ' Well,' I said, ' I hope I shall be able to do a hell of a lot for the Army before they do get me out.' "

Greatly heartened by the overwhelming approval given to the changes, Hore-Belisha attached little importance to Fabian Ware's warning. But time was to show how right Ware was : both in the method of operation and the time it would involve, it proved to be a remarkable prophecy.

CHAPTER VIII

His London Setting

IN THE summer of 1936, when he was Minister of Transport, Hore-Belisha had bought a small four-storied Georgian type house in Stafford Place, near Buckingham Gate. It had been built a hundred years earlier close to the Palace for Lady Catherine Coke, one of the Ladies-in-Waiting to Queen Victoria. As she lived until she was over ninety, Hore-Belisha was only its third occupant.

In December 1934 he had appointed Sir Edwin Lutyens,[1] the architect of New Delhi and designer of the Cenotaph, as the sole consultant to Colonel Charles Bressey,[2] to draw up, within a three-years time limit, a complete plan of Greater London's highways,[3] based on an expert forecast of the growth of traffic in the next thirty years. The survey was to cover a circular area of 900 square miles with a radius of twenty-five miles from Charing Cross. While there had been numerous bodies of inquiry into London's major traffic problems, no such comprehensive and imaginative survey had been undertaken since Sir Christopher Wren's abortive design after the Great Fire, two hundred and sixty years before. A model of the Bressey-Lutyens plan was displayed in the Royal Academy of 1937 and the Report[4] was published the following year, by which time Hore-Belisha was Secretary of State for War. It envisaged a new capital, with ringed roads round it, arterial roads crossing it, tunnels under the parks, and the reconstruction of narrow streets. But the

---

[1] Elected President of the Royal Academy in 1938.
[2] Sir Charles Bressey, C.B., Chief Engineer of the Roads Department, Ministry of Transport, 1928-1935.
[3] Circular No. 409 (Roads), 1934.
[4] Highway Development Survey 1937 (Greater London), H.M. Stationery Office.

outbreak of war in 1939 stopped any action on the project and no more has since been heard of it.

One evening, while dining with Hore-Belisha at Stafford Place to discuss the Highway Development Survey, Lutyens greatly admired the house and expanded on the advantages of altering it. His suggestions delighted Hore-Belisha. During the succeeding weeks they used to meet after dinner when the day's work was over and both were completely relaxed. Lutyens elaborated his plans, while Hore-Belisha put forward his own ideas. During the Parliamentary recess, Lutyens began the alterations, and on his return to London, Hore-Belisha rented a furnished house a few minutes away, so that he would be able to keep an eye on the reconstruction. It was not until the end of November 1937 that his house was ready for him.

A complete transformation had been effected. As you entered through a highly polished black front door, with its brass dolphin knocker,[1] you found yourself in a square, white-walled hall, the cornice picked out in gold leaf. Two marble busts by Nollekins on pine plinths, one of Pope and the other of Sterne, faced you. Opposite, under the window, was a Sèvres copy of Houdon's Voltaire, leaning slightly forward in his chair and smiling cynically. Pale-blue jasper Wedgwood tablets, depicting the Muses, old gods and heroes, had been inlaid in the walls and in the cross-section of the white Sicilian marble mantelpiece. In recesses in the walls were Wedgwood urns of the same colour.

Over the stairs, beyond the hall, a bronze *bambino* in a niche raised its hand in blessing. Attractive arched doors, a feature of Lutyens' architecture, opened on to the pine-panelled dining-room. There was a circular white marble-topped Empire dining-table, under which fitted white leather chairs with pointed fronts which Lutyens had specially designed so that they could be pushed right in, their backs forming an elevated circular frame. Two long french windows, with a stone bas-relief of an old Madonna let into the

---

[1] This was added a little later. " As a souvenir of my visit to Malta I have brought back a dolphin door knocker, which I have had fitted on my London house. It seemed to me to make a very happy link, as the Dolphin is incorporated into the arms of Devonport and represents fair weather and peace."—Hore-Belisha in an interview on his visit to Malta, given to the Lobby Correspondent of the *Western Morning News*, 26th April 1938.

wall between them, opened on to a patio, sheltered by a vine-covered trellis. It was here on a summer's night that Hore-Belisha often used to sit and talk with one or two of his colleagues who had come back with him after the House had risen.

Steps led down from the patio to a narrow stone-paved garden, bordered by flowering shrubs. At the far end, with three steps leading up to it, was a delightfully designed feature that suggested the well-preserved ruins of an ancient Greek temple. In the middle, on a Corinthian column, stood a marble bust of Apollo. Behind was a profusion of greenery, with a vine and fig tree among it, because the prophet Micah had used them as symbols of peace.

On the first floor of the house was the library, with arched doors leading into the study. The walls of both library and study were lined with books, which ranged over history, literature, poetry, *belles-lettres*, religion and philosophy. Hore-Belisha rarely read a novel. One side of the study was given to the Classics, both Greek and Latin literature and ancient history. In the middle of one wall of the library, opposite the Adam mantelpiece, was a marble bust of Disraeli, flanked by his novels, his letters and speeches, and Money-penny's and Buckle's six volume *Life of Disraeli*. The lighting was for the most part concealed and set off sea-green jasper Wedgwood vases placed in niches among the bookshelves. A letter from Lutyens sent during the reconstruction, expressed his alarm at the electric lighting. "To floodlight your Nollekins' busts would destroy them. I am jealous for my Minister. Do let's meet at the house one morning and you can hear what I say." To this Hore-Belisha, unable to spare the time, replied in a few lines at the foot of the letter : " Your word is law. Please have the lighting done as you like."

Some felt that the decorations and the furnishing were a little ornate. But those who had seen him in his rooms at Oxford were conscious of the restraining influence of the years. There was not much of the old flamboyance. There were no harsh colours. The house expressed the informed taste and the personality of the man as he was in his early forties.

Here over dinner with small groups of Generals and officials from the War Office he continued the more urgent discussions and the planning. Often he would work into the early hours of the morning, for he was undisturbed and it was then, he used to say, that his mind worked best. He spared no one, least of all himself, as those who worked with him have acknowledged. He tusselled with each problem, seeing it now from one angle, then from another, striving after the perfect solution. The process was exhausting, at times even exasperating to those who sat up with him. Even after they had left he went on making notes, retiring too late to bed to be up at the normal hour. In consequence he was often still in his dressing-gown or had just emerged from his bath, if an unexpected early caller happened to come in.

It was an easy distance along Birdcage Walk to the War Office and to the House of Commons and generally he preferred to go on foot.

The uniformed doorman at the War Office—the Pepper Pot building as it was called because of the domes on the roof—pressed the bell-button three times as the Secretary of State arrived. This alerted the messengers and secretaries upstairs. An impressive double staircase of marble led to the first floor, where enormous mahogany doors, confronting the stairs, opened into the Secretary of State's room. It was the room Kitchener had used during the early years of the First World War and his silver inkstand still adorned the desk. The room was panelled and three long windows looked out on to the traffic of Whitehall below. Behind the desk, on the Adam mantelpiece, rescued from the old War Office in Pall Mall,[1] was a gilt clock, flanked by ornate electric lights. On the mantelpiece at the other end of the room, stood a marble bust of Wellington—old Nosey as he was familiarly called. A long sofa between two of the windows had been put in by Lloyd George when he was Secretary of State for War. With its end lowered it formed a bed : here Lloyd George used to recline at times in the afternoon or sat when a barber was brought in to cut his hair. Suspended from the ceiling, by the Secretary of State's desk, were rolls of maps, installed by Hore-Belisha, who by pulling a cord could lower one or other of them and see at a glance where contingents of the Army were stationed in all parts of the world. The smaller conferences were held in this room. There was a long table

[1] The Royal Automobile Club now stands on this site.

and a number of chairs, recently covered in dark red—enough accommodation for a dozen or more.

Hore-Belisha, however, never regarded his as a desk job, to be conducted by files of correspondence passed from one room to the next. He went out to see for himself. He was on the move, inspecting troops, visiting barracks and troopships, attending Army exercises, flying to Scotland, or even farther afield. For a great many hours each day, as is required of all Ministers, he was on the Front Bench in the House of Commons, answering questions, taking part in debates, trooping out for divisions. It had all to be fitted in somehow: Cabinet meetings, committees, talks with the Prime Minister, occasional visits to the King; and there was the recurrent interviewing of officers for appointment to the higher posts.

Lieut.-General Sir Douglas Brownrigg, who was appointed to succeed Gort as his Military Secretary that autumn, gives details of one such interview which took place in Scotland. He writes:[1] " I first met Mr. Hore-Belisha in October 1937 at the Gleneagles Hotel. He had become Secretary of State for War in May of that year, and had very rightly made a point of meeting as many senior officers in the Army as he could. General Sir Charles Grant had succeeded General Sir Archibald Cameron as the Commander-in-Chief in Scotland, and he had arranged a gathering of Commanding Officers and Adjutants of Territorial units with the object of pooling knowledge and discussing military matters in general. The new Secretary of State decided to attend this gathering. . . .

" As I was in the room in my hotel changing for dinner I received a message saying that the Secretary of State would be very glad if I would sit at his table at dinner. Others had received a similar message, and five of us sat down to eat with the Secretary of State. . . . Mr. Hore-Belisha made himself extremely pleasant and ordered champagne. During dinner the conversation ranged over many aspects of soldiering. The Secretary of State, like a benign kennel-man, kept throwing bones of contention on to the table and retrieving them well gnawed to examine the toothmarks made by the different dogs. . . .

[1] *Unexpected* by Lt.-Gen Sir Douglas Brownrigg, K.C.B., C.B., D.S.O. (Hutchinson 1942).

" After the fruit had arrived on the table Hore-Belisha looked at our glasses and suggested more wine, while a waiter stood by with an unopened bottle in his hand. We all protested that we had had quite enough already, and Hore-Belisha turned his attention once more to whatever we were talking about when the waiter had hopefully suggested that we were still thirsty. I was sitting opposite the sideboard, and I saw the waiter deliberately commence to remove the tinfoil from the rejected bottle. I could not bear this and interrupting our host's talk by a touch on his arm (for I was sitting next to him) I indicated this nefarious act. He stopped the waiter opening the bottle, but once more acted as the perfect host and pressed us to change our minds ; but still we all refused.

" As we got up from the table Hore-Belisha said to me, ' That was pretty quick of you,' or words to that effect ; and I replied that I knew the form of the waiters at Gleneagles or something equally futile. But in the light of after events I believe that this trivial incident had a decisive effect on my life. I can only think that it impressed Hore-Belisha, in search for new talent, that here was an officer who had at least two of the qualities desirable in a Military Secretary, observation and a regard for other people's interests ! "

Brownrigg received a telephone call two months later, saying that Hore-Belisha would like to see him. An appointment was made for four o'clock the next afternoon and, despite the fact that snow was lying thick on the ground and trains from Scotland had been delayed, he managed to get to the War Office in time.

" The first thing remarkable about my interview was that it took place punctually ! It was about the only time I remember an officer having had such good fortune. . . . He began to ask me questions on all sorts of military matters. I recognised some of the bones I had already gnawed at Gleneagles two months before ! . . . After some time he said, ' I believe you are shortly to go to Sandhurst as Commandant ? ' I replied in the affirmative.

" ' That is a Major-General's appointment, isn't it ? '

" Again I signed assent.

" ' But I should like you to be a Lieutenant-General ! ' (with a beaming smile).

"I clutched the arms of my chair and swallowed hurriedly.

"'I should like you to come as my Military Secretary. Will you?'"

Brownrigg accepted. "I staggered out; and in a dream returned to Scotland by the night train."

CHAPTER IX

Preparing his First Estimates

THE GOVERNMENT, towards the close of 1937, influenced by the shifting events in Europe, formulated its Imperial Defence Policy. The cornerstone was the maintenance of the security of the United Kingdom, whose chief assets were man-power, productive capacity, and financial stability.

Two principal objectives, deriving from this policy, were the safeguarding of Britain against invasion and the keeping open of our communications for the bringing in of food and raw materials. A third objective was the maintenance of forces for the defence of Britain's territories overseas. This was additional to the provision of the normal garrisons stationed abroad on Imperial police duties.

Lastly, and only after the other needs had been met, was assistance, under Treaty obligations, to Britain's allies, if their territories were attacked.

The role of the Army was therefore fixed. As the main objective was the protection of Britain and the new peril was from the air, Air Defence of Great Britain was given first priority, and Anti-Aircraft defence was accorded precedence over the Army's other obligations.

It was with this background that Hore-Belisha began early in 1938 to prepare his Memorandum for the Cabinet on "The Organisation of the Army and its Role in War."

7th January 1938

Warren Fisher came to see me about the Army Estimates. The War Office and the Treasury had been in touch for some time about them. John Simon before leaving for the South of France wrote to me, turning down our proposals. This knocked me out.

87

Warren said he wanted to be helpful, but instead of discussing the Estimates, we talked about religion, philosophy and life after death. I told him that I had stayed for a few days at Christmas with the nuns who had nursed my mother, at Esperance in Eastbourne. He gave me *Verba Christi* and I sent him Renan's *La Vie de Jésu*.

Latent, but never far below the surface and ready to emerge, at times quite unexpectedly, lay this—one would not call it piety so much as an interest in religion in its widest non-sectarian sense, an inquiring into the purpose of life, a seeking after the verities of our existence. Into this he was to probe more deeply later.

The new Army Council was an improvement on the old and Hore-Belisha noted in his diary in December, soon after the change was made, his delight that " Gort is getting down to things." But barely a month later, their speed in achievement, and even in decision, did not appear to Hore-Belisha to be as great as he had desired and expected. Gort's reforming zeal, which had led to his selection as C.I.G.S., seemed to be tempered by caution. From the very outset there were arguments. Liddell Hart, over a lunch, was told by Gort : " We must go slow for a time. We must not upset the people in the clubs." To which Liddell Hart replied : " With war imminent the people of the country won't forgive you if you are not ready when it comes."[1] It was not so much opposition to the Secretary of State's proposals, but delays in overcoming difficulties that caused Hore-Belisha so much exasperation. Liddell Hart states :[2] " It became more difficult for the personally dynamic War Minister to apply a spur or press a differing view as strongly as he had done previously—lest it might be felt as showing a lack of confidence in the new team that had just been installed. And the changes recently made could not be lightly repeated. The months that followed brought out the fact, in itself a suggestive lesson, that it is easier to deal with an open objection than with a profession of agreement in principle which covers an underlying reluctance to translate it into practice. While clear opposition presents an obstacle that can

[1] Liddell Hart's note following lunch on the 21st January 1938.
[2] *Defence of the West* by B. H. Liddell Hart, 1950.

be surmounted, hesitant acquiescence acts as a constant brake." In part the appointment of Gort had been a piece of window-dressing: he was a Viscount and a V.C. and it was felt these added assets would make him an impressive figure in the public eye. But in time Hore-Belisha began to realise that he was far better fitted for a high command in the field than at a desk in an office, especially an office amid the hurly-burly of Whitehall. Two years later, after his own resignation, Hore-Belisha said: " My difficulty was that, having sacked the Army Council once, I could not do it again."[1]

With regard to the role of the Army in War, Hore-Belisha spent much time with Gort and other senior officials, preparing his Memorandum for the Cabinet. There were many arguments. Hore-Belisha insisted on the Memorandum being revised again and again. It was re-drafted five times before he would accept it and even then he was not fully satisfied. Notes indicate what he had in mind. " The strategical concept. Defence against air attack at home. Coast Defence and the whole question of our commitments abroad —in Gibraltar and Malta, Egypt and Palestine, reinforcements for Singapore, a garrison for the Anglo-Iranian oilfields—are all of immense importance. Then there are Kenya and Ceylon, Hong Kong and Malaya, the Sudan." To augment the available troops, he proposed to raise more local recruits for the garrisons abroad, but they would have to be supplied with arms from home. India and Burma, which absorbed the largest part of the Regular Army overseas in peacetime, were one of the biggest problems. How were the drafts to be made up ?

The Memorandum, finally revised, was sent to the Cabinet in February.

10th February 1938

I sent a copy to the Prime Minister, Warren Fisher, Duff, Swinton, Inskip, Sam Hoare. At 9.30 p.m. I saw the Prime Minister in his room at the House and discussed it with him for two hours. I told him that if he gave me two years at the War Office I hoped to get something done. He replied that he hoped I would be there longer than that.[2]

[1] In a statement to the author in January 1940.
[2] As events show he was not. He was out of the War Office more than a month before the two years had elapsed.

Warren Fisher wrote on the 11th February : " I am unfamiliar with the technical side, but at least I can see there has been considerable thought in place of traditional shibboleth."

12th February 1938
Inskip said he thought it was ' a beautiful paper.' Others told me it was ' real, concrete and complete ;' ' constructive ' and ' a realistic contribution.'

Hore-Belisha based his Army Estimates speech on his " Role of the Army " paper and on his proposals for recruiting, after they had been accepted by the Cabinet. Four weeks of hard work for him and for all concerned at the War Office were put into the speech. At meetings of the Army Council, at conferences and talks with principal officials, at discussions with military experts, every detail was gone into. Lights at the War Office were often seen burning until a late hour.

In his letter to the Permanent Under-Secretary, Hore-Belisha wrote :

" Rarely could a Secretary of State have been assisted by a Department so thoroughly and efficiently . . . and at great personal strain. I should be glad if you could let all concerned, whether military or civil, know that I retain feelings of admiration and gratitude for all they did.

" I had hoped that having a policy now defined, we could all work at less pressure, but I see that events are developing in Europe which must cause us to increase our efforts to attain national safety. Whether this be so or not, I am pleased to be co-operating with all at the War Office. They have tolerated the foibles of a rather restless Secretary of State in the knowledge that he is one of a team and conscientiously trying to improve the status and importance of the Department in every way and to intensify its contribution to the national needs."

A pleasant interlude occurred during the preparation of his Estimates Speech when an invitation came from the Duke of

Connaught's Equerry, Captain FitzRoy Fyers, asking him to have tea with the Duke at Clarence House.

1st March 1938

The Duke is nearly ninety and the oldest Field-Marshal. I felt as if I were being received by a past generation. The Duke of Wellington was his god-father. To be in Clarence House, with its lovely furniture, was like being in a box of souvenirs. The Duke was quite clear in mind, but he coughed a good deal and had two nurses in attendance.

He recalled that Disraeli was a great gentleman, but Gladstone was ill-mannered and dictatorial. The Treasury, he said, always takes money away.

He remembered the trees being planted in the Mall and Birdcage Walk, and because of his interest in trees King Edward VII had said to him, " If everything else fails, I will make you my gardener."

CHAPTER X

First Army Estimates Speech

HORE-BELISHA introduced his first Army Estimates in the House of Commons on Thursday, the 10th March. He spoke to a full assembly. The Prime Minister sat beside him and other Ministers occupied the Front Bench. His notes of headings lay on the red despatch box on the table in front of him.

The total sum allocated to the Army was £108,500,000, a record figure, the highest since the end of the 1914-18 war. Over £43 million was to be spent on military stores, mainly ammunition, guns and tanks. This figure alone was larger than the whole of the Army Estimates in any year from 1926 to 1934 and was a measure of how much later the Army started on the essential processes of modernisation.

Hore-Belisha began with an enumeration of the various forces stationed in various parts of the world, which led him to the military strategy upon which the organisation of the Army was based.

Only two extensive reforms had been carried out in the British Army since the time of Waterloo. Cardwell, Secretary of State for War from 1868 to 1874, had devoted himself to the distribution of the forces and Haldane, who held the same office from 1906 to 1910, had mainly concerned himself with their organisation. The time had now come, Hore-Belisha said, to examine afresh these two problems, the correct redistribution and reorganisation of the forces.

After briefly explaining how the Cardwell system of double-battalion regiments, aimed at creating an adequate strategic reserve, and how the strategic reserve of the type perfected by Haldane, no longer met the present needs, he asked this question:

" Would a commander to-day, having our Regular Army under his single control, and surveying the Imperial field at large, dispose his forces in exactly their existing proportions ? Would he not, having fixed his garrisons so that each one of them, when its communications could be interrupted, should be maintained in peace at a strength adequate to discharge its defensive duties at the outbreak of war, aim at holding a strategic reserve in a zone whence it could be directed most rapidly to those alternative places where security is most likely to be threatened ? The location of such a reserve would not be fixed, but would be liable to change in the light of changing conditions and requirements."

But, he went on, change in the system was blocked by the rigidity of the fixed relation between the forces and equipment of troops in India and at home. This had hampered the necessary modernisation and adaptation of the Army as a whole. " As in certain contingencies armies can determine the fate of nations, it is vital that they, above all other institutions, should adapt themselves to changing times." India must no longer govern Army organisation and distribution. For this reason the Prime Minister was prepared to initiate discussions between the War Office and the India Office. Meanwhile, pending the outcome of the inter-departmental enquiry, the best attainable form of organisation for that part of the Army outside India would be achieved without delay.

He then proceeded to define the role of the Army in its order of priorities.

Home defence, which included defence against air attack, internal security and coast defence, was to come first. The menace of air attack " in a form unknown in 1914 is a primary consideration." Because home defence counted for so much, the Territorial Army would assume an importance it never had before. Mainly through the Territorial gunners and sappers would Britain be protected on the ground from air attack.

Second to Home Defence came the discharge of British commitments overseas, including the defence of ports on trade routes. Additional local forces would be raised to take over the duties of Regular Army units and thereby reduce the garrisons at present required.

Next the uses to which this strategic reserve could be applied—a reinforcement to internal security and the defence from external attack of territories for which Britain was responsible overseas.

Lastly, the co-operation in the defence of the territories of any allies Britain may have in case of war. His reference to an Expeditionary Force was guarded. Haldane's pattern, six infantry divisions on the continental model created out of the strategic reserve—which, owing to his foresight had been found suitable in the Great War—had remained virtually unaltered. " History sometimes repeats itself, but rarely in the same context—the assumptions of an unforgettable past are not always the surest guide to an unpredictable future." Other tendencies, developments and modifications had to be taken into account. The extent to which we could assist an ally in war must be related to the priorities he had outlined, " and it must be remembered that support on land is not the only support we can offer."

The new Army was to be made more flexible. A reorganisation was being carried out of the existing stereotyped divisions and battalions, whereby the reduction of personnel to a minimum would produce a greater number of divisions. " Smaller divisions are easier to manage, to move, to supply, and to transport—important considerations for a country which has to operate overseas." There would be two main types of divisions, the motorised division based on the light machine-gun, and the mechanised division, based on the tank. He enunciated the principle that machine power not man-power was in future to be the gauge of strength.

" The strength of the Navy is assessed in ships and not in personnel, that of the Air Force in squadrons and not in ground staff. Following this line of thought, the strength of the modern Army is based, not on the individual, but rather on fire units which combine fire-power and mobility. Why alone in the Army should heads be counted and fire-power and mobility discounted?"

In regard to supply, he said, the fulfilment of the Army's programme depended on the 30,000 workpeople employed in Royal Ordnance factories and on an equally large number in private industries. Scientific research should be kept up to the highest pitch of inventiveness and a Director of Scientific Research was to be appointed.

He briefly referred to the recent Army Council changes and the promotion of the closest possible identity of purpose between the War Office and the Commands, adding that the central purpose of all these reforms was " to abbreviate the hiatus between considera- tion and decision." There would be less spit and polish. The progressive elimination from the soldier's drill of all superfluous postures and from his kit of all superfluous gadgets requiring polish, was a further evidence of the intention to make the Army in all respects " the embodiment of business-like practice."

He then went on, " with some pleasure," to what he called " the more human side," adding that " no one can remain long in association with the Army without conceiving towards it the warmest and most admiring feelings." He enumerated a list of improvements to be made in the conditions of service for officers. Merit was to be the test of promotion. Higher allowances for officers were to be given—" to ease wherever it is open to us such strains as affect the more domestic aspects of Army life. The same motives must inspire us in our treatment of the men, not to attract recruits, but to do justice." There would be progressive increases in pay, special proficiency pay, increased allowance to a wife, and a children's allowance for soldiers on the marriage establishment. There would be better opportunities for promotion from the ranks, and twenty- eight days' furlough on full pay to those soldiers discharged on medical grounds—to remove " a hardship with which we have been impressed."

He would build on the firm foundations laid by his predecessor (Duff Cooper) in the modernisation and construction of barracks and for this purpose £800,000 more would be spent in the current year than in the previous one.

His survey at this stage covered a mixture of proposals, from an extra half-pint of milk a day to recruits and to those men who, in the opinion of the Medical officer, needed this extra "stimulant," to the appointment of Sir Isadore Salmon[1] as Honorary Catering Adviser to the Army. There would be an extra meal a day as in the Navy.

[1] M.P. for Harrow, Chairman and Managing Director of J. Lyons and Co.

The Territorial Army would also share in the reforms. He was awaiting the report of the Committee set up to inquire into the finances and administration of the Territorial Army, but, meanwhile, to enable the Associations to play their full part, additional grants would be made to them, amounting to about £110,000. Later, on the Report stage of the Estimates,[1] he announced that the new rates of family allowance granted to the Regular Army would be extended to Territorials attending camps. The reorganisation of the Army will continue, he said, " until we have for its size the best and happiest army in the world."

In his summing up, he appealed for the assistance of the public in representing the Army always and everywhere in its true light. " There is no other industry in ordinary life, so far as I am aware, which offers to a man guaranteed employment for six or seven years on end and which offers so many varieties, both of scene and of occupation, so many opportunities of comradeship." He then concluded :

> " It will be our ideal in the War Office so to conduct our business that in all important matters there will be speed in decision, flexibility in action, and in administration not only thoroughness, but that humanity which will help to give in peacetime to the soldier the security which we expect from him in the blunt reality of war."

The speech was punctuated by " Hear! Hear! s " from Members on both sides of the House and he sat down after sixty-four minutes to loud cheers. There was some clapping in the public galleries which was instantly stopped.

Mr. J. J. Lawson,[2] speaking for the Labour Opposition, and himself later a Secretary of State for War, said : " The House naturally expected colour and virility in the speech of the Right Honourable gentleman and it has not been disappointed. Whatever department he is in, he knocks things about a bit. He had not been long at the War Office when certain people left the War Office on the ground of age. . . . He certainly bombed old areas of activity in this country. . . . The war-time soldier would hardly recognise the

---

[1] House of Commons Debates, 22nd March 1938.
[2] Later Lord Lawson.

modern Army. Even the officer who left the Army two or three years ago would find himself lost in it to-day. The most remarkable change that has taken place is in regard to the relations of the officer to the men."

Sir Archibald Sinclair,[1] Leader of the Liberal Party, after congratulating the Secretary of State on a speech " of rare power and clarity," added that the key elements of our national and imperial security remain the sea and, increasingly, the air. "An Expeditionary Force for a limited operation like the Shanghai expedition of 1927, or an expedition which could be regarded as an extension of our naval power is one thing, but an Army on a continental scale is quite another, and to attempt to organise it would, in my view, be a disastrous blunder."

That was the note struck repeatedly. Even Leo Amery, speaking from the Conservative benches, shook his head gravely at the prospect of an Expeditionary Force. " The mere addition of a large mass of British troops and a still larger mass of transport, say, to the French Army, would be of infinitely less help to them than the direct and immediate service of the whole of our Air Force at the disposal of, and in co-operation with, theirs."

One of the later speakers, Rear-Admiral Beamish, a Conservative, reminded the House : " The Prime Minister has pledged his Government against conscription, and recently, he has pledged it again against compulsory service." In a year Hore-Belisha was to change that.

The speech was well received by the Press. *The Times:* " Thirty years have passed since the House of Commons listened to a scheme of reform comparable in its comprehensiveness with that which the Secretary of State for War unfolded yesterday. And in many respects it offered a greater relative advance in outlook than that achieved by Mr. Haldane's measures."

The *Daily Mail* referred to his human touch, which was supplied " in full measure. .   . The concessions to officers and men and opportunities for more rapid promotion will act as a tonic to all ranks."

A cartoon in the *Birmingham Mail* depicted Bairnsfather's Old Bill, dressed in the uniform of the old British Tommy, saying to a new

[1] Later Lord Thurso.

THE PRIVATE PAPERS OF HORE-BELISHA

recruit : " Luv a duck, son. They ain't 'arf makin' a fuss of you."

The *Manchester Guardian* described the speech as the most notable speech of its kind since Haldane's day.

Among the many letters he received was one from Duff Cooper, his predecessor : " Heartiest congratulations on your great triumph yesterday. I am desperately sorry to have missed it. Many thanks also for your generous references to my own work. Nobody knows so well as I how much you have accomplished and how great your difficulties have been. I know also that I couldn't have done it—and I am not modest." Oliver Stanley, who was to succeed Hore-Belisha, wrote : " A real masterpiece." Samuel Hoare[1] sent this note : " More important even than the speech is the policy behind it, and I am sure that your energy and persistence have got it into the right direction."

Lord Gort, who listened to the speech with other members of the Army Council in the Distinguished Strangers Gallery, sent him a note by messenger to the Front Bench. " May I congratulate you on a magnificent oration which was wonderfully delivered. I have just been down to tea and those I was with were full of enthusiasm, as indeed all of us were who have heard you."

[1] Later Viscount Templewood.

CHAPTER XI

The Annexation of Austria

CHAMBERLAIN PLAYED a strong personal role in the conduct of international affairs, which his predecessor, Baldwin, had been content to leave entirely to the Foreign Office.

It was Chamberlain's practice to refer Foreign Policy to an inner Committee of the Cabinet. The Defence Ministers were not included. The broad lines of policy taken by the Committee were, as a rule, then put before the full Cabinet. Sir Horace Wilson had been installed at No. 10 Downing Street as the Prime Minister's principal official adviser. The role of *éminence grise*, ascribed to him in the post-war years, may be as fanciful as it is picturesque, but there is no doubt that he exerted an unusual influence for a Civil Servant in the handling of both home and external affairs.

From the outset of his premiership Chamberlain's double purpose was to rearm and at the same time to improve relations between Britain and the two dictator countries. To separate Hitler and Mussolini seemed to him the practical way of lowering international tension and he nursed the idea of dealing directly with them, rather than through the old established machinery of the Foreign Office.

Finding attempts at a rapprochement with Germany were fruitless, he decided to concentrate on Italy. In July 1937 after talks with Count Grandi, Italian Ambassador in London, he sent a friendly letter to Mussolini, recalling the " Gentleman's Agreement of Goodwill "[1] between the two countries.

The Duce responded amicably. But the better feeling created was dissipated by developments in the autumn. The Spanish Civil War was extended to the Western Mediterranean, where Italian

---

[1] January 1937. An Anglo-Italian agreement concerning the Mediterranean.

submarine piracy broke out. At Geneva, Britain opposed the recognition *de jure* of Mussolini's conquest of Abyssinia. Chamberlain, however, remained undaunted in his resolve to come to terms with Italy.

Events favoured him early in 1938. On the 12th February the Austrian Chancellor, Dr. Schuschnigg, was summoned by Hitler to Berchtesgaden and bullied into accepting conditions which violated Austria's independence as a Sovereign State. Ciano at this stage informed our Ambassador, Lord Perth, that he had instructed Grandi to press for a start of conversations with the British Government in view of " possible future happenings."[1] Reports reached Chamberlain from Rome that the Duce wanted an agreement and the restoration of the old relationship between Britain and Italy. This, decided Chamberlain, was the opportunity to show Mussolini that he had other friends besides Germany. Failure to act in the past had, he reasoned, led to a tightening of the bonds between the two dictators and had resulted in the Rome-Berlin Axis[2] and the Anti-Comintern Pact.[3] His mind was made up to open conversations without any more delay.

When an urgent meeting of the Cabinet was called on Saturday, the 19th February, Hore-Belisha, like many of his colleagues, was unaware of the rift between the Prime Minister and the Foreign Secretary. Not only did Eden disagree with his leader about the timing of the conversations (he was in general agreement that there should be conversations, provided certain undertakings were fulfilled by Mussolini), but there were other differences in outlook between the Prime Minister and himself. Eden, for instance, had strongly objected to the rebuff, given in his absence by the Prime Minister, to President Roosevelt's direct proposal in the preceding month to set up by stages a World Conference in order to agree on the principles of international conduct.

Eden's intimation that he intended to resign shocked his colleagues. Meetings of the Cabinet were adjourned and readjourned throughout Sunday in an endeavour to bridge the differences and avert his resignation, but all efforts were in vain.

The other members of the Cabinet approved of the Prime

---

[1] *Life of Neville Chamberlain.*   [2] 25th October 1936.
[3] 23rd November 1936 between Germany, Italy and Japan.

Minister's initiative and Grandi was informed that the British Government was prepared to start conversations immediately in Rome. A proviso was made that no agreement would be operative before Italy withdrew her legionaries from Spain.

20th February 1938

Anthony's going was a painful moment. I understand his reluctance to embark on conversations in view of his previous experience, but if, as is not disputed, we must have conversations, then why not now? Events in Austria have left the world breathless. We are losing the confidence of all South European States. Austria has shown them that they cannot count on France and ourselves to act.

If it be true that Hitler and Mussolini have made some deal over Austria, we should be able to clarify this by holding conversations with Mussolini, because if he has done such a deal, then he could not reach agreement with us. Who will benefit if we refuse to hold conversations? Not the Central and South European States, but only Hitler? If we are criticised for going tiger hunting with the Italians, the Germans are tiger hunting with them now. If we let Hitler assume he has an open field and that we will stand aloof, the result may be incalculable.

A peaceful Mediterranean was vital to Britain. The menace of an unfriendly Italy to our garrisons in Egypt (whose frontier adjoined Italian Libya), in Palestine, in Malta and in Arabia was of the greatest concern to the War Office. As Hore-Belisha noted : " Strategically, with Sicily, Pantelleria, Tunis, all in Italian hands, the Central Mediterranean would virtually be closed to us." He felt it was of paramount importance to try to break the Rome-Berlin axis and establish better relations with Italy.

Some months before Hore-Belisha had had conversations with Count Grandi.

22nd July 1937

Grandi rang me up and said he would like to come round and have a talk with me. He came to lunch at Stafford Place and he unfolded to me the purpose of his visit. His points were :

1. He brought a message from Mussolini, who, holding the

Portfolio of War in Italy and wishing to cement the relations between our respective Armies, addressed himself to me as Secretary of State for War, and said he would be glad to meet me personally.

2. Italy feared that Britain, strengthening incessantly her defences in the Mediterranean, was preparing to make war on Italy. The movement of Italian troops in Libya was to counter our preparations. Mussolini, and most Italians, thought that we were suffering from paranoia (a strange coincidence of phrase!).

3. There was no other power in the Mediterranean but Italy against whom our fortifications could be directed. Correspondingly, there was no other power in the Mediterranean but Britain of whom Italy could entertain fear.

4. The considerations in (3) could result in an intensification of preparations. Alternatively, they could be used as a basis of agreement. Such agreement must have a military character and that was why he addressed himself to me. It should take the form of an understanding to disclose to one another the nature of our defences ; in other words, it would be the sanction for confidential relations between our respective military staffs.

5. If the proposal of such an agreement were rejected, it could only result in our spending some millions of pounds unnecessarily in the Mediterranean.

6. If such an agreement could be made, Italy would feel that she had a line of escape from the " Germanic menace," and a relationship of the character suggested would, from a military point of view, make for a re-establishment of the Stresa front.[1]

7. He recalled the Protocol of the Triple Alliance, which relieved Italy of the necessity of entering a war against us.

8. He made the above proposals as a result of personal correspondence with Mussolini.

I discussed the above with C.I.G.S., who states that it confirms the view of the General Staff that Italy is not so much directing her measures against us aggressively, but in genuine apprehen-

[1] The Stresa Conference in April 1935 made provision for Great Britain, France and Italy to consult together as to "the measures to be taken in the case of threats to the integrity and maintenance of Austria."

sion, particularly concerning her line of communications to Abyssinia.

The General Staff feel that there would be every advantage in exploring such a proposal, particularly if it could lead to a removal of Italy's apprehension and thus liberate us from the anxieties caused to us by Italy's behaviour in the Near East, on the one hand, and by the concentration in Libya, on the other.

Later I saw Eden, informed him of the visit and gave him a memorandum of my notes, together with the comments of the C.I.G.S. and the views of the General Staff.

Lord Halifax succeeded Eden as Foreign Secretary. Early in March 1938 Hitler descended on Austria, with the same speed and brutality that had marked his ultimatum to Dr. Schuschnigg at Berchtesgaden a few weeks before. Unexpectedly the Austrian Chancellor had announced that he was holding a Plebiscite. The Führer, seizing the opportunity for which he had been waiting, instantly gave the order for Nazi troops to march over the border. Military force from without and subversion within the State sealed Austria's doom. It was Hitler's first success in his plan to establish German hegemony over Central Europe.

The Prime Minister heard the news during a lunch to von Ribbentrop, who was taking his leave as German Ambassador in London. German tanks were at that moment actually entering Vienna. Instructions were immediately sent to Sir Nevile Henderson, our Ambassador in Berlin, to call on Hitler and make the strongest protest on behalf of the Government. The French acted similarly. France was in fact without a Government when Germany invaded Austria. Italy, the third party to the Stresa Agreement, showed by the aloof attitude of her Government that she considered it was none of her business to interfere.

Three events had come hard on the heels of each other. Eden resigned on the 20th February, Hore-Belisha's Estimates speech was delivered in the House on the 10th March. The next day, the 11th March, Austria was annexed.

Hore-Belisha wrote in his diary:

Saturday, 12th March 1938
The Cabinet was summoned for an emergency meeting at

11 a.m. I went early to the War Office. I asked for a copy of *Mein Kampf*, but as there was no copy in the library, a messenger brought me mine from Stafford Place. I marked the passages I had in mind and took *Mein Kampf* to the Cabinet. We sat for two hours and are to remain within call. I asked for the expansion and acceleration of the Air Force and Anti-Aircraft defences to be announced in the next forty-eight hours.

Sunday, 13th March 1938

Talked to the War Office about the Memorandum for to-morrow's Cabinet. A messenger brought me the draft setting out the position of A.A. defences as they would be in three months' time (1) without taking special measures, (2) giving acceleration to A.A. equipment, (3) with acceleration on an emergency basis.

Informed that only six 3.7-inch guns have been delivered. *But they are in production!*

Hillman[1] rang after dinner and told me that within half an hour 300 German aeroplanes had arrived in Austria, bringing with them the equivalent of three war battalions of infantry with full armament.

Notes for to-morrow's Cabinet:

What we are seeing now in Austria is *Mein Kampf* in action. This is what Hitler wrote in *Mein Kampf*:

" A Germany stretching from the mouth of the Ems to the Danube, from Memel to Trieste, from Metz to the Bug, is in a position to impose peace on Europe. . . . Because the whole world wants peace, the whole world must want this Germany. . . .

" If the Germans alone understand the truths of political morality, it is better for the world that Germany, that is to say the truth, should prevail. Every question of foreign policy can be considered only from this stand-point : will this or will it not be to the advantage of our people? All considerations of internal politics, of religion, of humanity, every other point of view . . . must be eliminated. . . ."

One has only to look at the map to see that the Czechoslovak flank can be turned at any moment and the Germans can walk in.

[1] William Hillman, representative in London of the Hearst Press of America.

We are up against new methods.

There will be grave risk if our only reply to Germany is a dilatory expansion.

France is our only ally and she might have to defend an additional frontier, Spain. Her Air Force is weak.

Our Air Defences are terribly behind hand and there are serious deficiencies in the Field Force.

Months have been spent in review after review, but *examination* does not produce a programme.

I hope there is no illusion among my colleagues as to the extent of our ability to defend ourselves from the Air.

Defence programmes ought to be examined not from the point of view of paper programmes but from productive capacity.

At present we are trying to carry out our programmes with peacetime methods in industry and with the old-established Trade Union practice against a Power which is carrying out an armament programme on a scale never before attempted in peacetime, without any interference. Germany's whole financial, social and industrial system is mobilised.

What is wanted is a great intensification of our efforts.

It is all very well to have a five-year programme, but shall we have five years for it ?

A day after the Cabinet meeting Hore-Belisha had a letter from Sir Maurice Hankey :[1]

" The extract you gave from Hitler at the Cabinet yesterday awakened a chord in my memory. When I got home I looked up my books and found an almost exact parallel to it in Machiavelli.

" While I was about it, I hit on two or three other quotations from Machiavelli, which suggest that both Hitler and Mussolini model themselves on that astute Florentine statesman.

" The last of the series shows what a usurper should do when he seizes his state. It is exactly what Mussolini and Hitler did when they came into power. It is also what I suspect Hitler is doing and going to do in Austria.

[1] Later Lord Hankey, Secretary to the Cabinet, 1919-1938.

" The last part of it[1] illustrates what a new ' Prince ' at the War Office recently did ! "

There were reports in the Press of disagreement with the Prime Minister's policy within the Cabinet. In a letter dated the 20th March, Chamberlain wrote to Hore-Belisha : " I was never troubled by the foolish stories of divisions in the Cabinet. I should trust my colleagues to tell me first if they disagreed with me and your loyalty has always been beyond suspicion."

On the 24th March the Prime Minister announced in the House of Commons that, in the light of the changing international situation, measures were to be taken to increase production and to accelerate the rearmament programme, particularly in regard to the Royal Air Force and the Anti-Aircraft defences. " The full and rapid equipment of the nation for self-defence must be the primary aim," he said. He was in touch with employers and Trade Union leaders in order to devise practical methods for meeting the accelerated rearmament plans by mutual arrangements with the minimum of Government interference. But he made it clear that there was to be no compulsion or dictation.

---

[1] " Benefits ought to be given little by little, so that the flavour of them may last longer." (From Machiavelli's *The Prince*, Chapter VIII. " The Way Princes should keep Faith.")

CHAPTER XII

Visit to Malta and Mussolini

ARRANGEMENTS HAD been made for Hore-Belisha to visit Malta during the Easter Parliamentary recess in order to inspect the defences and military establishments.

5th April 1938

Lunched with Grandi. I told him of my plan to visit Malta during the Easter recess and I expressed the hope that there would be no difficulties about landing facilities for the plane in Italy. I said I would like to see the Duce. I had already talked it over with the P.M. and Halifax and obtained their permission. Grandi expressed his pleasure and said he would get in touch with Rome at once.

7th April 1938

Message came through from Grandi that Mussolini would see me in Rome on my return journey from Malta.

8th April 1938

Before leaving for Aldershot to lunch with Dill,[1] word came through that Reuters had sent out a report that I was visiting Malta and that I was calling on Mussolini. Our newspapers took up Reuters' report and pressed for confirmation. They were informed that a statement would be issued when arrangements had been fixed and that there was no authority for any announcement about my visit to Mussolini. A telegram was sent to Bonham-Carter[2] explaining the position.

Dill told me at lunch that the King, who is paying a visit to

---

[1] Lt.-Gen. Sir John Dill, G.O.C.-in-C., Aldershot.
[2] Lt.-Gen. Sir Charles Bonham-Carter, Governor and G.O.C. Malta.

Aldershot next Thursday, expects me to be there, so I cancelled my engagement to attend the Annual Meeting of the Liberal-National Association in Devonport on the 11th.

9th April 1938

I was informed about the Treasury's reduction of the Army's allocation in the Fifth Defence Requirements programme. I wrote to the P.M.: " As you discussed this matter with me and as the attached statement is of such grave importance, I feel certain you would like to see a copy. I have despatched the original to the Treasury with a heavy heart, but you will see the *extent* of our desire to co-operate."

On 11th April, an official announcement was made that Hore-Belisha was leaving for Malta on 14th to inspect troops and military establishments and that he would be accompanied by Major Charles Haydon,[1] who had been recently appointed his Military Assistant. This was the first time since Haldane's day that a Secretary of State had had a soldier on his personal staff. For Hore-Belisha it was of immense advantage to have a soldier so adept, understanding and eager as a helper. All his life, as a child in his mother's home and since, he had relied on others to render various services. Haydon arrived early each morning, after going through various letters and cables, and gave a summary of their contents while Hore-Belisha was being shaved, for he was never able to shave himself. Often, while travelling, if there was no one else to do it, Haydon helped with the packing, for in the everyday essentials such as these, Hore-Belisha was unpractical.

12th April 1938

Before I left for Aldershot Grandi rang up. He seemed a little disturbed and asked me why it was being persistently denied at our end that I was seeing Mussolini. He admitted that the Italian Embassy was responsible for the leakage to the Press and he said my visit had created a good impression in Italy and that I would be the first British Minister to visit the Duce for three years.[2] I explained that the reason for our discretion was not to cause embarrassment on the eve of the signing of the Anglo-Italian

[1] Later Major-General J. C. Haydon.
[2] Since Eden's visit after the Stresa Conference in April 1935.

Agreement.[1] He urged that my visit should be officially announced.

The Foreign Office was informed of Grandi's views and it was forthwith given out that " It has been decided, on his return from Malta, Mr. Hore-Belisha will stay the night in Rome and, as a matter of courtesy, he will pay his respects to the head of the Italian Government." If pressed, enquirers were to be informed that " no political significance " was to be attached to the visit.

The Diary continues :

Had lunch at Aldershot. H.M. present ; accompanied him in inspection of barracks. Went to Windsor and had a walk with the King before dinner. The King came over to me after dinner and said : " Does the Prime Minister know of your call on the Duce ?" I said he did, and instinctively followed it up by adding that Halifax approved. I asked him if he personally had any objection and he said he thought it would be a good thing. Slept at Windsor.

Printed on the invitation to Windsor was the order : " Evening Dress. Please bring knee breeches and trousers, white waistcoats. Decorations. Riband and star and miniature medals." In the brief span of time that has since elapsed, many of the traditions, the grace and the colour associated with such an invitation have receded into the museum show-case.

13th April 1938
Returned to London at 11 a.m. In the evening opened the new Drill Hall of the 315th (Surrey) Anti-Aircraft Searchlight Co. T.A. at Croydon.

The building was described as the biggest and best equipped in Surrey. It included eight lecture rooms, three canteens and messing-rooms for all ranks, a special dark room to assist in training, fitted with miniature searchlight equipment, several workshops and ample accommodation for cars and lorries.

In his speech Hore-Belisha said :

" If men are proud to wear the uniform of the Territorial Army, let every woman, whose son or husband or companion has not

[1] Signed later that week on 16th April 1938.

yet the right to wear it, covet it and urge him to acquire the distinction . . ."

After playing darts in the men's mess, he returned to the House of Commons.

Had an appointment with the P.M. at 10.30 p.m. I noticed he was slightly ' cold ' when I went into his room and I connected his attitude with the King's remark last night about my call on Mussolini. He opened : " So you are off to-morrow." " Yes," I replied and then I told him quite casually the facts about the leakage and that Grandi was responsible. He obviously had not known anything about the leakage and apparently had not liked it.

We had a long and friendly talk and I outlined to him my proposals about the Army in India. The delegates had just arrived from India for discussions. I referred to some other measures I had had to take and said they were not calculated to add to my popularity in some quarters, but I thought the Army would be pleased and that my one aim was to get a move on and do the job I knew he wanted me to do.

He remarked that popularity was a very ephemeral thing and that he had noticed that a man who was popular one day or was courting popularity, found that in a short time he had lost what he thought he had and that popularity did not matter at all ; what mattered was to do the job.

14th April 1938

Left Hendon with Haydon for Malta. After an overnight stay at Marseilles we flew down the Italian coast to Pisa, where we landed. I inspected the guard of honour and we had lunch in the officers' mess of the Commandant of the Airport. The atmosphere was frigid at first. I was told that none of the officers present could speak English or French well enough to converse with me. To relieve the tension I asked them to sing Giovenezza. I conducted ! We drank healths and before we left the atmosphere was warm and friendly.

In the late afternoon we flew over the Bay of Naples. Vesuvius was in eruption so we circled round and saw the glare of the crater and red-hot cinders spouting out of it. At Naples greeted by Major Giuseppe Ferroni, Commandant of the airport.

Next morning the aeroplane took off for Malta and, after lunching at Catania, Hore-Belisha arrived at Hal Far aerodrome. A salute of guns from the citadel greeted him. After being welcomed by Brigadier G. C. Stubbs[1] and inspecting the guard of honour, mounted by the 1st Bt. Green Howards, he drove to San Antonio Palace, where he was the guest during his visit of Sir Charles and Lady Bonham-Carter. He could not have chosen a more pleasant time to be in Malta. The gardens of the old Palace were at their best. Red-flowered lucerne lined the sea cliffs and the rocky beaches, and the scent of wild narcissi was everywhere. Sun and sky were azure.

Five crowded days of engagements followed. Accompanied by the Governor, he toured the island to see the land defences and had many conferences with representatives of the three services. He visited dockyards and ordnance factories. He paid surprise visits to troops in barracks, often during their meal hours, in order to see the conditions in which they lived and the arrangements made for the men's welfare. Details caught his eye. In the married quarters he noticed that there were no rugs on the cement floors by the bedside, as in the married quarters at home; he was told that rugs were more precious than gold in the Army in Malta. He invited suggestions for improving barrack amenities.

The locally raised troops impressed him. " The material is first class," he said. " It is a pity we do not make more use of it."

At the dinner given by the Royal Malta Artillery, he had an opportunity of talking to Maltese officers. The table had been decorated with Belisha beacons.

Later a call was made on the Archbishop.

Two engagements which he particularly enjoyed were the Old Cliftonian Dinner, which he attended, accompanied by the Governor, an old Cliftonian like himself, and a special visit at the invitation of Admiral Sir Dudley Pound[2] to H.M.S. *Devonshire*. He was piped on board this Devonport ship, manned by some of his constituents, and the entire ship's company marched past him on the deck.

[1] Assistant-Adjutant and Quartermaster-General in charge of the administration in Malta.
[2] Commander-in-Chief Mediterranean.

In a message of farewell given at Hal Far airport when he left, he said :

"I am very glad to have come to Malta, not only because I represent the War Office, but because I have had the opportunity of showing the interest which all my colleagues in the Government have in this island. I carry away with me decided impressions, one of pride that Malta is associated with the British Empire, and another strong impression I shall retain is the character and spirit of the Maltese. They are a fine and alert people and I am glad they are playing their part in the defence of the Empire, and I feel they should be given facilities in that regard in increasing degree.

"The Royal Malta Artillery is a splendid unit. I was struck by the fact that many of the officers are sons and grandsons of former officers of the unit, showing a great tradition of service.

"I was filled with admiration by the King's Own Malta Regiment, which is up to strength, setting a fine example to many Territorial Battalions at home. . . .

"The defences of these islands[1] are being actively improved and, as the days pass, they will become more and more formidable by land, sea and air. They are intended for protection, not for aggression, and it is right that the Home Government should see that in an island of this importance nothing is neglected for the security of such loyal people."

His visit had its repercussions on the Army Estimates of the following year. In his speech in the House of Commons on the 8th March 1939, he announced an addition of 1000 Maltese gunners to the existing establishment of the Royal Malta Artillery. Nine hundred recruits presented themselves as soon as the offer was open. Rates of pay for Maltese units serving on the island, formerly about half those applicable to British other ranks, were increased to about two-thirds of British rates, with equivalent higher rates of educational and military proficiency pay. The qualifying period of service for pension was reduced from thirty to twenty-one years and the rates were uplifted. Officers' emoluments were improved. A depot was formed on the island for the training of recruits on lines adapted

[1] Malta and Gozo.

to the needs of Malta. Further schemes for the recruitment of Maltese artisans for service with the Royal Army Ordnance Corps were launched. " Malta is thus making a greater contribution than ever before to the defence of the Empire, of which she is so important and patriotic a part."[1]

Nearly two years after his visit, Lord Mountbatten wrote to him :[2]

" By a curious irony of Fate, I have just received a letter from Colonel Borg, of the Royal Malta Artillery, saying that all Maltese officers will honour your name for ever for righting a centuries' old grievance. It was written just before your resignation, otherwise I expect it would have contained some even stronger sentiments."

Hore-Belisha arrived in Rome on the afternoon of the 22nd April and stayed at the British Embassy.

23rd April 1938
  In the morning I was met by General Pariani, the Italian Under-Secretary for War, and took the salute in the vast courtyard of the barracks at a march past in *passo romano* (goose-step) of the Regiment of the 2nd Sardinian Grenadiers, who wore ceremonial uniform. The band played *God Save the King* for the first time since economic sanctions were imposed on Italy by the League of Nations in 1935.
  The officers were particularly smart and extremely tall and well made, and the men, though not of more than average British physique, were alert and efficiently trained. They had done about a year's service. There was a display of gymnastics, which was characterised by daring feats, such as jumping at the run out of windows into nets and somersaulting over tanks. The exercises were designed to cultivate nerve rather than strength.
  The officers were the instructors and evidently play the part which N.C.O.s discharge in England. While standing to attention the troops sang patriotic and regimental songs, including the solemn traditional Sardinian hymn.

---

[1] House of Commons Debates 8th March 1939.
[2] 30th January 1940.

There is a museum of regimental history of the three centuries of the brigade, displaying trophies of various wars and engagements, and a chapel in which a gramophone plays a regimental tune.

I thought that the barracks were below our standard.

At lunch, given by General Pariani, the guests included Marshal Graziani, Marshal di Bono and the Governor of Rome. Other engagements, including a cavalry display, followed. Haydon, aware that Hore-Belisha's appointment with Mussolini had been fixed precisely for four o'clock, underwent considerable strain and anxiety to ensure that the Secretary of State arrived punctually for it, for Hore-Belisha had no sense of time. Although he always wore a watch, he never looked at it. So at intervals Haydon kept knocking at his door to suggest that they should start. " There's plenty of time," Hore-Belisha said, " why do you keep pestering me ? " When they did set out, Hore-Belisha stopped the car at a jeweller's and spent some time looking at cigarette cases. He asked Haydon which he liked best of three he had been examining. In order to get him out of the place Haydon quickly said : " This one." Whereupon Hore-Belisha bought it and presented it to him. There was hardly any time left now. Haydon was sure they were going to be late. " At every traffic block I had a fresh heart attack," he says.[1] " When finally we did arrive at the Palazzo Venezia, from the balcony of which Mussolini used to make his speeches, Hore-Belisha, just as he was getting out of the car, pointed to a clock in the road. The time was precisely four o'clock. ' There you are, Haydon. All that fuss was quite unnecessary.' "

Count Ciano greeted Hore-Belisha as he alighted from his car and escorted him in the lift to the first floor.

Signor Mussolini received me promptly at 4 p.m. He was waiting at the door of his study as I entered with Ciano. He gave me a Fascist salute and I bowed. He led me to his desk at the opposite end of the room, where he offered me a chair facing him. He spoke fluently in French, to which language we adhered throughout. He was dressed in a double-breasted blue suit and looked older than I had anticipated. He did not impress me as

[1] In a statement to the author.

a dynamic personality. He is certainly not a Winston, who has all the qualities of a dictator, but shows no desire to be one. His eyes were tired and rather lifeless.

He began by expressing an apology that he had not been present at the review of the Sardinian Grenadiers in the morning. It had been his intention to welcome me there, but he had been prevented as there was a Council of Ministers. I complimented him on the appearance and efficiency of his soldiers.

He then passed to a criticism of our Army organisation and informed me that he was proceeding on opposite lines. In his view, battalions should have more men and not less, owing to the losses which they are liable to sustain from gunfire. He thought 1,000 was the correct number. He also thought that more and more artillery was required.

He asked whether our Army was being trained for the Continent. I answered that it was being trained for general purposes and explained that our problem was different from his. We had India and other parts of the world to consider and our units must be mobile and easily shipped. We had to have a flexible organisation.

He informed me that in his view the machine-gun must be the central weapon in all theatres of war and that defence was impregnable when infantry was liberally equipped with these weapons.

A criticism of our decision to create a Fleet Air Arm was then delivered. In his opinion the air should remain an independent organisation with its own schools. He would decide how many machines should be allotted from time to time to the two other Services and they would always, even when based on aircraft carriers, be manned by Air Force personnel. He said the Italians were born aviators and that the largest proportion of pilots came from his own district in the north.

He was interested in our Army Council changes and asked me how these had been received. He remarked that in France Joffre had had to superannuate 90 per cent of his generals after the war had broken out in 1914.

It was subsequently explained to me by Colonel Ruggieri, the Italian Military Attaché, that Mussolini's stressing of his point of view on military matters was an attempt at self-justification, the advice he had received from the Italian General Staff to reorganise on our lines of economy of man-power having been recently rejected by him.

I paid him a tribute on the reconstruction of Rome and particularly on the Foro Mussolini[1], which I had visited in the morning. This pleased him and he said, "I am the greatest destroyer that Rome has ever known," to which I made the rejoinder, "Yes, but the greatest builder"—an obvious retort, but one which gave him an even more obvious satisfaction.

I delivered to Mussolini an assurance of the personal satisfaction of the Prime Minister at the conclusion of the Anglo-Italian Agreement and stated that the restoration of Anglo-Italian friendship had always been the Prime Minister's objective. I added that Mr. Chamberlain intended that for his part the Agreement should be loyally observed.

At this point he became very emphatic. He thumped the table, opened his eyes wide and said: "I know the desires and the character of Mr. Chamberlain. Will you assure him that I shall carry out the Agreement in letter and in spirit and that never, never will I do anything that is contrary to the idea which underlies it."

On my asking him how he envisaged the future, he recalled that before Stresa, he had been responsible for bringing the four principal European Powers together. There had been criticism on the ground that the Congress of Vienna was being revived and that the great nations were putting themselves in a position to dictate to the small. He believed, however, that only by a union of the four great nations could peace be made secure and the necessary readjustments of boundaries be effected from time to time without bloodshed. He had made the attempt before Stresa to secure such an organisation, but he would never take the lead again in trying to secure it.

I enquired whether he did not think that Italy's connection with France should be made closer. He was evidently feeling some annoyance with France and he answered that the French were formalists and were always raising juridical points. "They

---

[1] Now the Foro Italico.

are the most formalistic country in Europe." I observed that France was nevertheless a great country. It was true, he retorted, that Daladier had received a large majority in the Chamber and in the Senate, but in France the larger the majority a Minister received, the more imminent was his danger. Had I not noticed that the Bourse had fallen despite the majority? He said the French officers were good, but the soldiers were not so good as the officers. He asked me whether the French generals thought the Maginot Line to be insuperable. I answered yes, and he agreed.

On my enquiring whether he thought it was not just as important to come to an understanding with the French as with the Germans and that perhaps the Germans were also difficult people to satisfy, he became pensive. He stated that while, in his belief, war would come, it would not come in the near future. The Anglo-Italian Agreement[1] had made hostilities less likely.

Throughout the interview he played with a pair of spectacles and this is apparently the first occasion on which he has been known to use them. His manner was patiently didactic. He spoke slowly, with frequent noddings of the head, as if to make his points plain. He was extremely courteous.

I was interested to see that his desk and a considerable expanse of the floor were covered with newspapers.

The interview which lasted forty minutes, terminated with an expression of regret that he was not able to attend the dinner at the Embassy in the evening as he rarely went to social functions.

At a reception at our Embassy in the evening the American, Portuguese and Turkish Ambassadors were at pains to express their congratulations on the Anglo-Italian Agreement. The Russians alone failed to make any comment on it.

Herr von Mackensen, the German State Secretary, especially asked to see me and he too evinced pleasure at the Agreement. He informed me that he was in the German Foreign Office at the time when Germany annexed Austria and that none of them knew that it was going to happen. It was, in fact, he said, a sudden decision of Hitler's.

[1] 16th April 1938.

On my asking him what could be done about relations with Germany, he answered, " Nothing now. It is an ideal to be kept in view."

M. Blondel, the French Chargé d'Affaires in Italy, asked me to take any opportunity that might occur in speaking to French Ministers and asking them to be less pedantic in issuing instructions to him in the negotiations with Italy. He realised, but Paris did not, that all that was wanted was to set down the matters on which there was common agreement, and to leave out any matters on which there was reserve.

Everywhere in Rome there seemed to be great satisfaction at the Agreement. I felt that it had brought a sense of relief after a period of strain.

I was told that the prospective visit of Hitler was most unpopular, and that there was even a fear of hissing and hostile demonstrations. I heard that there are many German police in Italy. The preparations for the Hitler visit are on a grand scale and the principal streets in Rome and Naples are all studded with pillars and posts, adorned with swastikas.

Ciano, in the course of a long conversation which I had with him at our Embassy, spoke freely on almost every aspect of international affairs.

Among his points were :

He emphasised that Italy had no territorial ambitions in Spain. Their intervention had been purely idealistic. They had never had more than one soldier, Bonaccorsi,[1] in the Balearic Isles.

He would not prophesy when the conflict would end, but Franco's victory was so certain that any proposal for arbitration was too late.

Russia was no longer a military factor to be considered. She was too weak to intervene anywhere. If Poland had invaded Lithuania she would not have taken part.

Japan would in time take Vladivostok from Russia as it was a danger, aerially, to Japan.

The absorption of Austria by Germany was not premeditated, but the result of a sudden decision taken by Hitler.

[1] A filibuster of whom many stories were told under the title of *Count Rossi*.

Benes[1] ought to make the right concessions before it was too late.

Italy must digest her new Empire before proceeding with further Imperial aims, and the digestive process in Ethiopia would take 20 years.

I asked him about Germany. He said that all we could do was to restore her colonies. I asked him whether Germany really desired them at this moment. He received this with surprise and observed that if Hitler had indicated that he was not ready to discuss the Colonies it was most interesting. He (Ciano) had noticed the omission from recent speeches in Germany of any reference to the Colonies. It was possible Germany had changed her attitude in the last few months or so.

I asked him whether, and if so when, he thought the Germans would try to take Trieste. He answered that Trieste was an Italian city and not a discussable question. I observed that the Germans did not always pause to discuss. He said he was more afraid of the Upper Adige, where the population was German. He was obviously apprehensive of the German intentions.

He hoped very much that the French would prove more reasonable than they seemed at the moment in the negotiations for an Italo-French Agreement.

He did not appear to have much confidence in Daladier and praised Herriot, who, he said, had a superior intelligence and a great sense of humour.

He spoke with warmth of Perth and described the Ambassador as a great friend with whom his relations had always been most easy and friendly.

Ciano is typical of the younger generation, vigorous, full of life, and he talked English perfectly. He wore a double-breasted suit and kept his hands in his pockets.

Before leaving Rome I was presented, on behalf of the Minister for War, with a large medallion as a memento of my visit.

The following day Hore-Belisha flew to Paris.

[1] President of Czechoslovakia.

24th April 1938

At the British Embassy, Phipps[1] gave me the opportunity of meeting Daladier[2] at a quiet dinner. I told him about the feeling of the Italians concerning the Italo-French negotiations and he quickly understood the point of not stressing difficulties. While holding the Italians to be unreliable, he obviously does not take our view of the importance of good relations with Italy, but he seems ready to fall into line with us in this and other matters.

In the course of conversation, Daladier said that the King of the Belgians was becoming more and more pro-German and he doubted whether the Belgians would resist the Germans.

25th April 1938

Gamelin called to see me at the Embassy before my departure. He made a strategic *tour d'horizon*. His points were :

The French would have difficulty in holding Indo-China in the same way that we would have difficulty in holding Hong Kong. It was because of their weak position there that they had refrained from allowing munitions to pass over the frontier to the Chinese.

In the event of our being attacked anywhere in the Far East, the French would be ready to help us from Indo-China.

In the event of our being attacked at Gibraltar, the French would be ready to advance into Spanish Morocco and, having taken Ceuta, they could give us protective fire at Gibraltar.

He spoke of coming events in Europe on the assumption that Italy would be hostile. He said the Italians were quite unreliable and that although the French Government would follow our suit, as a soldier it was his duty to prepare for all contingencies.

He thought it highly possible that the Germans would try and pass through Belgium again and he was doubtful of the Belgian capacity and intention to resist.

He hoped we would hold available some mechanised units to assist in the defence of Belgium, but I led him—not to his surprise—to appreciate the improbability of our being able to do this at the beginning of hostilities.

[1] British Ambassador in Paris.   [2] Prime Minister of France.

He was applying to Daladier for authority to increase the strength of the French Army by 200,000.

He said that it was impossible for France to give military assistance to Czechoslovakia.

He was, on our principle of making garrisons self-sufficient, in view of the risks of the Mediterranean passage, holding large forces, albeit native, in Tunisia, where the defences had also been strengthened. He would like me to see these. If the forth-coming agreement with Italy were sincerely regarded in Rome, he would bring more Algerian soldiers to France.

He thought that the Russians were capable of fighting in the Far East if Japan attacked, but in Europe he hoped they would be kept neutral.

He said that anything that we wished to see of the French fortifications was open to us, and he felt that there was an advantage, fundamental in the preservation of peace in Europe, in our relations being close and candid.

He was interested in our Army reorganisation but had not yet studied it closely enough to reach decisive opinions.

He thought that we should take precautions in Spain against the Germans acquiring the principal industries.

We landed at Hendon. Before the Cabinet meeting at 5 p.m., I called at the Foreign Office, and saw Halifax and gave him an account of my interview with Mussolini, and of my talks in Paris.

After the Cabinet meeting I saw the P.M. and gave him a similar account.

CHAPTER XIII

The Sandys Affair

WHILE HORE-BELISHA was at the Ministry of Transport he spent
most week-ends by the sea near Angmering, where his mother had
a cottage. It was an escape from the full routine of a Government
department, a mass of correspondence, Parliamentary duties, engagements, and it gave him an opportunity to read and to consider
plans and problems undisturbed.

He continued to go to the cottage after his mother's death, but
in the spring and early summer of 1938, after the Austrian crisis, his
week-ends were constantly cut short by sudden calls for Cabinet
meetings. He therefore decided to find a quiet spot somewhere
nearer London, and at the end of May found just what he wanted
in the Old Warren Farm, which stood in the heart of Wimbledon
Common. Two 17th century shepherds' cottages had been converted
into a charming house set in a small garden. It was completely
secluded among the trees and about thirty minutes' drive from
Whitehall.

Returning to the War Office after his second week-end there, he
saw a letter among his papers which was to cause a prolonged and
" thoroughly wearisome " distraction, and was to take up considerable time of senior officials at the War office and of the House
of Commons. The letter was from Duncan Sandys, Conservative
Member for Norwood, who was at the time a Second Lieutenant
in a West London Anti-Aircraft battery. It was not marked
Private or *Confidential* and had been opened by David Roseway,
Hore-Belisha's principal private secretary, who acknowledged it and
as was customary, sent it to the appropriate department " for an
early and detailed report " for the Secretary of State.

The letter read :

" When we had a talk the other day about the anti-aircraft defence position I told you that before taking any further action in the matter I would consult with you again. I am accordingly sending you a copy of a question which I am thinking of putting down for answer on Tuesday 28th June. As, however, I do not wish unnecessarily to create alarm, I am anxious before doing so, to give you an opportunity privately to contradict the statements contained in this question."

The statements Hore-Belisha had been asked specifically by Sandys " to contradict " gave precise figures of deficiencies known only to a comparatively small number of senior officers of anti-aircraft units in London. The appropriate department, which was the General Staff, in their minute back to the Secretary of State wrote :

" We are greatly concerned that Mr. Sandys should have been in possession of such information. Not only does it appear that he was conversant with the details of a secret scheme but that he was kept up to date in the subsequent changes agreed to by the Air Officer Commanding-in-Chief, such as the diversion of guns. It was quite unnecessary to impart such information to a junior officer, and, further, it is obviously not in the public interest that a question of this nature should be asked."

The secret scheme referred to in the General Staff's minute was the Emergency Plan for the Defence of London. It indicated the exact dispositions of our guns, the exact number of these guns, and the sources from which they were to be provided.

That there was a shortage of anti-aircraft guns, searchlights and other instruments concerned with the defence of London was known to units. Military correspondents of newspapers and some Members of Parliament were also aware of this. There was in consequence a certain anxiety, but the public as a whole had only a vague idea that there were shortages. Hore-Belisha, busily engaged in encouraging recruiting for the Territorial Army and in opening new drill halls, was careful not to reveal in his speeches the extent of these shortages, which he had been trying desperately to overcome, but spoke chiefly of the improvements that were being made in the hope that this might reassure the public. In the same way, in his answers to Parliamentary questions, he was careful not to mislead the House, but in the condensed reports published in the Press of both speeches and answers his guarded phrases were apt to be either omitted or blurred.

Hore-Belisha, aware of the General Staff's concern and alive to the fact that Sandys, although a serving officer, was also a Member of Parliament, went to the Prime Minister to seek his advice. That Sandys was the son-in-law of Winston Churchill, at this time a stern critic of the Government, was not overlooked. The Prime Minister, in view of the gravity of the matter, suggested that Hore-Belisha ought to lay the facts before the Attorney-General, Sir Donald Somervill, before seeing Sandys himself.

Later that day, the 23rd June, in the course of a talk with Somervill, Hore-Belisha told him of " my desire to see Duncan Sandys myself, although I felt some difficulty in doing so, because of the terms of his letter to me which virtually made it a condition of the withdrawal of the question that I could deny the facts."[1] But the Attorney-General took the view that, it was clear from the memorandum of the General Staff " a serious breach of the Official Secrets Act had been committed[2]," and he, as Attorney-General, ought to see Sandys himself. This he did on the same day. Their talk was reported to Parliament by Duncan Sandys on the 27th June.

" At this interview," he said, " the Attorney-General informed me that the question which I had sent to the Secretary of State for War showed, in the opinion of the War Office, a knowledge of matters covered by the Official Secrets Act, and he asked me to reveal the sources of my information. He added that I was under a legal obligation to do so.

" When I enquired what would be the consequences were I to refuse to comply with his request, he read me the text of Section 6 of the Official Secrets Act, and pointed out that I might render myself liable to a term of imprisonment not exceeding two years.

"In view of this I asked my Right Hon. and learned friend not to

[1] House of Commons Debates 30th June 1938.
[2] Report from the Select Committee of the Official Secrets Acts, 28th September 1938.

press me for an immediate reply, as I felt I must have an opportunity of taking advice in regard to my position."

Sandys added that the Attorney-General had later informed him that he was under a misapprehension, and gave him the assurance that there was no intention to take any such action. But Sandys was not satisfied. He told the House that " an intention might subsequently be changed." He added that the Attorney-General was prepared to write him a letter " giving an unqualified promise that, in no circumstances, would these powers of interrogation be enforced against me."

The Speaker advised that the proper course was to give notice of a Motion so that the House might fully discuss and decide what action it proposed to take. The Motion, that a Select Committee of the House should be appointed " to enquire into the substance of the statement[1] made on the 27th June . . . and the action of the Ministers concerned, and generally into the question of the applicability of the Official Secrets Act to Members of this House in the discharge of their Parliamentary duties," was debated and agreed to on the 30th June. The Select Committee consisted of members of all three Parties.

Meanwhile the General Staff, having completed their preliminary enquiries on the 27th June, in accordance with normal procedure ordered a Court of Enquiry to be assembled.

There was a fresh development when this military Court of Enquiry, proceeding with its investigations, summoned Sandys to appear before it and give evidence. Sandys reported this to Parliament on the 29th June and contended that the Court's action constituted a gross breach of privilege of the House. The Speaker ruled that a *prima facie* case had been made out and the Prime Minister moved that this should be referred to a further Committee, a Committee of Privileges. This was agreed and the second Committee was set up. Of this Committee Winston Churchill was a member.

Hore-Belisha immediately instructed the Army Council to suspend proceedings until the Committee of Privileges had met and reported. On the 30th June, the Committee of Privileges found that a breach of the privileges of the House had been committed by the military

---

[1] Made by Sandys.

court in summoning Sandys to appear and give evidence. The Army Council announced on the same day that their Court of Enquiry would be adjourned until after the Select Committee had reported.

The Select Committee sat for seventeen days. Hore-Belisha appeared on three days before it and gave evidence for eight and a half hours. In the course of his examination he said : " I want to

**CHARLES I TRIES TO PUT IT ACROSS
THE COMMONS**

Evening Standard, 1 July 1938

make it plain to the Committee that I should be glad if they would call any member of the War Office, whether Army Councillor or other, whom they may desire to see ; but if they desire to see people for whose actions I accept responsibility, I think it only fair to them that I should have an opportunity of explaining to the Committee the position of the Army Council, and the fact that I take complete responsibility."[1]

[1] Minutes of Evidence taken by the Select Committee on the Official Secrets Act.

On the 28th September, the First Report of the Select Committee was published. Referring to Sandys' " somewhat disingenuous " letter to Hore-Belisha, the Report stated " he knew that the information contained in the draft question was accurate and could not be contradicted, and yet affected to be anxious to give the Secretary of State for War an opportunity of privately contradicting it. . . . While your Committee fully accept Mr. Sandys' explanation, they do not think he was justified in threatening to do what he would not have considered himself justified in doing, and they must call attention to the fact that in the course of events, which was largely a series of misunderstandings, here at the outset was an element of misunderstanding introduced by Mr. Sandys himself." It added that the Prime Minister's conduct was not open to the slightest criticism. He was quite justified in giving Hore-Belisha the advice he gave him. Criticism was assigned to the Attorney-General for insisting that he and not Hore-Belisha should see Sandys—"it was unfortunate that Hore-Belisha took this advice "—and also for mentioning the Official Secrets Act to Sandys if he had no intention of applying it. Hore-Belisha was held responsible for failing to postpone the assembly of the Court of Enquiry by the Army Council after proceedings in the House of Commons were started on the 27th June. " For both act and omission the Secretary of State must, and does, take full responsibility."[1]

In this long drawn-out " Sandys Storm," as it was called, the only light intervention came from A. P. Herbert, Independent Member for the City of Oxford. In a characteristic speech he set the House laughing with this diverting dig at Winston Churchill :

> " Only last Monday Mr. Churchill used these burning words :
> " ' I think this report of the Committee of Privileges will be read with the greatest interest abroad, and admiring and serious eyes will turn to this country from many lands.'
> " I understand Mr. Churchill is shortly going on a well-deserved holiday in Paris. I hope when he arrives he will send us a telegram to report on how many envious and admiring eyes are turning

[1] Report of Select Committee.

in that city on that report which he now assures us is absurd and wrong.[1] . . .

" I cannot understand," Herbert went on, " how Mr. Churchill reconciles it—I will not say with his conscience, but with considerations of taste and dignity—that he should sit on this Committee of Privileges in this matter at all. He seems to be attempting to combine the incompatible and separate functions of the centre-forward and the referee. One minute he is bounding forward to the attack, shooting goals in all directions, and the next moment, with dignity but still bounding, he is blowing the whistle."

He added that " some surprise would be felt if it were now proposed that the Secretary of State for War should be added to the Committee of Privileges. That is perhaps the best way I can explain my meaning."

The whole business had been most frustrating to Hore-Belisha. During many weeks much time had to be given up not only by himself but by Army Councillors and others at the War Office when urgent rearmament problems were pressing. He had to abandon his idea of visiting Gibraltar to confer with the military authorities there about the defences. There was growing tension in the area, because of the Civil War in Spain and Hitler's reported designs on it.

Several months later Sandys buried the hatchet with, Hore-Belisha commented, a " generous testimony."[2] Speaking in the Army Estimates debate Sandys said :

" It may be within the recollection of the House that last summer I made certain criticisms of the anti-aircraft equipment situation. I think, therefore, that it is right that I should say something on this occasion about the great improvement which has undoubtedly taken place in that connection since then. . . .

" I wish to testify to the notable improvement which has taken place during recent months. As I think my Right Hon. friend the Secretary of State made perfectly clear in his speech, the equipment of our anti-aircraft units is still not fully up to war establishment. But what I wish to emphasise to-night is that the change for the

[1] Churchill had earlier in the debate stated that "the decision of the Committee of Privileges was taken on a misleading representation of facts," and in consequence "censure had alighted on persons completely innocent."
[2] House of Commons Debates 14th March 1939.

Hore-Belisha's London House
(*above*) *Entrance hall, Library* (*below*) *Dining-room, Part of the garden*

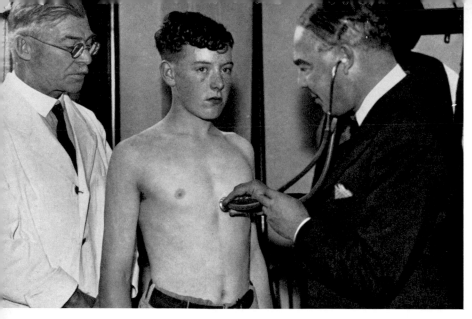

Hore-Belisha inspects recruiting centres,
15 October 1937

Hore-Belisha talking to members of the newly formed militia,
15 July 1939

better which has taken place during these last few months has been very remarkable indeed."

A week later Winston Churchill, with paternal approval—he was nearly twenty years older than Hore-Belisha—said: " The Secretary of State takes great pains with his work. I have watched his career with much sympathy—except on some occasions—and I should like to remain one of his supporters;" Hore-Belisha, acknowledging the " equal grace with which my Right Hon. friend carried the blunderbuss and the olive branch, which he sometimes presents to the victim simultaneously,"[1] accepted the olive branch.

Hore-Belisha was eleven years old when he first met Churchill, who had just left the Conservative Party and had called[2] to see Hore-Belisha's uncle, a prominent Liberal in Manchester. " The maid opened the door," Hore-Belisha writes,[3] "and showed in a masterful, yet slightly stooping figure. The pink face was topped with reddish fair hair. He was dressed in a frock coat with silk facings and below his chin was a large winged collar with a black bow tie. He strode into the room talking with an unmistakable lisp. Then he walked up to me, patted me on the head and said : ' What a nice little boy ! Would you like to come for a drive in my carriage ? ' "

Churchill was being considered at the time for nomination as the Liberal candidate for North West Manchester.

" I never went for the drive," Hore-Belisha adds.

Later that month the boy, listening to Churchill address a big political meeting, had his attention particularly attracted by the use of the words *chocolat Menier*, introduced to illustrate the argument for Free Trade. Churchill was in due course elected.

That meeting left an enduring impression. " I followed everything Churchill did. I watched the papers for his speeches . . . I even went so far as to buy—and to wear in private—a large winged collar. Thus the imagination of a small boy was captured."

During the fifteen years they had been together in the House of Commons, although they belonged to different parties, for Churchill

---

[1] House of Commons Debates 14th March 1939.   [2] In 1904.
[3] *Churchill: by his Contemporaries*, edited by Charles Eade. (Hutchinson 1953.)

had returned to the Conservative benches in 1924, Hore-Belisha's regard for his brilliance as a speaker and his quick thrusts in repartee grew. From time to time they lunched or dined together and Churchill, for his part, must have been considerably impressed by Hore-Belisha's ability, for, some months after Chamberlain replaced Baldwin as Prime Minister, it was to Hore-Belisha that Churchill confided his readiness to serve under Chamberlain, which is surprising in view of Churchill's sustained opposition to Chamberlain's foreign policy. Feeling that Churchill's inclusion would be of immense advantage to the Government, Hore-Belisha had a talk with Chamberlain, but the Prime Minister was quite adamant in his refusal. " If I take him into the Cabinet," Chamberlain said, " he will dominate it. He won't give others a chance of even talking." Churchill was not informed of this conversation, for Hore-Belisha hoped that in time he might succeed in wearing down Chamberlain's resistance. When later he again broached the subject, the Prime Minister with renewed emphasis remarked : " I won't have anyone who will rock the boat." To Churchill, Hore-Belisha's silence may have suggested a reluctance to have him as a colleague in the Government. A coolness developed and, from time to time, there were clashes as in the course of the Sandys case. But now, in the Spring of 1939, the hatchet appeared to have been buried.

CHAPTER XIV

2,500 Officers Promoted

It was a change, after the " Sandys Storm," to hear the House cheering Hore-Belisha. On the 28th July he announced far-reaching reforms affecting officers in the Army. He referred to Lord Willingdon's Committee, which had been set up by his predecessor Duff Cooper, to enquire into the causes of the shortage of officers. In March 1938 a new class of warrant officer had been created to take over a number of commands previously held by subalterns. In the circumstances, he explained, the shortage of officers into which Lord Willingdon's Committee had enquired ceased to exist as a problem. Nevertheless, in order to make the Army career as secure and attractive as possible, inter-Service discussions had taken place, over a wider field than that covered by Lord Willingdon's Committee.

As a result, a new system of direct commissioning from the ranks would be introduced in place of the existing system of passing candidates from this source through Woolwich and Sandhurst. In addition, it would be possible in future for a qualified candidate to obtain a completely free education at Woolwich and Sandhurst. Wherever a parent's means called for a reduction or remission of fees, no charge whatever would be made on them for their son's upkeep, scholastic material, uniform or equipment. This was Hore-Belisha's first step towards the democratisation of the Army.

In 1871, promotion by purchase had been replaced by promotion by vacancy. Under that system an abnormal situation had arisen, owing to a block of officers of approximately the same age having obtained their commissions within a few years of each other during and immediately after the 1914-18 war. In consequence fifty per cent of officers had failed to reach the rank of major.

It was this block in promotion, Hore-Belisha said, which his proposals were designed to remedy. Henceforward, there would be guaranteed continuity of service, subject to efficiency. Promotion by vacancy would be abolished up to the rank of major. It would come automatically, subject to efficiency, at stated intervals of time[1] and there would be increases in pay.

Promotion above the rank of major would in future only be made for the purpose of filling a particular appointment. Regulations were being amended so as to ensure that never again would the Army see officers of the rank of colonel and upwards waiting for years on the half-pay list, unaware if or when they would be re-employed and losing the whole of that time on half-pay towards the period reckonable for their pensions.

The upper ages of retirement for the ranks of general had been materially reduced, with lesser reductions in the ranks of major, lieutenant-colonel and colonel. No officer would suffer any form of " axe " and no officer would lose one penny whilst he continued to hold his existing appointment.

" Perhaps," Hore-Belisha concluded, " the immediate effect of these proposals can best be illustrated by the statement that over 2,000 officers will receive promotion with effect from the 1st August. In one day over one-quarter of the subalterns and captains in the combatant corps of the Army will be promoted."

The *London Gazette* of the 5th August contained the names of nearly 2,500 officers. They filled twenty closely-printed pages. It was the largest single list of promotions in the British Army. Telegrams reached Hore-Belisha from officers in remote stations in different parts of the world, expressing appreciation and gratitude.

Field-Marshal Sir Philip Chetwode, in the *Yorkshire Evening Press*,[2] wrote : " It would be ungracious to say that the Army reforms have come because the Secretary of State has a frightened country behind him, which has got to get officers, and a Treasury who dare not go against the will of the people. Perhaps it is something to do with that, but not many people would have taken advantage of it in the way he has done, for all his reforms have been directed towards the

---

[1] Eight years to captain, seventeen years to major (Hore-Belisha wanted it to be fourteen years, but the Treasury would not agree).
[2] 14th September 1938.

betterment of the conditions of the officers and men in the Army, to whom the country owed so much in the past, and for whom the country has done so little."

When Parliament rose for the summer recess, Hore-Belisha resumed his visits to training establishments and military camps. Whenever he could he went by air. This form of travel was a new departure for Ministers in those days. Early on the morning of the 9th August he set out for Lympne. The weather was misty and reports reached the units he was to visit that his flight might have to be cancelled. He was most anxious to keep to his arranged schedule and the plane after some delay took off.

On arrival at Lympne, he inspected the training in progress and later went on to Larkhill and Bullford, where the troops were engaged on exercises. Territorials were encamped alongside Regulars. John Gordon, Editor of the *Sunday Express*, who was at Lympne at the time, has recalled that the men were given leave to fall out after inspection, and they gathered round the Secretary of State. " He talked with them ; he didn't seem to miss one of them," Gordon recalls. Many asked him for his autograph. The sergeants bore him off to their mess, where he had a drink with them and joined them in a game of darts. He went from canteen to canteen while the men were having their meal. He saw tanks in action and a demonstration by the Worcestershire and Oxford Yeomanry Field Brigade.

On his return to London Hore-Belisha received the following letter[1] from John Gordon : " I would like to tell you something which most of the men might feel diffident about saying or which, if said by them, you might regard simply as just a normal politeness. You would be astonished, and I am sure very gratified, if you knew how great a success you were not only with the officers but with the men.

"I had spent the morning, before you came, out at exercises with scattered groups of men representative of the whole battalion. I know, as an old war soldier, how visits of bigwigs are usually regarded as an unmitigated nuisance because they cause a lot of fuss, inconvenience and hard work. The difference at Lympne was extraordinary. For a day and a night beforehand all these fellows

[1] 10th August 1938.

133

were talking of nothing else but your visit. They were obviously determined to be right on top of their job for you, and they took endless pains to be ready.

" You have clearly captured their imagination and that is a thing of which any man may justly be proud. When the news came that your visit might be cancelled their disappointment was really deep and genuine. I am glad for their sakes that you came after all, and the march past put them right on top of the world again. You might like to know also that after you left, the camp rang with your praises. Both officers and men alike ' fell for you.' They think you are the greatest Secretary for War for generations. They think—what is more important—that you are the Army's best friend ; that you have the ability and the desire to make the Army a thorough, modern and effective weapon, and that at the same time you want to make it a happy service. Their appreciation of you in free conversation is much warmer than anything you are likely to hear directly from them, because there is a natural awe of those fellows in high places. I thought you might like to know that. It is a great feat to have done in so short a time."

CHAPTER XV

His Feelings Before Munich

UNCERTAINTY and tension grew in Central Europe after Hitler's annexation of Austria. The danger spot was Czechoslovakia, whose flank lay wide open, if the Führer chose to attack. France was pledged under a Treaty of Mutual Assistance to go to the aid of Czechoslovakia in the event of German aggression. Russia had a similar Treaty, but it was dependent on France fulfilling her obligations.

In a speech on Foreign Affairs, on the 24th March, the Prime Minister reminded the House of Britain's commitments. She was bound, he said, by the Treaty of Locarno to go to the defence of France and Belgium against unprovoked attack. While emphasising the importance of maintaining the most cordial and close relations with the French Government, he explained the reasons why His Majesty's Government felt unable to give a guarantee that Britain would go to the aid of France and employ her full military strength, if France were called upon, by reason of German aggression, to implement her treaty with Czechoslovakia. But, he added:

" Where peace and war are concerned, legal obligations are not alone involved, and if war broke out, it would be unlikely to be confined to those who have assumed such obligations. It would be quite impossible to say where it might not end and what Governments might not become involved. The inexorable pressure of events, revealing threats to vital interests, might well prove more powerful than formal pronouncements, and it would be probable that a Government, not party to the original dispute, would also be immediately involved. This is especially true in the case of the two countries with long association, like Great Britain and France, which are devoted to the same ideals of democratic liberty and are determined to uphold them."

Measures were taken by the Government to accelerate the rearmament programme, which had hitherto been carried out so as not to impede normal trade. Firms engaged in munitions production were asked to give full priority to Government orders, but there was still no question of changing over from the peacetime economy and taking compulsory powers.

Towards the middle of May political and military developments gathered momentum in both Germany and Czechoslovakia. Day after day the Nazi Press clamoured for the incorporation in the Reich of the Sudeten Germans, a minority group inside Czechoslovakia. Konrad Henlein, the Sudeten-German leader and Hitler's puppet, was actively engaged in fomenting dissension among his fellow-countrymen. Rumours filtered through to Whitehall of German troop movements towards the Czechoslovak frontier and of the calling up of certain classes by President Benes' Government. Ugly incidents were reported. Everything pointed to the danger of some precipitate action which might result in a conflagration.

It was in this disquieting situation that Mr. William Strang,[1] the head of the Central Department in the Foreign Office, was sent first to Berlin to consult our Ambassador, Sir Nevile Henderson, and thence to Prague, to observe the atmosphere and confer with Mr. Basil Newton, the British Minister. In the shifting events of the next few weeks and, as a result of Strang's report to the Cabinet, the idea of sending out an investigator was formulated.

On the 26th July the Prime Minister announced in the House of Commons that a British Mission, led by Lord Runciman, would be proceeding at once to Czechoslovakia. Before agreeing to undertake this mission Runciman had stipulated that it should be acceptable to both the Czechoslovak Government and to the Sudeten German leaders. Chamberlain made it clear in the Commons that Runciman would be acting on his own responsibility, " not in any sense as an arbitrator, but as an investigator and mediator, and not under instructions from His Majesty's or any other Government." Mr.

[1] Later Lord Strang.

Ashton Gwatkin, who had the reputation among his colleagues in the Foreign Office of knowing more about that part of Europe than anyone else, would accompany him.

From his own personal experience at the Board of Trade, Hore-Belisha was in no doubt about Runciman's skill as a negotiator. But he was concerned about the conditions of his assignment and about the difficulties that must inevitably confront him. Runciman had told him that he felt as though he was putting out in a dinghy in mid-Atlantic. Hore-Belisha was convinced that it was only the highest sense of service that had induced his former Chief to undertake such a mission.

His association with Runciman had been a close one ever since his appointment as Parliamentary Secretary to the Board of Trade. In the formation of the second National Government in October 1931, Walter Runciman (as he then was) President of the Board of Trade, had asked the Prime Minister, Ramsay MacDonald, for the young Liberal to be his assistant. It was Hore-Belisha's first Government post. During the ensuing months, when the country's economy was being turned over from Free Trade to Protection, the Board of Trade was very much in the public eye.

During the passage in the autumn of 1931 of the Abnormal Importations Bill, which empowered the Government to levy duties up to 100 per cent on manufactured goods, Runciman gave Hore-Belisha a full share in carrying through the legislation—a most valuable experience. While Runciman was at Ottawa, in the following summer, he kept him fully informed of the proceedings at the Imperial Economic Conference.

Runciman continued in office as President of the Board of Trade until May 1937 when, on Chamberlain becoming Prime Minister, he left the Government. In a letter[1] to Hore-Belisha on his appointment to the War Office he wrote :

" You have written me a very warm-hearted letter, which has been a comfort and a consolation. To be offered a sinecure office[2] and to be taken from the Board of Trade in the middle of discussions with the Dominions on economic relations and while the contacts with Washington are of first-rate importance, made one

[1] 31st May 1937.   [2] Runciman was offered the office of Lord Privy Seal.

reply and only one possible for me. I was bound to refuse the offer.

" I am delighted that you step into a seat of a Secretary of State and I shall always rejoice in your progress. It has been pleasant to remember that from the earliest hours of our comradeship we have trusted each other implicitly. I carry with me these happy recollections. With an abundance of good wishes to you."

Hore-Belisha never forgot his indebtedness to his old chief, as his diary of the 25th February 1939 shows :

I had a letter from Runciman[1] in reply to a cable which I had sent him, wishing him good recovery and discovery on his voyage to Australia. He is a gentle fellow. I owe him everything.

On the 30th August 1938, while Parliament was in recess, the Prime Minister called a conference of Ministers.

30th August 1938

A conference of Ministers at No. 10 lasted several hours. The position in Czechoslovakia has worsened and the Prime Minister called us together because he wanted to tell us how matters stood. Nevile Henderson came back from Berlin and reported to us. I was against any threat being made that we would declare war if Germany attacked Czechoslovakia, unless there was an overwhelming public demand first, and on the facts no such overwhelming demand exists. Opinion at home is very much divided and we have been given strong evidence to show that the Dominions would not come in.

I am alarmed at what it means for the Army. All we could do at the outset would be to provide a force of two divisions which would be inadequately equipped for any offensive operations. The whole of our anti-aircraft resources would be required for A.D.G. B.[2] Our rearmament programme is based on what is necessary for our own defence and we have concentrated on the Navy and Air. We cannot at present put an army into the Field large enough to have any decisive effect.

We are to meet again at short notice.

[1] Written on board SS. *Strathnaver*, 19th February 1939.
[2] Air Defence of Great Britain.

12th September 1938

Another long meeting of Ministers this morning. Two meetings with Inskip, discussing precautionary measures. Held up for Treasury approval.

I asked for speedy decisions so that the War Office can act. Someone from the Treasury is to attend future meetings, so I hope there won't be any delay.

During the whole of the crisis the Inner Cabinet, " the Big Four " as they were called, consisting of the Prime Minister, Sir John Simon (Chancellor of the Exchequer), Lord Halifax (Foreign Secretary) and Sir Samuel Hoare (Home Secretary), met in constant session.

13th September 1938

Another meeting at 6 p.m. of Service Ministers and Chiefs of Staff at No. 10 to discuss precautionary measures. The P.M., Halifax, Simon and Hoare were there. Feeling against any premature action.

In the evening of the 12th September Hitler in an important speech at Nürnberg, while not committing himself, had referred to a plebiscite among the Sudeten Germans.

14th September 1938

The Cabinet met this morning to consider Hitler's speech. Neville put before us his plan to go and see Hitler. It came as a bombshell. He said he had been turning it over in his mind and had mentioned it to one or two of his colleagues and to Nevile Henderson, who was in favour. Since our last meeting events had become more critical, so he, Halifax, Simon and Sam Hoare had decided that his plan, Plan Z, should be put into operation at once and a telegram had already been sent to Nevile Henderson. It is to be kept a dead secret until a reply is received. Apparently the P.M. had not found it possible to consult us all.

I said that his plan was an adventurous one, which might appeal to the imagination of the world, but it was not without risk. Hitler may say he is not interested in the autonomy of the Sudeten Germans and that he wishes to incorporate them in the Reich. If so, what action do we propose to take? It should be made plain to Hitler how we stand. The present episode is all part of a relentless plan on the lines of *Mein Kampf*. Whatever the result of the P.M.'s plan, we should at once intensify our rearmament programme.

Saturday, 17th September 1938

Cabinet met at 11 a.m. to hear the P.M.'s account of his visit to Hitler at Berchtesgaden. Runciman was present during the first part of the meeting. He had just returned from Czechoslovakia. He said he had found it impossible to get any solution between the parties concerned, there was close contact between Sudeten leaders and Berlin. The main opposition centres were in N.W. Bohemia, where there were about 800,000 Sudeten Germans. There was serious economic depression in parts and a grievance existed among Sudeten Germans that they were being pushed out of Government posts and Czechs were being put in their places. They wanted to be incorporated in the Reich. A plebiscite was their only solution. The Czech Government would be against this. He said there was a complete impasse at present about any plan. He felt it would be unwise for him to submit a plan himself, as the onus would fall on the British Government. His view was that Czechoslovakia could not remain as she was to-day.[1]

The Prime Minister told us about his stormy interview with Hitler. The upshot was that Hitler insisted on self-determination for the Sudeten Germans. The P.M. said he could not give him any assurance about this. He would go back and consult his colleagues and the French Government. He would then return and resume the conversations. Hitler agreed and promised that he would meanwhile take no action against Czechoslovakia. The P.M. said it was most important that no time should be lost in deciding whether the principle of self-determination should be accepted. He felt sure Hitler meant a plebiscite.

My view was that if the principle of self-determination were agreed to, a committee of experts should be called together to examine the possibilities of improvising a workable scheme.

The General Staff have prepared a paper on the military forces needed to exercise control. At least three divisions would be required. There would be difficulties in protecting our troops, if they were attacked by Czech forces.

[1] White Paper CMD. 5847. No. 1. House of Commons Debates 28th September 1938.

Daladier and Bonnet[1] have been invited to come over as soon as possible so that we can reach a joint decision.

We adjourned until 3 p.m.

We are to hold ourselves available at two hours' notice.

Among Hore-Belisha's papers are some notes made by him after the meeting :

We must have a clear foreknowledge of the problems raised by the principle of self-determination and of the terms of the principle.

It is Hitler who has asked for self-determination and we must know the kind of options to be offered to the voters.

By accepting self-determination we are not committed to accepting the surrender of areas to Germany, which would make the maintenance of the Czech State economically impossible, and strategically indefensible.

This is all the more necessary if we are to give a guarantee. We would be guaranteeing something which could not be defended.

Hitler says that he is attached to the principle of race. Ethnologists affirm that in Bohemia it is impossible to tell who are Czechs and who are Germans by race. But if he is attached to the principle of race, we are attached to the principle of democracy.

Hitler will be confirmed in his theory that democracies are feeble if we have to dispute with France as to which of us really let the Czech democracy down.

Surely it has never been intended to give a reply to Hitler without giving the Czechs an opportunity of adequate consideration. Otherwise the impression will be given that the Germans are giving them a more straightforward and comprehensible deal with a sporting chance of defending themselves than we are.

Let us remember the gust of public feeling that swept up after the Hoare-Laval Agreement.

The public does not yet know what it is that is proposed. And we have not tested the reactions of Parliament. We are not committed to go to war. We have to judge that matter in the light of events.

[1] The French Prime Minister and Foreign Secretary.

141

What we need not do in this is to force the Czechs to yield helplessly what they are prepared to defend.

Most of us agreed with the same reluctance as the P.M. to the principle of self-determination.

None of us, however, I imagine, has ever contemplated a simple announcement that we accept self-determination without a clear tabulation of the conditions in which it is to be applied.

I still feel that before an answer is given to Hitler some Committee of Ministers or experts should give us a scheme.

We still do not know whether one of the options is to be the cession of territories or whether it is to be a transfer of population.

The more I reflect on the transfer of territories, the more I feel we are bereaving Czechoslovakia of its power to exist.

19th September 1938

The Cabinet was called to hear the P.M.'s account of the conversations which he, Halifax, Simon and Sam Hoare had had with Daladier and Bonnet. They had flown over early yesterday and talks had gone on all night. The French stonewalled. They were against a plebiscite, but said they could get Benes to agree to a transfer of Sudeten territory, provided we gave a definite guarantee to Czechoslovakia. P.M. up against it. Vital to reach agreement with French—and he cannot return to Hitler until he has the agreement of the Czechs. There wasn't time to call the Cabinet, so he, Halifax, Simon and Hoare had decided in favour of a guarantee. A joint British-French message has already been sent to Prague.

Most of us disliked the idea, but in the end there didn't seem to be any alternative because of the time factor and we and the French have to be in agreement. The proposed guarantee filled me with apprehension. I pointed out that Czechoslovakia would be an unstable State economically after the Sudeten-German areas had been transferred. It was difficult to see how it could survive. Czechoslovakia would be strategically unsound and there was no means by which we could implement the guarantee. How could we fight the Poles or the Hungarians if they attacked Czechoslovakia? I was afraid that the solution proposed was no real solution. It might only be a postponement of the evil day.

21st September 1938

Halifax brought us up to date. No reply from Czech Government until late last night, when a telegram came saying there was no alternative but to accept the British and French proposals.

Henderson had sent a message that things might get out of hand unless a date were definitely fixed for the P.M. to see Hitler again. This was fixed for to-morrow at Godesberg.

The P.M. is going to press for a joint guarantee by us, France and Russia, and that Germany should sign a separate pact of non-aggression with Czechoslovakia.

We were all dead against any proposal to allow German troops to cross the frontier during the transitional period and it was agreed that there should be some form of international force.

When I returned to the War Office I wrote a note to the P.M. as I wanted him to be in no doubt as to what I had told him about the employment of our troops in Czechoslovakia. I explained that if we were to send troops to Czechoslovakia on police duties, we would diminish our capacity to deal with any emergency that might arise, not only in Europe, but in Egypt and Palestine. If ugly incidents were to arise in Czechoslovakia while British soldiers were there, that might create a dangerous situation for them. I told him that I thought I ought to mention these points again to him in fairness to the War Office.

On the 22nd September the Prime Minister flew from Heston airport to Godesberg for his second meeting with Hitler.

22nd September 1938

11 a.m. I went with Gort to No. 10. Halifax, Simon and Sam Hoare, also Inskip present—about sending British troops to Czechoslovakia if it is decided to send an international military force there.

23rd September 1938

Heard from Duff that things were not going well at Godesberg. Very anxious. At the War Office all day with Gort, on defence preparations. But we can't get a move on until we get definite instructions. Everything shrouded in secrecy.

Saturday, 24th September 1938

Had a note from Simon in pencil when I got to the War Office. It was from his home, dated " 8 o'c., Sep. 23."

" My dear Leslie,—I have just come in to take my wife out to dinner—a special party as it is her birthday—and am sorry to hear from her that you had a message from the W.O. ' that I wanted to see you urgently.' No such message was sent by me —I merely sent word to say that I would tell any Cabinet Minister who was in London, if he cared to look in at the Treasury, what I knew of the position at Godesberg. You will now see this in your night's telegrams and if you care to drop in to-morrow, I will add anything I know. So sorry for mistake—Yours ever, John."

I heard from Duff that Simon had seen him, Walter,[1] Kingsley Wood and others yesterday afternoon at 4 o'clock. Telephoned Simon, who told me P.M. was coming back.

Cabinet met in the evening. P.M. back from Godesberg. Hitler has turned down flat British and French proposals, and insisted that Sudeten German territory should be handed over at once, that there must be general plebiscite and that the whole of the transferred territory should be occupied by German troops ! ! He would not conclude pact with Czechoslovakia as other minorities were involved.

P.M. told Hitler his proposals were impossible. After long arguments P.M. went back to his hotel and discussed the position with Horace Wilson, Nevile Henderson, etc. They decided to write a letter[2] to Hitler and ask him for his definite proposals in writing. Hitler replied next day.[3] The proposals were the same as orally given the day before to P.M.

The P.M. saw Hitler at 10 p.m. and told him that if his proposals were his last word, there was nothing for him to do but to leave. During the talks a message was brought in that the Czechs had decided to mobilise. The P.M. said he would send Hitler's proposals to the Czech Government. He would return at once to consult his colleagues and the French Government. Hitler told

---

[1] Walter Elliot, Minister of Health.   [2] White Paper CMD. 5847. No. 3.
[3] Hitler's reply: White Paper CMD. 5847. No. 4. Chamberlain's reply: CMD. 5847. No. 5. P.M.'s report to Parliament 28th September 1938.

Hore-Belisha and Lord Nuffield

Hore-Belisha visits a Territorial Army Sergeants' Mess
22 March 1938

Hore-Belisha with Mr Duff Cooper, at the time of the Munich Crisis

him he would not invade Czechoslovakia while negotiations were going on. P.M. seems convinced there is no other chance of getting a settlement on peaceful lines.

I asked what would happen if Czechoslovakia rejected Hitler's proposals? Would he still hold out the hand of friendship to Germany? The P.M. said ' No.' The position remained the same, if France carried out her treaty obligations to Czechoslovakia. I said we ought to mobilise at once. It was the only argument Hitler would understand. We would never be forgiven if there were a sudden attack on us and we had failed to take the proper steps to put ourselves in a proper state of protection. If we did not mobilise at once, we should be handicapped in carrying out a number of measures of reinforcements, for instance in Palestine and Egypt. It would take 48 hours before the Anti-Aircraft Artillery and Searchlights could be fully deployed. This portion of the T.A. could be embodied by a proclamation signed by me without general mobilisation. We left at 7.30 p.m.

Meeting to-morrow morning at 10.30. Daladier and Bonnet are coming over.

I returned home. I wanted to clear my mind in readiness for to-morrow's meeting.

He drew up the following notes :

I never believed that there was any obligation upon us to declare war on Germany on account of Czechoslovakia, but I have always believed that if France were involved, we should be involved too. This was the definite implication of the P.M.'s speech on 24th March.

I understand the purpose of the P.M.'s visit to Hitler was to convince him that the advice he was receiving from Ribbentrop and others of his entourage that he could walk in with impunity and without risk of bringing in France and ourselves was un-founded.

In examining the proposals that might be offered to Hitler, the Cabinet had accepted, as the last stage to which we were prepared to go, a plebiscite in principle.

In the event the P.M. went to Berchtesgaden and accepted the principle of self-determination. The terms which gave affect to this principle were accepted with extreme reluctance by the Czechs.

When the P.M. went to Godesberg Hitler refused even these terms and said in effect in his Memo : " I am going to do what I like," which is what the P.M. went to Germany in an endeavour to prevent.

In my judgment we have incurred a moral obligation to the Czechs and we are no longer the free agent we were before the matter started.

Czechoslovakia is a democracy. She shares our opposition to Nazi tyranny. When the P.M. and Foreign Secretary see Jan Masaryk,[1] let them tell him that the British Government takes the view that Czechoslovakia would be justified in refusing to accept Hitler's proposals.

It is quite clear that Hitler only understands one argument and that is the argument he has been employing—a display of force. Why should we not display the might we possess ? Why should we not mobilise the Fleet ?

The P.M. yesterday spoke to us of the horrors of war, of German bombers over London and of his horror in allowing our people to suffer all the miseries of war in our present state. No one is more conscious than I am of our present deficiencies. Chiefs of Staff view—to take offensive against Germany now would be like " a man attacking a tiger before he has loaded his gun."

But life is only worth living for certain things : respect for law, liberty and the decent treatment of human beings towards one another. Europe is at present littered with the wrecks of lives of good people who have nothing to hope for while these methods prevail. We are the trustees of that civilisation which is being abruptly assaulted over ever-widening areas. If Czechoslovakia accepts the proposals, there is little more to be said. But then, our bounden duty, having been warned, will be to rearm with vigour, put our industries on a war footing and set up a Ministry of Supply, so that we may never allow this situation to occur again.

Sunday, 25th September 1938

Cabinet met at 10.30 a.m. Halifax gave a fine moral lead.

[1] Czechoslovak Minister in London.

I spoke on the lines I set out last night.

We met again at 3 p.m. Daladier and Bonnet are coming at 5 p.m. I thought it vital we should know the French intentions before making our decision. If the French were prepared to support Czechoslovakia, we must let them know the stand we would take.

I passed a note across the table to the P.M. :

" Why should not the French Ministers meet the whole Cabinet ? "

And he wrote in pencil at the bottom of my note :

" Perhaps at the 2nd meeting, but not at the first."

At 6 p.m. the Service Ministers with Chiefs of Staff met at the Admiralty. We discussed further defence measures to be taken, including the reinforcement of Singapore and Egypt. Dined at the Savoy with Duff, Walter Elliott, Shakes Morrison[1] and Oliver and Maureen Stanley.

We all went to No. 10 at 11.30 p.m. Apparently the French had been very evasive and were putting the responsibility and initiative on us. Gamelin is to come over at once. I do not think it likely that he will disclose his military plans to us unless he is sure that Britain will stand in with France. Gort told me that Gamelin's view is that the Siegfried Line is not finished and that in many respects it is improvised.

The discussions went on for a couple of hours. As a last effort to avert war the P.M. is to make a final appeal in a personal letter[2] to be taken by Horace Wilson to Hitler, asking him to agree to a Joint Commission, including German, Czech and British representatives. If Hitler refuses, he has authorised Wilson to give a personal message from him that Britain would stand by France if France went to war.

We agreed. I pressed for further precautionary measures to be taken. It was most urgent to call up the Anti-Aircraft.

As we left I saw Daladier for a moment in the passage. I said " Courage," and he replied, " Il faut tenir."

26th September 1938

First thing on arriving at the War Office, I sent a note by messenger to the P.M.

---

[1] Later Lord Dunrossil.   [2] White Paper CMD. 5847. No. 10.

" I assume that in any conversations which Ministers may have with General Gamelin, I shall be invited to be present and I should like to bring the Chief of the Imperial General Staff."

General Lelong[1] rang me up. He said things were going better, but that Daladier and Bonnet had been furious about the cross-examination they had been put through on technical military matters with which they were not *au courant*.

We met at noon. A message came from Roosevelt urging the P.M. to continue his negotiations to the last minute in order to avert war.

The French were in complete agreement with the P.M.'s letter to Hitler an[1] his personal message that we would support France if Germany attacked Czechoslovakia.

Horace Wilson has already left for Berlin. Parliament is to be recalled on Wednesday. I was authorised to call up Anti-Aircraft personnel.

3 p.m. Inskip called a conference of Ministers about defence measures. All brakes were off. More decisions were taken in an hour than in weeks.

[1] French Military Attaché in London.

CHAPTER XVI

Call up

At 6 p.m. on the 26th September a State of Emergency by Order in Council was declared. The Fleet was mobilised. The machinery which the War Office had been setting up since the beginning of the crisis was immediately put in motion. Orders were sent out by telephone and telegram to all Territorials of the Coast Defence units and the 1st and 2nd Anti-Aircraft Divisions to report at once for duty to their Headquarters. Fifty thousand officers and men answered the call. Never before had Territorial Army units been called out in advance of a general mobilisation.

Records of the time reveal the thoroughness of the arrangements made by the local T.A. organisations all over the country. At the signal, men hurried from their homes, offices and workshops to their drill halls where quartermasters issued equipment, stores, blankets, steel helmets, cables, telephones, and all the other impedimenta. Roll calls were taken. Then Army lorries and hired transport drove off into the darkness to isolated searchlight detachments in fields and to battery positions in parks and on golf courses. Overnight the citizen army, having changed from lounge suits into khaki, manned the defences of the country from the east of Scotland to the Channel coast.

The next day, the 27th September, Hore-Belisha, accompanied by Major-General L. R. Hill, toured the defences of London. In a telegram to all General Officers Commanding-in-Chief, the General Officer Commanding London District, the General Officer Commanding Northern Ireland District and the Commander A.A. Corps, he expressed his appreciation

" of the spirit displayed and of the remarkable results achieved in

149

the minimum of time and in difficult conditions. The fact that the full strengths of the Anti-Aircraft and Coastal defences of the country were in position and manned by officers and men, who a few hours before had been at their work or otherwise carrying out their civil avocations, is a splendid and most encouraging fulfilment of the confidence the country places in them as the first line of defence Recognition is also due to those employers who, through the readiness with which they released their men, have contributed to the results achieved."

On the 29th September Chamberlain met Hitler for the third time. The meeting took place at Munich. Mussolini, greatly disturbed at the prospect of being drawn into a general war for which he was not prepared, had urged Hitler to have a further meeting with Chamberlain and Daladier, which Mussolini proposed to attend too. His purpose was, if possible, to achieve a compromise.

Chamberlain arrived by air from London. Mussolini's train was met at the German frontier by Hitler, and the two dictators travelled to Munich together. The meeting began at 1 p.m. and went on until 2 a.m. From the outset it was clear that there would be no war. Sir Ivone Kirkpatrick, who was one of the British officials at the meeting, has placed on record[1] his impression that the French " were resolved to reach an agreement at any cost," and that, while Mussolini and Goering were jubilant that an agreement had been reached, Hitler's face was " as black as thunder." He was by no means pleased that war had been deferred.

Chamberlain, returning to London the next day, was cheered by wildly excited crowds, who believed as he waved the Agreement of Anglo-German friendship, signed by him and Hitler before he left, that he had brought home " Peace with Honour." He appeared later with the King and Queen and Mrs. Chamberlain on the balcony of Buckingham Palace and was enthusiastically cheered again.

There is no record in his diary of Hore-Belisha's feelings at this moment. He was greatly preoccupied with the Call-up. He had urged a stiffening of our attitude in the notes sent to Hitler. But there is no doubt that the breathing space granted by the settlement

[1] *The Inner Circle* by Sir Ivone Kirkpatrick (Macmillan 1959).

was accepted by him with relief. One has, as a guide, his later comments when he said, frankly and unequivocally: " I fully supported the Prime Minister over Munich."

The British officers and men called up stood by their action stations for nearly a fortnight. The anti-aircraft organisation was put to the test. Gaps in the system were revealed. Serious shortages of equipment of all kinds were brought to light. The people of Britain awoke to the country's insecurity from the horrors of bombing. The sense of national relief and gratitude to the Prime Minister for having averted war, was soon turned to a grave uneasiness as to what would have happened if war had actually come. Was Britain ready to meet the Nazi onslaught ? The answer was on every lip. Quite clearly she was not. The vulnerability of London and the industrial areas had been made manifest.

The Press vociferously expressed the country's disquiet and clamoured for the deficiencies in the defence system to be made good without delay.

When Parliament reassembled on the 3rd November, Herbert Morrison[1], for the Labour Opposition, moved a Vote of Censure, condemning the Government for their lack of preparedness " to protect the civil population when the country was brought to the brink of war."

The debate was in two parts. Sir John Anderson,[2] newly appointed Minister directly responsible for Civil Defence, concentrated on Air Raid Precautions. On Hore-Belisha fell the main task of dealing with the Opposition motion. He had been warned by Lord Elmley[3] of the concerted attacks that were also to be made on him by back benchers on his own side.

Since 1931 Elmley had been his Parliamentary Private Secretary —Hore-Belisha used to say that he was the perfect P.P.S. He was also a staunch friend.

There was hard hitting on both sides of the House. Some of Hore-Belisha's critics went so far as to assert that " there was hardly a gun anywhere " during the emergency. But this was disavowed by Lt.-Col. Gandar-Dower,[4] who, speaking from his own recent

[1] Later Lord Morrison of Lambeth.　　　[2] Later Viscount Waverley.
[3] Viscount Elmley, later Earl Beauchamp. He was at the time P.P.S. to Hore-Belisha.
[4] M.P. for Penrith and the Cockermouth Division of Cumberland.

experience in command of a London A.A. battery, said that, while this might have been true twelve months before, it was a travesty of the existing situation.

Hore-Belisha wound up the debate :

" The subject," he said, " which we are discussing must be treated fearlessly, candidly, without exaggeration, and, above all, without complacency. No one must be allowed to minimise the real sense of apprehension of the people and their legitimate concern with our air defences. That feeling of apprehension is attributable, I think, to the sudden and overwhelming realisation that our island security was open to be violated. Henceforward, we must pay the same attention as a nation to our anti-aircraft defences as we have always paid to the maintenance of the Fleet."

Then he unfolded a list of shortages, which the War Office, at his request, had obtained from every Territorial unit which had taken part in the emergency. Every step, he emphasised, would be taken to remedy them. He went on :

" It must be realised that in 1935 we had virtually no organisation at all for anti-aircraft defence on the ground. In the latter part of that year we entrusted the task of forming such an organisation to the Territorial Army. On 1st January 1936 the First Anti-Aircraft division was formed and its strength at this time was about 5,200 all ranks. Recruiting was bad and by the end of the year its strength was still only 7,700 men. In June 1936 we formed a Second Anti-Aircraft division. Recruiting was still bad and the actual strength of this division was still just under 7,000. It may be said that the popular imagination had not then become fired with the necessity for providing ground defence against air raids.

" In 1937 for the first time the tendency of recruiting changed for the better and by the end of the year the strength of the two divisions was 27,000. By June of this year the numbers had risen to 45,000 and, profiting by this hopeful increase, the Government decided to create five Territorial Divisions, numbering 100,000 and covering the whole country. . . .

" We decided to take the risk of getting the men in advance of the equipment. It was a risk with a definite time limit, for in 1937 the final design of the new 3.7 inch anti-aircraft gun had been approved and new plant had been planned for its production. I therefore knew, as surely as day would follow night, this gun would come into issue, and I felt very strongly it was better to have the men who could be trained in advance of the full equipment than to have the full equipment at a later stage, but not to have the men who could handle it. It would have been easier and more comfortable to have taken the reverse course. . . . I have never said that more than training equipment existed. . . ."

He continued :

" I do not think I need authority to say that a programme is a developing and not an instantaneous phenomenon."

Turning to Winston Churchill, who was sitting in his accustomed place at the end of the first row below the gangway, he added :

" As has been stated in this House in vivid language which may perhaps be recalled, ' in these sombre fields in the first year you have to sow, and in the second year you have to harrow ; the third year is your harvest.' . . . I hope the House will remember that some of the factories where this production is in progress were, less than two years ago, empty shells for which all the plant and tools had to be made and assembled. There has further been recruitment and training of labour, of which there is still a shortage on this work. It must be borne in mind that practically the whole of the armament industry in this country was closed down after the war."

Then he concluded :

" Nothing, of course, could atone, or will atone until our programme is complete, for the shortage of war equipment. . . . I have dealt frankly with the present state of our deficiencies and it is not a state which will endure. . . . The country has a right to know that His Majesty's Government are resolved to see that the legitimate fears at present entertained shall, so far as is humanly possible, be averted and in the shortest possible time."

His sincerity and determination were obvious. The House

divided and the Opposition's motion of Censure was defeated by a large majority.

No time was lost by the War Office in putting into effect measures to implement Hore-Belisha's pledge to the Commons. Already on the 14th October, six days after the emergency ended, a scheme was launched for the local protection of industrial factories, in order to supplement the defence of the country against low-flying aircraft. The new force was to form a Territorial Army Reserve, and was to relieve anti-aircraft divisions from having to defend places isolated but essential to the economic life of the country. Selected firms were asked to co-operate by allowing their employees to put in thirty drills a year and eight days annually in camp. The response was immediate. Training of the " Dungaree Brigade," as it was called, started at once. Not for many years had Britons at home " stood at arms " in this fashion.

In a broadcast the same night Hore-Belisha explained the working of the scheme. In the event of war, he said, men engaged at these " vital points " would remain at their work, but, if an emergency arose, they would be ready to drop their tools and man the guns. The country would thus have a further safeguard. Four divisions of Territorials would stretch from Land's End to the Orkneys, but wherever men were employed in vulnerable places, there would be weapons and crews to fire the guns against low-flying attack.

He then appealed to all concerned in the construction of factories and the manufacture of armaments

" to exceed anticipation in the months ahead. It is essential to build up fresh munitions capacity, which since the war has been lacking in the country. It takes longer to make a gun than to enlist a man."

Progressively the anti-aircraft organisation was re-planned and enlarged. Six months later, in his second Army Estimates speech, Hore-Belisha reviewed the comprehensive measures that had been put into effect by the War Office. When the test came in the Battle of Britain a magnificent job was done by the gunners and sappers of the Anti-Aircraft Command and the Coast Defence.

CHAPTER XVII

Need for a Ministry of Supply

IT WAS not until after Hitler's invasion of Austria on the 11th March 1938 that the British Government formally accepted the possibility of preparing and equipping a Continental army. The great expansion this would involve made Hore-Belisha see more and more clearly that the Supply system at the War Office was unable to cope with such a development and he was resolved that a Ministry of Supply should be set up as quickly as possible.

It was not only our own needs that had to be considered, as the Dominions looked to Britain for the supply of their armament requirements. It was also of the utmost importance, on political as well as economic grounds, that Britain should meet the orders for munitions placed by her Allies, particularly as Germany was making a bid for some of these markets.

24th March 1938

At the C.I.D.[1] this morning we discussed the supplying of artillery equipments to Portugal. The importance of preventing this order going to Germany was pointed out. But at this stage of our rearmament programme, in my view, we cannot give Portuguese requirements priority over our own. We have made no provision of capacity to meet this type of order, which comes not only from Portugal, but from Egypt, Iraq and Belgium. I said I thought it would be advisable to set up a pool of capacity for this type of order.

Weir[2] was right about this country always being able to accept foreign orders for warships, because there was a steady demand

---

[1] Committee of Imperial Defence.   [2] Lord Weir.

for the Navy, which has always had therefore a strong shipbuilding industry as a background. But it is not the case with our small Army. We have no industrial background for orders for field artillery and there is no inducement for private firms to go into that kind of business.

18th May 1938

The question of a Ministry of Supply was raised at the Cabinet this morning. I said I hoped the P.M. would not close the door to that possibility even in time of peace. I was sure that before long we would be forced to take drastic steps. Germany is deliberately building up a system of selling arms to foreign countries. It is part of her policy to bring them into her orbit and get a footing in them. Our position is being undermined. Yesterday the Press reported a speech by the Minister of Defence in Canada about his difficulties in obtaining from us their defensive requirements. I am going to have a disappointing story to tell Australian Ministers about their orders when I see them during the week. The same is true of Portugal, Egypt, Iraq and other countries.

20th May 1938

Reports of German rearmament are alarming. It is stated that it is possible for Germany to redouble her production within a year, not only of aircraft, but armament stores—guns. We are told that it is not possible to bring new capacity into production within a period of two years.

The setting up of a Ministry of Supply had been for some time a political issue. Churchill was the main protagonist. The Opposition, Labour and Liberal, were in favour, but with reservations. The Government throughout the controversy maintained that to establish a Ministry of Supply in peacetime, with all the dislocation it would entail, would result in a delay in fulfilling the rearmament programme.

On the 25th May, in the course of a debate on the Air Defences, the Prime Minister set out his views:

"Although in actual war a Ministry of Supply would be essential—and indeed we have all the plans ready which could be put into operation at once—I do not believe that a Ministry of Supply in peacetime will be as effective as the Ministry of Munitions was in the Great War unless you give that Ministry the same powers as the Ministry of Munitions had."

Mr. Dalton[1] intervened to say that the Ministry of Supply should have powers over industry—over all stages of processes of manufacture, design, inspection, testing and delivery. The Prime Minister retorted that the powers would have to be more extensive if there was to be an improvement on the present system. A great deal was being done by persuasion, by voluntary effort and co-operation with labour and employers, but if the supporters of a Ministry of Supply in peace wanted the sort of effect there had been under the Ministry of Munitions in the Great War, then there would have to be not only the power of controlling factories, but the power of relaxing Trade Union practices and regulations, the power over strikes, the power over dilution of labour.

Mr. Kirkwood's[2] interruption at this point " You are not going to get that " expressed the uncompromising stand taken by many in the Labour Party and the Trade Unions.

After the annexation of Austria Hitler intensified his war of nerves in Central Europe. Anglo-French Staff conversations were started, at first on a limited scale.

Early in July a report appeared in the *News Chronicle* of a lecture given by General von Reichenau, Commander of the Fourth Army Group, to the National Socialist leaders at Leipzig on " the German attitude towards events in Spain." The German Ambassador in London, Herr von Dirksen, promptly called at the Foreign Office and denied the authenticity of the reported lecture and said his Government were issuing a formal *démenti*.

That Hore-Belisha took the lecture seriously seems clear from his note on it and the passages he marked with a red margined line and a cross :

12th July 1938

Reichenau's lecture is a revealing document. It is another evidence of what we are up against : Germany's military advantage by her intervention in Spain. Reichenau sums it up :

[1] The Rt. Hon. Hugh Dalton, Labour M.P. for Bishop Auckland.
[2] Labour M.P. for Dumbarton Burghs.

" Two years of real war experience have been of more use to our yet immature Wehrmacht, to the efficiency of our new army and hence to the offensive power of the people as a whole than ten years of peacetime training could have been. For systematic and careful war preparations it is necessary to devise means whereby long beforehand one may get at the enemy, his commercial routes, his sea routes, his means of transport, his fixed movable potential *de guerre*, everywhere where serious war operations may be expected."

Shortage and inefficient distribution of skilled men and the inability to secure absolute priority for Army orders impeded the further measures which were taken after the Munich crisis in September to accelerate the anti-aircraft defences.

6th October 1938

At the C.I.D. meeting this morning I pointed out that the capacity at present available for the manufacture of guns was fully taken up. Increased capacity for anti-aircraft production could only be obtained under the present system at the expense of some other requirement of the Field Army. In my view we could only get substantial acceleration if skilled labour was provided and if powers were taken which would give Army orders in private factories effective priority over civilian orders. If we are to have any material improvement in the near future these powers should be taken immediately and we must face the political and economic consequences involved.

A Ministry of Supply with the necessary powers, Hore-Belisha determined, was fundamental to the whole scheme of preparedness for war. Only by this means could the Army obtain in a given time the guns, tanks and every other kind of equipment it needed.

Early on the 21st October he flew to South Wales, where a Territorial Army Week was being held. He opened a new Drill Hall at Merthyr Tydfil. In the evening he spoke at a dinner at the City Hall given by the County of Glamorgan Territorial Army and Auxiliary Air Force Association. In his speech he made his views clear about the need for a Ministry of Supply and intimated what its scope should be.

" From the crisis[1] lessons are to be learned, and the problems must be stated with candour if they are to be solved with courage. ... The omissions of nearly two decades could not, unfortunately, even with a complete upheaval of our economy, have been rectified in two years.

" When impatience is expressed with the fulfilment of our armament programme, which, be it remembered, is a programme and not an instantaneous creation, it must be recognised that under our present system nothing can guarantee appreciable acceleration of it, nor can there be an appreciable enlargement of it in the given time. ...

" To obtain an appreciable acceleration, or an appreciable enlargement within the given time, of our armament programme it would be necessary to revive the wartime method under which every other consideration is subordinated to this.

" A Ministry of Munitions to be effective must have full powers to allot orders, to assign priorities, to control the supply of materials, and to make arrangements for the diversion of skilled labour. These would be fundamental changes."

The next morning he toured the munition works of Edward Curran & Co. and then flew back to London.

The Press took up the implication in his speech that the country must either accept unpreparedness for defence or consent to a radical change in our economy in peacetime.

The Beaverbrook papers, which had been highly critical of Hore-Belisha at the time of the Munich crisis, supported him and urged that the Government should take powers to conscript factories, material and labour.

There were hints in the Press of a division of opinion in the Cabinet.

24th October 1938

The P.M. sent me a message that he wanted to see me. I guessed it was about my speech at Cardiff. He asked me if I minded Horace Wilson being present. He made his points against setting up a Ministry of Supply in peacetime, which I endeavoured to demolish. I assured him that I did not wish to make things difficult. But I

[1] Munich.

felt I must make my conclusions clear. I asked him, if he could not see his way to setting up a Ministry of Supply, if he would tell the House that he was exhausting all other means, seeing employers and Trade Union leaders in order to persuade them to do everything they could to expedite production of armaments.

26th October 1938

At the Cabinet meeting this morning we had a post-mortem on the Call-up. Kingsley, Stanhope[1] and I had put in statements to Inskip showing what the progress of the Defence Programmes would be by 1st August 1939.

I pointed out that the present programme of equipment was quite inadequate to enable the Territorial Army to train effectively on embodiment. It was therefore absolutely necessary to increase its scale.

We were again reminded about straining the country's financial resources. I agreed with Kingsley that safety and security should come first and I referred to the time which had had to be taken by the War Office in review after review of the Army programme they had had to make, because of the limitation on what could be spent. I pressed for a prompt decision.

A Cabinet Committee is to be set up—Service Ministers, Inskip, Simon, Sam Hoare, Ernest Brown[2] to go into the priorities of the three Defence Departments and the aggregate cost.

In December an Advisory Panel of Industrialists was set up to assist in the execution of the armament programme, but Parliament rose at the end of the year with an uneasy feeling among some members over the delay in establishing a Ministry of Supply. The Secretary of State for War shared their disquiet. Events in the early months of 1939 were to reinforce the stand he was making.

[1] Earl Stanhope, First Lord of the Admiralty: he succeeded Duff Cooper in October 1938.
[2] Minister of Labour.

CHAPTER XVIII

Junior Ministers' Revolt

NOT ONLY criticism but concerted opposition from a quite unexpected quarter became apparent on 19th December. Hore-Belisha's diary discloses what happened.

19th December 1938

I was working in my room at the War Office and at about 5.30 a copy of the *Evening Standard* was brought to me. There was a front-page story in big headlines " Junior Ministers in Revolt. . . . Hore-Belisha as Chief Target." The three Junior Ministers were Hudson,[1] Secretary of Department of Overseas Trade ; Dufferin,[2] Parliamentary Under-Secretary for the Colonies; and Strathcona, Parliamentary Under-Secretary of State for War.

Lord Strathcona and Mount Royal, about two years Hore-Belisha's senior in age, had occupied this office since 1934 and was consequently at the War Office for over three years before Hore-Belisha came in. Their relations had always been very friendly. Strathcona dealt mainly with the Territorial Army and Hore-Belisha had worked closely with him on this, and had advised and helped him. It puzzled and surprised Hore-Belisha and others at the War Office that Strathcona should be a party to this rebellion.

I thought it was a canard and asked at once to see Strathcona. I never for a moment thought he could be implicated, nor do I think did anyone else at the War Office. I expected him to make a public denial at once, but he admitted to me that the report was true, but that he was shocked it had got out. I suggested to him

---

[1] Later Viscount Hudson.   [2] Marquess of Dufferin and Ava.

that it was a pity he had not come to me first with his complaints and that, while I might not have been able to convince him, I could at least have put my point of view. He said he had not thought of that. I asked him to tell me frankly what his grievances were. He mentioned the delay in the publication of the Territorial Army Organisation Report, of which he was Chairman. I told him this was awaiting Treasury approval. He said he wanted conscription and a Ministry of Supply, at which I intervened and remarked that if he had mentioned those matters to me, he might have heard I was in agreement with him, but in any event they were matters of high policy. He told me that he had not approved of my appointment as Secretary of State for War, though he liked me personally He disapproved of my methods of publicity. I suggested to him that perhaps I had to do many things which I myself did not like. I could not, for instance, have got the great increase in recruits during the past year if I had just remained in my chair at the War Office, reading and signing papers. I asked him what he was going to do and he said he liked being at the War Office.

I asked to see the Prime Minister and did so at 9.30 p.m. in his room at the House. I told him about my conversation with Strathcona. He said that about a fortnight ago Rob Hudson had been to see him and had made complaints against various Ministers, including Inskip, Winterton[1] and myself. Among his complaints he said I was incompetent and that it was owing to me that the plans for rearmament were ineffective. He threatened, as did the other Junior Ministers associated with him (he said he had only been authorised to mention two out of the alleged eight to the Prime Minister) to resign if the Ministers concerned were not dismissed. Our interview was cut short on the Prime Minister hearing that A. V. Alexander[2] had risen in the debate. I arranged to see him the next evening at 7 p.m.

20th December 1938

Morris-Jones[3] rang me up and told me that at a meeting of the Liberal-National M.P.s[4] called by him and Beechman a vote of

---

[1] Earl Winterton, Chancellor of the Duchy of Lancaster.
[2] Later Viscount Alexander of Hillsborough.
[3] Sir Henry Morris-Jones, M.P. for Denbigh.
[4] Hore-Belisha was Chairman of the Liberal-National Parliamentary Party.

confidence had been passed in me and that it had been decided that a deputation should see Simon[1] and give him their view of Hudson's attack on me.

When I saw the P.M. at 7 I said I was ready at any time to answer for my record. He replied that I had no need to do that, that I had done extremely well at the War Office and that he considered me the best Secretary of State for War since Haldane.[2] I mentioned that perhaps I had imperfectly understood a reference he had made in his conversation the previous evening about a reconstruction of the Cabinet which might affect me. He replied that he had meant no such thing and that I had clearly misunderstood him.

21st December 1938

I again saw the P.M. and he told me that Crookshank,[3] who had been reported in some paper as having been associated with Hudson, had written to him, repudiating any connection with the revolt and that Dufferin, whom he had seen, said he wanted to have no more to do with the business, and Strathcona likewise. He said he had not seen Hudson again and he was now the only one left in the revolt. Hudson, he added, was reported to be going round the lobby saying that either Hore-Belisha must go or he would. The P.M. said, " So we shall now see who will go." He ended by saying he was having something inspired given out to the Press.

The two days' political sensation ended as suddenly as it had begun. Some contemporary commentators probed below the surface and suggested motives and influences underlying the revolt.

Who was really behind it ? Was it a group of disgruntled and hostile Army officers working along the lines Fabian Ware foresaw ?

The *Birmingham Post*[4] referred to " an active whispering campaign directed against Mr. Hore-Belisha." Was it a prominent political opponent ? The *News Chronicle*[5] traced the trouble to the " long campaign waged against Mr. Hore-Belisha, War Minister, and several other Ministers by Mr. Winston Churchill and a group

[1] Leader of the Liberal-National Parliamentary Party.
[2] Recorded also in Keith Feiling's *Life of Neville Chamberlain*.
[3] Later Lord Crookshank.   [4] 21st December 1938.   [5] 20th December, 1938.

of rebel Conservatives." The *Yorkshire Post*[1] expressed a similar view.

A deeper significance was attached to the revolt by the London correspondent of *Il Giornale d'Italia*:[2] " The criticism of Mr. Hore-Belisha as War Minister by Junior Ministers is due to the growing feeling in Britain against Jews." He was not alone in this view. Many saw with increasing dread the growth of Mosley's anti-Semitic movement in Britain, so long renowned for her tolerance and love of freedom.

In lighter vein the *Glasgow Herald*[3] printed a barrack-room ballad :

" We was sad for 'Ore-Belisher, wiv that smilin' face we know. There was rumours, there was rumblin's, and they said 'e 'ad to go. But we're glad to 'ear 'e's stayin', for 'e's good to blokes like me, since 'e told the sergeant-major orf to bring us pots o' tea.

" 'E's the friend o' common soldiers, and our solid ranks was shook, when they told us that no longer 'e would 'ave his photo took. But we're glad it's just a rumour, and there won't be no disputes, for the bloke 'as told the Curnel orf to black the privates' boots."

Years later on 21st February 1957 Harry Boardman, Parliamentary correspondent of the *Manchester Guardian*, wrote in that paper : " I affirm this of my own knowledge, that a group of Tory Junior Ministers, of both Houses, engaged in an intrigue against Hore-Belisha. My knowledge of the intrigue came from the leader of it. He attained Cabinet rank, but died recently.[4] He left me in no doubt that the intrigue was inspired from within the War Office."

After his interview with the Prime Minister, Hore-Belisha had a talk with Strathcona and then wrote to Chamberlain asking if Strathcona could remain at the War Office. He renewed the request in a further letter dated the 23rd January, 1939, saying : " Strathcona has done some good work, notably on the Territorial Committee, and it will be a wrench for him to go." But the Prime Minister replied that his decision to replace Strathcona at the War Office could

---

[1] 20th December 1938.   [2] 22nd December 1938.   [3] 22nd December 1938.
[4] Viscount Hudson died earlier in February 1957.

not be reversed, as it was bound up with other changes he had in view.

Before leaving the War Office, Strathcona in a letter dated the 31st January 1939, wrote : " Once again thank you for all your kindness and thoughtfulness, which have removed any feeling of bitterness or disappointment that may be mine : as it is, I leave the War Office, feeling that everyone there was and is my friend, not least among all those friends, yourself."

On the 6th January Hore-Belisha went to Devonport, and in a forthright speech to his constituents replied to the charges that had been made against him. " Criticism," he said, " was the breath of political life and every Minister must be ready to answer for his record. But justice demands that where charges are made they should be open and precise. They were not so against me."

After reviewing his administration over the nineteen months he had been at the War Office, he claimed that the results could not have been achieved by a masterly inactivity, as had been suggested, or " by an amateurish superficiality or by a faltering courage." Some of the measures he had taken had to be drastic and decisive, for instance—the comprehensive changes in the Army Council and in the Higher Command.

" I was not unconscious of the risks I ran. I had no illusions when I went to the War Office of what I should have to do. My knowledge that the Prime Minister was equally acquainted with the character of the task and of the repercussions which must follow the measures that had to be taken has throughout sustained me. There are still things to be done if the nation is to have the Army it merits."

He recalled the humanising aims of his reforms and that their stimulating effect was shown in the higher recruiting figures. He referred to the handicaps imposed on the production of munitions owing to the existing system.

He took up the theme of his speech at Cardiff.

" The Supply Branch of the War Office," he said, " was under-taking a duty incomparably greater in variety and extent than had ever been entrusted to a Defence Department in time of peace.

The same Minister who is responsible for organising an Army and for obtaining recruits is responsible for this most intricate mechanism which has branches all over the country and in addition has to negotiate patents and purchases abroad. Just as the Army has to be raised on a voluntary system . . . so have the supplies to be obtained on a war scale from a peacetime economy."

CHAPTER XIX

Christmas in Alsace

Two DAYS before Christmas Hore-Belisha left for Alsace. Snow was falling on the Hohwald. Pictures of him appeared in the Press, ski-ing, sleighing and snow-balling in the Vosges. There were some raised eyebrows. It was unbecoming of a Secretary of State to be photographed in this way. To-day a picture of a Minister of Agriculture leaning over a sty watching his pigs, or of a Chancellor of the Exchequer boiling his egg for breakfast is a common feature in the Press. It was not so in pre-war days, but everything Hore-Belisha did was a news story. He and his beacons were a gift to Low and Strube and other cartoonists.

It was said that he courted publicity, and that he made no pretence about it. He never minded such criticism. It was part of his set purpose to identify himself with the Army and make the country more conscious that it had an Army. Journalists respected his natural and frank way with them and Hore-Belisha never failed to acknowledge the assistance he owed to Fleet Street, both as Minister of Transport in his campaign to reduce road accidents, and at the War Office in his efforts to stimulate recruiting.

After a few days' holiday in the mountains, he arranged with General Hering, Military Governor of Strasbourg, to have a close-up view of the Siegfried Line.

31st December 1938
I travelled with General Hering on a tug up and down the Rhine to see the fortifications the Germans had constructed since March last.

The remarkable feature was the very close concentration of

pill-boxes, some only 20 yards the one from the other. Besides being all along the German bank of the Rhine they were set back for some distance in further rows.

Hering told me this was the case along the length of the frontier for which he was responsible. They had been put up with remarkable rapidity and some were still in construction. He said from his military knowledge the close concentration was quite superfluous if they were merely to be used for machine-guns, and he thought that the Germans intended to use them for some new invention of flame-throwing, to smoke out and destroy the occupants of the French pill-boxes, and in any event to blind these pill-boxes as eyes of the French heavy artillery. The wooded character of the country on the French side would make landings more easily possible than on the German side. He estimated the strength of the Siegfried Line opposite him as being stronger than his by 12 to 1. The whole of the German side of the Rhine is now thickly covered with barbed wire.

The Siegfried Line, the depth of its defences and the speed with which they were being constructed made a startling and forceful impression on Hore-Belisha. These two aspects were obviously in his mind when, in the winter of 1939, after the B.E.F. went to France, he urged that " a bigger conception should be taken of the defences on the British line. What the Germans had done in a few months on the Siegfried Line could and should be accomplished by us, if as it looks now, the Germans do not launch an attack before the spring.[1]"

1st January 1939
I saw Gamelin in Paris and he told me that much time and money would be required to complete the Maginot Line north and south and to strengthen it in those parts where it was weak. It was difficult, he said, to obtain the money necessary now that concentration was centred on the air.

Both Hering and Gamelin were far less optimistic than when I saw them last. They both expressed the view that German troops would be on the Alps, and that Italian troops would be in the Siegfried Line. Hitherto they had regarded the Italian front

[1] *Diary:* 18th November 1939.

as a simple proposition because of the weakness of Italian soldiers, but they had reason to believe that it would not only be Italian soldiers that they might have to meet.

Gamelin said that there were German concentrations on the Dutch frontier and he thought that they might occupy Holland without necessarily going on through Belgium. He thought they would use Holland as an air and submarine base.

I was informed on good authority that Italian aircraft were concentrating on the Eastern Mediterranean. The danger to our Fleet in Alexandria from sudden bombing attack was pointed out.

I lunched with Bonnet at the British Embassy. He said that Chamberlain's policy at Munich was right and that it would have been a mistake for us to have gone to war with Germany in view of our weak condition. That was the principal reason why he had opposed intervention at that time. But if the Italians or Germans made any attack on the French that would be a different story. He hoped that no concessions would be made to Italy.

Bonnet said that he had had an inquiry from an emissary of Franco, asking what would be the French attitude in the event of an appeal for an armistice being made by Spain. I said I imagined he would support it.

On the subject of Spain, Colonel de Lattre de Tassigny, Chief of Staff of the 6th Region, told me that it was his view the Italians did not really wish to bring the Civil War in Spain to an end. The more unsettlement there was in Spain, the better pleased the Italians would be, as they could more easily use Spanish bases in the event of hostilities with France.

During the middle of January, the Prime Minister and the Foreign Secretary paid a visit to Mussolini.

18th January 1939
The Cabinet met this morning. The P.M. reported on his visit to Mussolini. Horace Wilson after the meeting asked me how things were going. I told him I was bearing up in spite of recent slings and arrows.[1] He said he would like to have a talk with me. Lunched with John Simon at No. 11.

[1] The Junior Ministers' Revolt.

19th January 1939

Horace Wilson came to lunch at Stafford Place. He spoke about the debating strength in the House. I said I did not think any lack of it came from the Government Front Bench. But the attitude of the Whips' Office was to get through everything quickly and this resulted in inadequate discussions. Back-benchers felt frustrated, and it was difficult to know who was coming on.

I talked to him about the need for a Ministry of Supply. We had started with a small programme over a long term, and we now have a big programme over what may be a short term.

I told him that on 9th January, I had asked every member of the Army Council to let me have separately a frank statement of any difficulties which, in his opinion, had hampered the progress of the Army's rearmament programme. I had asked for their statements to cover difficulties due to external administration, such as Treasury control, negotiations with other departments, Cabinet decisions, and difficulties arising out of administration in the War Office or under the control of the War Office.

I had told them that I had no intention of using their statements to apportion blame. I was only anxious to be informed of any hindrances so that I could help to remove them.

Yesterday I had received the reports of each Army Councillor and I gave Wilson the gist of their criticisms. I told him I was in general agreement with them, in fact they reinforced my own views, which I elaborated to him. Variations in policy had repercussions throughout the whole military machine and in the Commands. Indecision regarding the scale of war provision was definitely responsible for the delay in increasing factory construction.

I illustrated to him the retarding effects of the strict financial control exercised by the Treasury on the execution of the Army's expanding programme. Every item had to be subjected to meticulous examination before sanction was given. Every project had to be 100 per cent right and full value was squeezed out of every halfpenny. The whole procedure became so involved that it was almost brought to a standstill before authority was given to go ahead. There could be no real progress until there was some relaxation of the system at any rate while the emergency lasted.

With regard to difficulties within the War Office I told Wilson that steps were being taken to reach speedier decisions. The cumbrous machine of the Finance branch at the War Office needed decentralisation. I was appalled by the increase in 'paper' work and I had no doubt that the habit of writing minutes from one to another had a great deal to do with it.

On my way to seeing the P.M. I ran into James Rae.[1] He has always been very helpful, particularly over the Marriage Allowance. I half jocularly referred to the dead hand of the Treasury and he good-humouredly retorted that if he had received a penny for every time the Treasury was damned, he would be a very wealthy man.

I had a long talk with Neville, and told him about the Army Councillors' reports. I repeated what I had said to Wilson. Feel a bit depressed.

21st December 1938

In my Memorandum to the Cabinet on the effectiveness of the role of the Army in the light of Munich, I asked for increased provision of equipment and war reserves for the Field Force. I also asked for increased equipment for the Territorial Army. I attach considerable importance to this, but priority for the manufacture of A.A. guns still holds absolute. The French have been pressing for military assistance from us, but they have been told that our Air Defence requirements must come first.

26th January 1939

At the C.I.D. meeting this morning I said if we were involved in war it would be a struggle for our very existence and not a war in which we could limit our liability. The assumption, therefore, on which the role of the Army was based in March 1938, that there would be no such expansion of the Army and therefore of military supply as occurred in the 1914-1918 war, was out of date and that it should be referred to the Cabinet for reconsideration. The impact of the next war, I said, would be so overwhelming that if a Ministry of Supply were not already in being at the outset, there was a danger that the war would be lost before the organisation could be set up. Again I urged that a Ministry of Supply

---

[1] Sir James Rae, Under-Secretary, Treasury; Chairman, Inter-Service Committee set up in 1938 to examine the award of marriage allowances in the three services.

should be set up at the earliest possible date. I was supported by Halifax and Ernest Brown. Inskip is to put our views before the Cabinet.

2nd February 1939

The C.I.D. approved of the proposals in my Memo on the effectiveness of the Army, involving complete equipment and reserves for the first and second contingents of the Field Force, also for war equipment and reserves for four divisions of the T.A. Field Force and full training equipment for the remainder. This means of course much more productive capacity will be required. I said it was quite true my proposals modified the role of the Army laid down last March. The policy then was that land forces would not be needed for a Continental war, but Hitler changed all that a day after my Estimates speech.

I was asked whether a reduction in the cost could not be made. The upshot was I got general approval for all twelve infantry divisions of the T.A. to be provided with a full-scale training equipment. The Treasury and War Office are going to get together to work out the details. The rest of my proposals are being reviewed.

CHAPTER XX

His Second Army Estimates

HORE-BELISHA introduced his second Army Estimates in the House of Commons on the 8th March. The speech was comprehensive in its range from the fundamental principles of strategy to the soldier's clothing and food. It was divided into two parts, which were inter-related : Home Defence and plans for the Army's contribution in the event of a Continental war. Times had changed since his last Estimates speech and public opinion was changing too.

" I recognise," he said, " that this year the question uppermost in the minds of the House is to what extent we should be prepared, in the event of war, to intervene on the Continent of Europe. The question is a searching one, and can be adequately discussed only within the context of our strategic problems. . . . The foundation of British strategy has been to maintain land forces which, in conjunction with sea power, will be sufficient to safeguard our territories. . . . No organisation can be economical or effective, least of all a military organisation, in the absence of a clear appreciation of the purposes which it is to fulfil. For the con-venience of the House I propose to examine these purposes and the manner in which we are discharging them."

In a historical survey he showed how Army policy had changed with the beginning of the century from keeping the shores of Britain free from invasion, to the " Blue Water School " principles of Mr. Balfour. He recalled how the military centre of gravity had shifted and that in 1906 Haldane, rejecting the Army's traditional policy and basing his reforms on the new hypothesis that the Navy, with a lesser degree of military support, could look after Home defence, had dismantled the defences of London and scrapped everything that had formerly been thought necessary for the local protection of the country against attack. He had "got rid of things, root and branch, by the aid of a firm principle." Now we are back, Hore-Belisha said, where we were before Haldane's time, and "as we are proceeding in precisely the opposite direction, we may claim that history, so often alleged to be repetitive, is here, at any rate, in a self-contradictory mood."

More than thirty years before, Haldane had introduced to the Commons, in a speech of three hours, the military changes so long associated with his name, which were now recalled by his successor in 1939. Fewer than half a dozen of those who heard Hore-Belisha had listened to Haldane's speech. Among them were Simon and Churchill. Haldane's total expenditure on the Army was under £29 millions a year. Hore-Belisha was asking for just over £161 millions.

In the changed conception, that the invader would come not by sea but by air, Hore-Belisha explained how the new system of protection against air attack had been created and how it had recently been developed. A separate Anti-Aircraft and Coast Defence Army had been raised out of the Territorial body, adding great increase to our military strength. Two Anti-Aircraft divisions had been increased to five and he proposed to add two more. "They will repel invasion by sea and air." The whole would be organised into an Anti-Aircraft Command under a Corps Commander, who would become General Officer Commanding Anti-Aircraft Command under the Air Officer Commander-in-Chief, Fighter Command. A new directorate would be established at the War Office under a Deputy Chief of the Imperial General Staff for Anti-Aircraft and Coast defence. The importance and enhanced prestige of anti-aircraft defence had stimulated recruiting, he said, and in the last twelve months the number of officers and men had doubled and the new financial year opened with a strength of 75,000. "No provision which we can make for training seems enough to satisfy their enthusiasm."

With a glance back to the Munich crisis, Hore-Belisha enumerated the measures taken by the War Office to improve the defence system. All the gaps had not yet been filled, but the aim was to perfect the machine so that in any emergency "it would be less likely to omit some essential detail or overlook some requisite appliance."

Munitions capacity had been expanded and a new factory for making additional 3.7 inch anti-aircraft guns had been started. Production should begin in the autumn.

Further National Defence Companies were being formed, composed mainly of ex-Servicemen, whose duties would be to guard vulnerable points.

"Home Defence, once again our foremost obligation, was therefore being developed so as to give the people of this country, so far as humanly could be contrived, that security against invasion which they were determined to achieve."

He turned to Imperial Defence. "Have we also a principle to guide us in the increase of our garrisons overseas ? We find again and again, when we think we have evolved some new principle, that we are only reverting to an old one." And he referred to a recommendation[1] of the Caernarvon Commission of 1882. A start had already been made in stiffening British garrisons abroad by the recruitment of local troops. Recalling the heroic defence of Gibraltar and the fate of Minorca in former years and the Navy's task in relieving the fortresses, because they had fallen below strength, Hore-Belisha underlined the necessity, due to the submarine and the bomber plane, of accelerating the scheme of self-contained local forces. In Singapore, in Hong Kong, in Ceylon, more native personnel were to be enlisted. In short, the establishment of Indian and local troops in defended ports outside India was being raised in the coming year to 9,500, as compared with 3,766 in 1937.

Then he came to future plans for the Strategic Reserve. "We no longer intend to rely upon a single strategic reserve situated in the centre of the Empire." An additional strategic reserve was already being formed in the Middle East, with its nucleus of two divisions stationed in Palestine. The Middle East Reserve was to

---

[1] " The stations far distant from the United Kingdom and in close proximity to the stations of foreign Powers are liable to sudden attack and cannot be reinforced without delay; their garrisons therefore must be kept up to war strength." Para. 157, Report of the Caernarvon Commission.

be a separate, self-sufficient force, with its own reserves, and it was to be held for use anywhere within the radius of British interests in that part of the world. The area, which included Palestine, was crucial enough even in those days to warrant such a development. In the event of a satisfactory re-adaptation and re-arming of the forces in India, the Middle East Reserve would be geographically well placed to meet the emergencies of Imperial defence, without impinging on the strategic reserve in Britain. In this scheme of redistribution a link was being added in the middle between the United Kingdom and India. The Army would be flung right across the Imperial lines of communications and, when the scheme was completed, it was envisaged that no part of these communications could be threatened which would not have troops nearby for speedy reinforcement. The strain on the Navy would thus in a measure be relieved and the calls on it for escorts would be reduced. As with the first obligation of the Government's policy, Home Defence, so Hore-Belisha said, with the second obligation, the protection of our sea communications, the Army was endeavouring to fulfil its role.

He then proceeded to the preparation and equipping of the Field Force in the event of war in a European theatre. He outlined the size of the potential Army the War Office was planning. It would be composed of nineteen divisions, six Regular (two of them armoured), nine Territorial infantry divisions, three motorised and one armoured division and a number of unbrigaded units both Regular and Territorial. This compared roughly with the Field Force of six Regular and one cavalry division planned by Haldane, which was the size of the " Contemptible Little Army " that crossed to France in 1914 and acquitted itself so valiantly in Flanders.

Every fighting arm of the Service, he continued, had been remodelled and would be supplied with modern weapons. The Territorial Army would be on the same basis—a new decision, modifying the existing one which allowed the Territorial Army only a quota of equipment for training purposes. Many of Hore-Belisha's statements about the Field Army and production were couched, as the *Observer* of the 12th March pointed out, in the future tense and "would not be realised if 'the day' were to supervene say, to-morrow." " The day " turned out to be only six months away.

Referring to the progress of the mechanisation of the Army, he announced that an additional armoured division, Britain's third, was to be created. The first armoured division had been formed in the autumn of 1937 ; the second, known as the Seventh Armoured Division, had been formed in 1938 in Egypt, where Hore-Belisha felt mobile troops should predominate. Just before Munich, Hobart was sent out to command that division. Hore-Belisha admitted that tanks were the "most recalcitrant element in production." While the delay in the prototype of the heavier, or 'cruiser,' tank might have the advantage of learning from other countries' experience, he emphasised that it was "only now coming into production." In the light tanks "we were well ahead."

Woolwich, with its "treasures and historic possessions," was to be moved to Sandhurst, a difficult decision to make because "one touches on understandable susceptibilities which one desires to treat with reverence." The two colleges would each preserve its identity. There would be no lowering but a raising of the standard. Military training and education should be attuned to new tactical developments.

"My idea of democratising the Army was to throw Woolwich and Sandhurst open to any cadet from whatever school, irrespective of his means, provided he has the necessary qualifications. I preferred that to a system which would make promotion exclusively from the ranks."

Shortly he would announce a further improvement in the existing system.

"What numbers can we muster ? " he continued. Exclusive of British troops in India and Burma—531,355. Forty thousand men had been recruited into the Regular Army in the current financial year. With an intake of 83,000 men in the past twelve months, the Territorial Army had beaten all records since its formation. For the first time in peace it was over its establishment, which was being raised to 250,000.

"How shall we expand in emergency? " he asked. Comprehensive plans were being made at the War Office to speed up the machinery of mobilisation, and he explained how it would affect the embodiment of the Territorial Army. A nation-wide network of recruiting centres and training units was being organised. Buildings for new centres had been selected and additional recruiting officers had been nominated. Medical boards had been appointed and the medical code had been agreed. Preparations were afoot to call up in peacetime a number of reservists, both officers and men, for brief retraining. As far as possible the War Office was realistically gearing the organisation of the Army for all eventualities.

This led to his examination : How could the Field Army be despatched and maintained in war ? The whole Force could not arrive, he said, simultaneously in a theatre of war, where continental armies might already be in position. It would have to be despatched and it would have to arrive in echelons at serial dates. Shipping calculations had been made, but the problem, owing to the heavier and complex armament, was more difficult than in 1914.

A week later on the Report Stage of the Army Estimates,[1] when questioned for greater detail about the despatch of the Field Force, he confessed that he could not give exact times as in Bradshaw, because that would be a guide to interested countries, but he made it clear that the expedition would not be an operation in fits and starts, but a steady process, worked out in an orderly sequence. In this debate he referred to the Air component of the Field Force, which was to include a definite allotment of Fighter Squadrons. Before long he was to be engaged in a struggle for the Field Force to have its own separate Air Arm.

Britain, he said, had to fulfil her inescapable obligation to assist her Ally in case of war, and he quoted the Prime Minister's declaration of the 11th February that " the solidarity of interests by which France and this country are united is such that any threat to the vital interests of France, from whatever quarter it came, must evoke the immediate co-operation of this country."

While admitting that conversations with France had not committed us militarily, he rejected the idea that there could be any limited liability on Britain's part. The Army was not being planned for the purpose of aggression, it was a natural complement to the Prime Minister's pledge. There should be a common defence for common diplomatic interests. " Prudent minds should be ready for any eventuality," he commented. In the new order of things the role of the Army, defined in his Estimates of a year ago, was changed

[1] House of Commons debates 14th March 1939.

and the last priority, aid to an ally, had become a major commitment.

Hore-Belisha then posed a crucial question : " Can we also find a principle to guide us so that we can make the fullest contribution that necessity would impose ?

" The principle which we lay down is this. In order that it may be possible for us to deliver our maximum effort in a continental war, should need arise, the productive arrangements which we should make in peace, together with accumulated reserves and the new capacity which could be created and brought into operation, must be sufficient to equip and maintain each echelon of the force as it is deployed. By the time the last of the serial dates is reached, new forces should be trained and the necessary additional provision for their equipment and maintenance made. It is in accordance with this principle that we are proceeding."

Six days later on the Report Stage of the Estimates he poignantly said :

" I recognise, no man more, that the essence of our effort depends upon production. The strength of the British Army is not only in Aldershot and on Salisbury Plain; it is in Woolwich and Nottingham "—by which he meant in the munition factories.

Turning to the conditions of service he continued : " The Army is being mechanised. I hope it is being humanised." Following the pattern of the reforms that had been instituted a year before to make the Army better fed, better housed, better educated, better paid, to give to every soldier, without a trade, training, if he so desired it, before he left the Army, he announced "one or two measures for the benefit of the soldier." Service in India, a hardship many felt, was to be reduced from six and a half years to four. Seven million pounds were to be spent on barracks in the coming twelve months —a large increase on the preceding Estimates—" but there was much leeway to make up."

Under the auspices of Sir Isadore Salmon, the Army's honorary catering adviser, improvements were being made in the highly skilled craft of cooking and in catering, and a highly qualified cook had already been promoted to commissioned rank. His continuing aim, was to bring the standard of living of the soldier more into accord with modern conditions ; to enable him to make a career in the Service ; to make the Army more attractive to the youth of the country, instead of a lost opportunity to the actual and potential unemployed. The flow of recruits had shown that the Army had been invigorated with a new spirit. For the officer the aim was better prospects and a more assured career. Two years before it had been impossible to fill the number of vacancies, but as a result of the improvements in pay and allowances, the guaranteeing of careers by time-promotion, subject to efficiency, and the abandonment of the old device of keeping officers on half-pay while waiting for employment, the situation had completely altered.

He concluded by recalling a type of soldier of forty years ago, Joe Pepper by name. He had come across him recently in a book entitled *The King's Service*. As the author described him, his appearance was unimpressive. He had a pasty complexion and hair cropped close to his scalp, except for his quiff. He was a friendly sort and ripe for conversation at any time. A good soldier in the making. The people at the top displayed no particular interest in him beyond keeping him rigidly efficient as a fighting machine. He was given no opportunity to learn the simplest trade and his future prospects after discharge appeared to be a matter of complete indifference to everybody.

He added :

" Joe Pepper died. He was killed, in fact, and his type has passed away. The author of the book, Major-General Ian Hay Beith, is now Director of Public Relations at the War Office.[1] His task is to make the soldier known and the Army understood. Joe Pepper's successor is more fortunate in the conditions of his service. He resembles him, however, in certain unchangeable respects ; he will carry on into the unknown future of our history what is quite independent of circumstances, the imperturbable spirit and the good-humoured courage of those who belong to the proudest of professions and march onward with the regiment."

[1] He succeeded Major-General Alan Dawnay on his death.

He sat down after one hour and fifteen minutes. During the speech it was noticed that he took an occasional sip from a glass on the table. Lady Simon, wife of the Chancellor, had prepared a concoction and had sent it over from No. 11 to ease his relaxed throat, following an attack of influenza.

Uppermost in Members' minds was the significance of his statement that there could be no limited liability on Britain's part if war broke out, and the military plans he had outlined to meet the eventuality. Only a year before the Liberal Leader, Sir Archibald Sinclair, had been but expressing the general view when he said that " to attempt to organise an army on a continental scale would, in my view, be a disastrous blunder."[1]

The official Labour Opposition made no protest. Conservatives welcomed the Government's new approach. The Press on the whole took a realistic view, but there was still some questioning about the wisdom of sending an Expeditionary Force to France. " Willingness to send this heavy complement of land power across the water can only prescribe our strategy and shackle our finances."[2] And " Our help to France would best be rendered in the air, not by the Army. . . . To undertake this military burden is unnecessary and unwise."[3]

Duff Cooper said that his speech was " probably the most satisfactory statement with regard to the Army that had ever been made in the House." Churchill[4] complimented him on the " very excellent and carefully considered statement . . . which will be looked upon as one of the definite pronouncements on behalf of the War Office on military policy. . . ." " Churchill ends the war on Hore-Belisha," announced the *Daily Herald*,[5] apparently sharing the view, expressed from time to time by other newspapers, that Churchill was one of Hore-Belisha's foremost assailants, and it invited its readers " to cast their minds back to last autumn, when Winston was launching the great attack upon Hore-Belisha, in order to get the full flavour of these Churchillian embraces."

The Times :[6] " It may justly be said that if there is still a good deal that could be realised in the way of Army reforms, Mr. Hore-Belisha

---

[1] House of Commons debates, 14th March 1938.
[2] *Evening Standard*, 9th March 1939.   [3] *Daily Sketch*, 10th March 1939.
[4] House of Commons debates 14th March 1939.   [5] 15th March 1939.
[6] 9th March 1939.

has done more in less than two years of office than has been achieved before in a generation." The *Birmingham Post* : " The biggest and most important speech since Haldane explained his policy and organisation. No War Minister could have done more, many would have done less." The *Scotsman* :[1] " It may without exaggeration be said that the Army has not known such a reformer since Mr. Haldane's day and the problems with which Mr. Hore-Belisha has to deal are both more extensive and complex than those which confronted his illustrious predecessor."

In France there was a feeling of relief in political and military circles. The French Ambassador, M. Corbin, who had listened to the speech from the Diplomatic Gallery, was instructed by his Government to convey a message,[2] of very sincere appreciation for the recent statement in Parliament of the Secretary of State for War. " This evidence of the determination of Britain to make all its resources available and effective in the event of trouble had had a great effect in France, just as no doubt its significance would be readily appreciated in all quarters." But there was some disappointment also that Hore-Belisha had made no mention of conscription in Britain. In French opinion a community of effort should entail a common sacrifice. Moreover, M. Fabry, a former War Minister, had stated in Paris on the same day as Hore-Belisha's speech that the Maginot Line was undermanned by twenty per cent.

In Italy, Gayda, Mussolini's mouthpiece, in *Il Giornale d'Italia* commented that " The rearmament of the democracies had assumed an offensive character . . . but they will not discourage Italy, Germany and Japan from proclaiming their legitimate aspirations." The German newspapers printed the text of Hore-Belisha's speech with little comment and a Nazi propaganda spokesman said that it was only of interest as a news report. The reaction, however, of the German Military Attaché in London appeared otherwise. In a letter to Hore-Belisha of the 9th March, Major-General Sir Edward Spears[3] wrote :

" What I think will interest you is that last night I saw the American Military Attaché. He was sitting next to the German Military Attaché during your speech and said the latter was

[1] 9th March 1939.   [2] 11th March 1939.   [3] M.P. for Carlisle.

completely stunned, and in fact, when he left on his way to get a bus, he had not recovered enough to carry on ordinary conversation. Colonel Lee, the American, was very much amused and immensely interested in the extraordinary effect of what was apparently a completely unexpected blow to the German."

No letter of congratulation pleased Hore-Belisha more than the one[1] he received from Major-General Sir Gerald F. Ellison, who had been private secretary to Haldane at the War Office :

"I trust you won't think it presumptuous on my part my offering you my most sincere congratulations on your statement in the House. It was a truly masterly pronouncement of policy. If Haldane's spirit is still in touch with mundane affairs, it must have given him undiluted pleasure. . . ."

On the morning after his speech Hore-Belisha wrote to Liddell Hart :

"I do not forget that you it was who first directed my mind on to the constructive lines which it has since followed. The task of fulfilling ideals is not so easy as you, with your dynamic conceptions, have sometimes imagined. There is much on the road and it is sometimes wiser to steer round obstacles rather than, on all occasions, crudely to try and crush them.

"You have not known sometimes how much preparatory work, psychological as well as material, has been required. We are engaged, you and I, in our different ways, in trying to obtain recognition for the Army and a clear understanding of the purposes for which it exists. Our mission must take time and I think we are nearer to carrying everyone with us than ever before.

"Changing circumstances, arising from political developments, cause us also to adjust the emphasis which we place on one aspect or another of our role, but I have endeavoured to show the historical continuity of the Trunk Road down which, despite turnings, we are trying to make our journey.

"During these last days I have longed for an opportunity of exchanging ideas with you and having the benefit of your counsel, but I have had the 'flu on me for a month and I have been almost

[1] 10th March 1939.

completely voiceless. I knew, however, that you were a silent companion on the journey.

" My gratefulness to you. Stick to your last and don't become that more confused personality, known as a politician.

" P.S.—We have at the War Office really as good and well-related a team as human affairs permit."

CHAPTER XXI

The Fight for Conscription

ON the 15th March 1939, Hitler struck again. German troops invaded Czechoslovakia and a second sovereign state was forced to surrender to his terms. Emergency meetings of the Cabinet were held during the next few days.

In a speech at Birmingham two days later the Prime Minister upbraided Hitler for his breach of faith and recounted the pledges, public and private, the Führer had given. " How can the events this week be reconciled with those assurances ? " he asked. He warned the German leader that if this was a step in the direction of an attempt to dominate the world by force Britain would take her part " in resisting the challenge to the utmost of her power."

18th March 1939

At the Cabinet meeting this morning we all warmly approved the P.M.'s speech. I said that hitherto Hitler's expressed aims had been to incorporate the German population in the Reich. The Prague coup shows his determination to absorb non-German peoples. There was a danger of speaking in terms of military attack on this or that country. We are now faced with a technique which brought the collapse of States from within. Hitler has seized in Czechoslovakia massive potential for equipping the German Army. We need to take steps vastly to increase our military strength. I was in favour of alliances with Poland and Russia.

International tension increased and there were rumours and reports that attacks on Rumania and Poland were imminent.

THE PRIVATE PAPERS OF HORE-BELISHA

From Sir Horace Wilson, 10 Downing Street, 28th March 1939:

" My dear Secretary of State—The Prime Minister is to address the 1922 Committee at the House of Commons this evening. He understands that many of those present will wish him to say something about the greater use of the Territorial movement and especially to say what it is proposed to do to take advantage of the recent flow of Territorial recruits.

" I see that the D.G.T.A.,[1] speaking on Saturday, referred to the 'spring tide.' There are reports that in some areas recruits are being turned away, perhaps because complements are already full. This naturally raises the question whether it would not be possible at once to decide to form new units so that, at any rate, the men might be enrolled and given some sort of training, even if, for the time being, equipment is not available for them.

" The Prime Minister would like to make some reference to the rush of volunteers for the Territorial Army and to go on to say that steps are being taken to utilise all those who are coming forward.

" If there is difficulty in quickly turning them into 'pukka' Territorials, one suggestion that has been made is that they might, for the time being, be formed into Voluntary Training Corps, attached to Territorial units, and be given instruction from the Territorial instructors. (If there is a shortage of instructors, can some of these be brought out from among the ex-Territorials?)

" Another suggestion that has been made is that it would be a good thing if Army Reservists were called out from time to time (including the officers) so that they might be trained in up-to-date methods.

" The Prime Minister would like a note on the Territorial points as early as possible this afternoon, so that he may consider what line to take this evening.

" When we meet at lunch perhaps we could discuss some other points which arise."

28th March 1939

Horace Wilson came to lunch at Stafford Place and we dis-

---

[1] Director General of the Territorial Army, General Sir Walter Kirke.

THE FIGHT FOR CONSCRIPTION

cussed the suggestions in his letter, which had come by hand during the morning. I told him we ought to go much further. Recent events had convinced me that we would have to have conscription.

He said it was out of the question, that the Trade Unions were adamantly opposed to it. I remarked that it would be a poor sort of Government that would jeopardise the country and the Empire for fear of political opposition.

After lunch I went straight to the House and saw the Prime Minister in his room. He told me Halifax was insistent that some forthright action should be taken as immediate evidence that we meant business in resisting aggression. An announcement of a bigger military effort on our part would be the most convincing gesture we could make in the present international tension.

I used the same arguments I had put to Wilson about conscription, but he said that on political grounds it was impracticable. What did I propose, to secure a large increase in the Territorial Army? I suggested doubling it. He liked the idea. I told him it was not all plain sailing. I had not been able to consult the Army Council and I saw difficulties from the military point of view, which might land the War Office in for criticism. The capacity of drill halls would be overstrained until new ones could be provided. There would be a shortage of equipment, instructors, uniforms, etc. He was anxious to have an announcement made in the next twenty-four hours.

I returned to the War Office, called a meeting of the Army Council and explained the whole position. The plan is to raise the peacetime strength (130,000) of the Territorial Field Force to war strength (170,000) and then to double it (340,000). The method proposed is to over-recruit in every unit so as to form a cadre from which a duplicate unit can be built.

In order to secure the maximum effect abroad, it was decided that the Prime Minister himself, instead of the Secretary of State for War, should make the announcement in the House of Commons on the following day, 29th March.

" The House will remember," the Prime Minister said, in reply to a Private Notice Question put by Arthur Greenwood,[1] " that in a recent statement I announced that every aspect of our national life including the National Defence programmes would be examined anew.

" In the course of this review His Majesty's Government have been impressed with the need for availing themselves still further of the spirit of voluntary service which is manifest throughout the country. In particular they feel that they cannot allow would-be recruits for the Territorial Army to be refused because the units to which they apply are already over strength."

He then announced the doubling of the Territorial Army. A similar statement was made by the Leader in the Lords. This suggestion, made by Hore-Belisha on the spur of the moment and without, as he records, any chance of his consulting the Army Council, now that it was set in operation involved, as he foresaw, a succession of problems. The existing drill halls were overstrained. There was a great shortage of instructors, of equipment and of uniforms. But the task was undertaken and the difficulties faced; and the doubling of the Territorial Army has since come to be regarded as one of Hore-Belisha's greater successes. Its effect was widespread. It encouraged the nation and indicated to the world Britain's determination to take every step in her power to resist aggression.

On the 31st March, Chamberlain informed the Commons of the Government's guarantee to Poland. " In the event," he said, " of any action which clearly threatened Polish independence, and which the Polish Government accordingly considered it vital to resist with their national forces, His Majesty's Government would feel themselves bound at once to lend to the Polish Government all support in their power. They have given the Polish Government an assurance to that effect." He added : " The French Government have authorised me to make it plain that they stand in the same position as His Majesty's Government."

5th April 1939

I again raised at the Cabinet the urgency of increasing the strength of the Regular Army. I pointed out that changes in the

[1] Speaking from the Opposition Front Bench.

international situation and in the role of the Army made it imperative to do this without delay. We will require an intake of about
100,000 in the coming year. Simon said it was impossible to
accept this further large commitment and I was asked to reduce my
proposal.

Albania was seized by Italy on the 7th April and the guarantee
which had been given to Poland was shortly extended to Rumania
and Greece. Against none of these Government declarations did
the Opposition raise a dissentient voice. It was only in later years
that criticism was made.

On Tuesday, the 11th April, following the bombardment of
Albania by Italy, on the previous Good Friday, the Army Council
met.

11th April 1939

A message was brought to me during the Army Council
meeting that Winston was on the line and had asked if I would
go to Chartwell as he had a bad foot and could not come to
London. He said he particularly wanted to have a talk to me.
I guessed what he was feeling, being out of it all. I sent a message
that I would go down as soon as the meeting was over.

Reached Chartwell about 10 p.m. He opened the door himself.
He had a felt slipper on his bad foot. We had dinner alone
together. He recalled the difficulties he had had during the war,
how he had advocated measures in the Cabinet, which had been
turned down by his colleagues, and then had suffered violent
opposition because those measures had not been carried out. I
arrived back home about 2 a.m.

Hore-Belisha's notes at this time indicate that the Government
was anxious to include Russia in their efforts and negotiations to
secure a common front against aggression. But Russia insisted on
her terms, which were incompatible with those of Poland, and the
Polish Government refused to enter into any military arrangement
that would embrace Russia. The Polish attitude was influenced by
historic memories of Russian invasion, but uppermost was its
contention that the one thing likely to provoke Hitler would be a
close association of Poland and Russia. Rumania also shared with

Poland a deep-seated hostility to Communism. The British and French Chiefs of Staff advised that, if war came, it was essential that Germany should be made to fight on two fronts. Poland, they maintained, was the master key in the situation and her support in any international defence scheme was therefore paramount.

Britain's commitments, as a result of the guarantees she had given, spread far across Europe. But without a Ministry of Supply and without conscription, she was not in a position to give the military assistance expected of her, if called upon to fulfil her pledges.

Hore-Belisha put off his visit to Gibraltar and to Portugal. On the 11th April the Prime Minister wrote him :

" I had hoped to have been able to see you to-day, but it has been quite impossible for me to do so.

" In the light of developments since the Cabinet last considered the question of a Ministry of Supply in peace and in war, and especially having regard to the decision about enlarging the Territorial Army, I have come to the conclusion that the matter ought to be considered afresh. I have therefore asked Chatfield[1] and Morrison[2] (who prepared the report which the Cabinet considered two weeks ago) to review the question again. and to prepare for consideration by the Cabinet—if possible at their meeting on the 19th April—a fresh paper with their recommendations as to what might be done to meet the needs of the new situation. I have asked them to consider the scope of the Ministry and, of course, the question as to its powers. I have no doubt that Chatfield will be communicating with you."

Hore-Belisha replied on the 12th April :

" I was more than pleased to have your letter and it is a great relief to know that the establishment of the Ministry of Supply is likely to be ready for settlement—I hope favourably—by the 19th April.

" It was encouraging to learn what is in your mind, because as you know, I have for some time urged the necessity for such a Ministry and it now seems to me that there will have to be wider

[1] Minister for Co-ordination of Defence.
[2] The Rt. Hon. W. S. Morrison, Chancellor of the Duchy of Lancaster; later Speaker of the House of Commons, then Lord Dunrossil.

powers than were contemplated when we first discussed the proposal.

" The question of assuring priority for Government orders has become overwhelmingly important in view of the pressure of events. Machine tool makers, for instance, are quoting fifty to sixty weeks delivery to us, but this is twice the time that it should take to obtain results.

" You will not mind my drawing your attention to another requirement of the Army. The absence of trained man-power is a weakness which I regard with more and more apprehension. As you are aware, I put in a scheme to Chatfield a little time ago and I had hoped that it was being considered. I learned only yesterday, however, that this was not the case, and I agreed with Chatfield that I should approach you. I accordingly do so, and I hope you will give instructions that it can be examined without delay.

" Our new foreign policy carries the inevitable implication that, should war break out, the land forces will have to bear a heavy part, and the scheme which I have propounded could be brought quickly into operation.

" I fervently hope that we may be able to overcome any opposition to compulsion at this time."

A *Times* editorial of the 13th April on the two problems, Recruiting and Supply, stated :

" It is small wonder that the Secretary of State for War, speaking in Bermondsey on March 31st ' from a purely military standpoint ' sighed for ' the inestimable advantages—in the simplification of training, of administration, and of immediate power—which conscription would bring.'

"It is only five weeks since, in the debate on the Army Estimates, the Army was given, for the first time, a definition of its new functions. Even that part of it which is concerned with anti-aircraft defence has been increased in a year from two divisions to seven. So great an expansion both in numbers and in functions renders obsolete the arrangements previously made for supply.

" The industrial background which sufficed for the Army as conceived in 1937 must clearly be quite insufficient to-day, though only last February the Industrial Panel[1] reported that the arrangements made for all the Services showed a scope and a foresight which the public did not fully appreciate. Supply for the Army, and for an Army of the size now contemplated, is a different question from supply for the other Services. . . . The Air Force to-day is generally recognised to have overcome its supply difficulties, and to be well ahead of its programme. But it took a long time and it was not faced so suddenly with a vast programme of expansion as the Army is to-day.

"As Mr. Hore-Belisha said in the speech already quoted, 'we are operating under a system which gives us no power to assure completion of our orders with urgency or in precedence.'"

12th April 1939

I saw Horace Wilson after Questions. I said I hoped the P.M. would not give any impression in the House on Thursday that he was continuing to accept Mussolini's word. The country would not stand for it; what was wanted was strong action.

I told him of my relief that a Ministry of Supply was to be set up. I am taking it for granted now that it must be.

Just before he left me to see the P.M., he said he was astonished that the P.M.'s suggestion to employ the Territorials from three to six months, that is to let them continue in their jobs during the day and man their guns and searchlights at night, could not be carried out. I told him that it was absolutely impracticable. The General Staff had advised me that it would completely dislocate the Territorial Army.

14th April 1939

Chatfield's paper on the Ministry of Supply, which the P.M. told me in his letter of the 11th April he had asked him to draw up, recorded the complex problems with which I was suddenly confronted, that it was my opinion that the task involved would necessitate the carrying out by the War Office of functions quite outside the scope of a normal Defence department, and that it was imperative to detach supply responsibility from the War Office and place it under a separate Ministry. Chatfield's conclusion was that my view should be accepted.

[1] The Prime Minister's Advisory Panel of Industrialists, set up in December 1938.

Saturday, 15th April 1939

Conferences all day at the War Office. I sent a letter by messenger to the Prime Minister at Chequers. I asked for his authority to circulate papers to the Cabinet on Monday morning.

" As I have always discussed with you and agreed in advance with you any proposals which I have had to make for the Army, I would like to let you know the present situation at once.

" Yesterday the C.I.G.S. suggested to me that it was advisable at once partially to mobilise the Regular Army. He advanced this proposal on three grounds :

(1) That the Field Force and the garrisons are short of men at a time when every country in Europe is in some state of mobilisation.

(2) That the shortage of men in the Regular Army makes it impossible to train the forces properly.

(3) That there is no means of keeping the anti-aircraft defences in a state of continuous readiness without some regular nucleus which could not in the near future be provided except from reservists.

" I subsequently with him saw all the Commanders-in-Chief who were in conference[1] at the War Office and they stressed the advisability of immediate partial mobilisation.

" It is only this morning that I have had an opportunity of seeing a paper on the subject, and, had you been in London, I would have immediately visited you. As it is, should you desire it, I am at your disposal to come anywhere, although I imagine it will be sufficient if you have this note in writing.

" At the same time—this morning—I was able to examine a paper which has been prepared on Anti-Aircraft Defence and quite independently my advisers upon this subject have come to the following conclusions :

(1) That the only immediate method of manning our defences is to call up the Territorial Anti-Aircraft Army by the declaration of an emergency.

(2) That we should utilise this period during which they are called up to provide a regular nucleus ; and that, it being

[1] The System of Commanders' Conference was set up in February 1938.

impossible to obtain the 26,000 men—the minimum number necessary in addition to all our other requirements— we should call up our reservists. You will see how this proposal dovetails into the earlier part of my letter.

(3) That while the reservists are called up we should build up a regular nucleus by means of compulsorily trained men so that when this last stage is reached, we should definitely have a permanent defence.

" As I am pressed to get my proposals in, in accordance with Cabinet instructions, as soon as possible, I would not like to do this without your having an opportunity of examining their nature. I have no alternative but to send them to you forthwith. If I can have your authority to circulate, I will see that the papers are issued first thing Monday morning."

Attached to the papers Hore-Belisha sent to the Prime Minister, was this note by him :

" As we cannot in the circumstances of the present day rely any longer solely on a Citizen Force for our permanent defence against air attack, it follows that a permanent force must be enlisted for the purpose. As it is quite beyond the capacity of the existing voluntary system, unless great inducements are offered, to provide the regular personnel, even for the existing Regular Army, it behoves us to take steps which will remove the present deficiency by a compulsory scheme.

" I should be hopeful that, if the situation were frankly explained to Parliament and the people, our needs at this time would not be denied."

During the week-end at the farm Hore-Belisha awaited a telephone call from the Prime Minister at Chequers.

Monday, 17th April 1939

First thing this morning I had a telephone message from the P.M.'s private secretary to say that the P.M. was considering the War Office papers, but that he did not wish me to circulate them to the Cabinet, and, if they were not taken at the next Cabinet meeting, he would call a special Cabinet meeting. In the meantime he wished Chatfield and the Treasury to consider them. I sent copies of the papers to Chatfield, the Treasury, and also Halifax.

Warren Fisher came over to the War Office to see me. I had kept him informed of all the developments during the past weeks. I told him I had come to the end of my tether and I was going to resign.

He was very understanding and pressed me strongly not to take any decisive step that day.

In the afternoon the P.M.'s secretary again telephoned and gave a message to Roseway that the P.M. was still considering the War Office papers and that he did not wish me to circulate them. He asked Roseway if there was any urgency, and he was told there was.

Later in the afternoon an appointment was made for me to see the P.M. to-morrow morning at 11.15. I saw Halifax at the Foreign Office at 6.50 p.m. He said he had only been able to read through the War Office papers quickly. I explained them to him. He said he had good reason to believe that conscription was the only course that would have any effect on Germany.

Reports, he said, were reaching us of France's restiveness at our holding back on conscription. I said we were entering into so many pacts and military commitments all over Europe and that we must make full preparations to fulfil them, just as a man who offers to guarantee another man's overdraft must have the money in his own bank to redeem the obligation.

He asked me what I thought of the idea of inviting Attlee, T.U.C. leaders, Churchill, and others to attend the C.I.D. I said it was a good idea, but I refused to believe that we would not stand up to opposition to compulsory military service from whatever quarter it came.

He said he would speak to the P.M. about the War Office papers and that he would not mention that I had shown them to him, but I said I preferred him to tell the P.M. I had shown them to him.

In the evening Churchill rang up. He was apprehensive about Gibraltar. I told him we were sending the Welsh Guards and that two battalions were on their way from Palestine and that they could be disembarked at Gibraltar. A reinforcement of guns and material had been dispatched there. He urged me not to resign.[1]

18th April 1939

At 11.15 a.m. I saw the P.M. It was not a pleasant interview. I said I understood he wished to see me and he answered, " You wished to see me." I said it was so, that I felt it was my duty to do so about the War Office Papers, which I had sent him to Chequers on Saturday.

He said I was adding to his difficulties and that I had made up my mind ; that I had a bee in my bonnet about conscription ; that the War Office wanted it and that I had therefore a biased view ; that I mentioned it in my speeches and so on. He referred to the repeated pledge Baldwin had given that conscription would not be introduced in the present Parliament, but it seemed to me that what really influenced him was the attitude of the Labour Party and the Trade Unions. From his enquiries, he said he felt it would be a very dangerous course to pursue. He then went on to say he refused to believe that the Territorials could not be called out at night to man the searchlights (his proposal was that they should volunteer to do this for about three to six months).

I pointed out to him that the regulation was they could only be called up in an emergency. The papers I had sent to him to Chequers had explained the position in full, but he did not seem to have grasped it.

I again told him that Lord Derby, the Chairman, and the Council of the Territorial Association, and also employers had been consulted and that they had unanimously agreed that the proposal he had made was impracticable, that it would not achieve the result desired, and that it would do harm to the Territorials.

Unless an emergency existed, I said, it would be an intolerable burden on Territorials to be called upon to serve whole time for indefinite periods. It was impossible to combine the duties in question with civilian work, more particularly in the case of

---

[1] Winston S. Churchill: *The Second World War*, Vol. i. " On April 27 the Prime Minister took the serious decision to introduce Conscription, although repeated pledges had been given by him against such a step. To Mr. Hore-Belisha, the Secretary of State for War, belongs the credit of forcing this belated awakening. He certainly took his political life in his hands, and several of his interviews with his Chief were of a formidable character. I saw something of him in this ordeal, and he was never sure that each day in office would not be his last."

searchlights, which were situated at considerable distances from the headquarters of units.

I argued that our defence system should be considered as a coherent whole and that all the integral parts of it should be manned, including the balloon barrage and the Observer Corps. Any attempt to obtain the necessary personnel by voluntary methods would fail and would deal a shattering blow to the voluntary system.

I said my task was impossible if he rejected some form of compulsory military service, but he refused to take 'No' for an answer to his proposals, and in reply to my asking him what he wanted me to do, he said I was to go back and consider them again.

John Simon on the bench in the House told me that he had read the War Office papers with an eye prepared to pick holes, but he was bound to admit that the case I had presented was unanswerable and that he was in agreement about conscription.[1]

At 5.30 I called a meeting of the Army Council and again put before them the P.M.'s views. They unanimously agreed there was no alternative to what we had submitted.

I got home late and there was a message that Churchill had telephoned. I rang him and he said from information he had received about Gibraltar, he felt something was going to happen there. I told him that everything possible the War Office could do, had been done, that extra gunners had been sent and that all personnel and material that could be spared had been despatched. I mentioned to him the difficulties I was having and he again advised me not to resign, that events would justify my objectives and that he would support me.

19th April 1939

Shortly after 9 a.m. a telephone message came from the P.M.'s secretary that the P.M. wished to see me and that he had something to tell me which he thought would please me.

I went across to No. 10 at 10.45 a.m. His manner had completely changed from yesterday. He seemed concerned that some members of the Cabinet had seen the War Office papers and others

---

[1] In 1916 Simon resigned his office as Home Secretary on this very question of conscription to which he was then opposed.

THE PRIVATE PAPERS OF HORE-BELISHA

had not. He said he was quite willing that I should submit the papers verbally to the Cabinet, but he did not wish me to circulate them.

I told him what was worrying me was that we cannot man our garrisons abroad, or our anti-aircraft defences, and we cannot mobilise the Field Army. I had reached the stage when I did not care a damn about his concern as to who saw the papers and who did not.

He said he agreed we had to go into these important matters and, after he had dealt with the international situation at the Cabinet Meeting, he would give me an opening.

At the meeting, after I had set out the steps we had taken to reinforce Gibraltar, I gave particulars of the extent to which our garrisons overseas were under strength. I said that partial mobilisation should be adopted immediately in the Army. Virtually all other nations in Europe had now taken substantial measures of mobilisation. It was only by mobilising reserves that we could provide the artillery personnel required.

Then the P.M. asked me to explain the 'defence against air attack' position. I did so on the lines of the War Office papers and concluded by insisting that some form of compulsory military service was absolutely essential and that it should be introduced as soon as possible. I was convinced that there was no other way of obtaining the manpower required.

About a Ministry of Supply—it was still being argued—I said the proper test, in deciding the powers such a Ministry should have, should be what effort this country would have to make, if war broke out. The right principle was that the Army, both Regular and Territorial, should be provided with equipment and reserves ready to proceed overseas by echelons within a fixed date. It was essential now to have a fixed programme and a Ministry of Supply to carry it out.

The Rae Committee was still considering the lowering of the age for granting the marriage allowance to the Forces. Hore-Belisha had pressed for this reform for some time.

During the Cabinet meeting he passed the following note across the table to Lord Stanhope, First Lord of the Admiralty :

" For goodness' sake, insist at the Rae Committee on marriage allowance from the age of twenty-one. It is vital to our recruiting and can't hurt you. Your representative is opposing this. Air Ministry and War Office are pressing."

20th April 1939

At 6 p.m. I addressed the Army Committee in the House. Mainly confined my remarks to explaining the difficulties in getting guns, tanks, equipment and everything else the Army needed without a Ministry of Supply. Our original Army programme had been expanded by more than six times and there had been a tremendous increase in manpower, but production had proceeded on the normal basis.

Heard that Horace Wilson wanted to see me. He told me that it had been decided to introduce conscription and that it was to be kept very secret. I insisted that the whole Army Council should be informed at once.

21st April 1939

Cancelled my engagement to open an Anti-Aircraft Drill Hall in Truro, called an Army Council meeting. Bridges came over at 11 a.m. and we spent the day thrashing out the scheme for compulsory military service.

22nd April 1939

At lunch time I saw the draft War Office paper which was to be circulated to the Cabinet. I made one or two small amendments. Conscription at last, and only a few days ago the P.M. upbraided me for adding to his difficulties.

Cabinet discussions on the scheme continued until the 25th April.

Meanwhile, in the House of Commons on the 20th April, the Prime Minister announced that the Government had decided to set up a Ministry of Supply. The legislation was to be so framed as to enable a Ministry of Supply " in the full sense" to be established at any time it was thought desirable. For the present, the scope of the new Ministry was to be confined to the problems of Army supply and to the taking over of certain branches of the War Office. A statutory right was to be embodied in the Bill to enforce on industry the acceptance of, and precedence for, Government orders. A Ministerial Priorities Committee was to be set up for the purpose.

Forecasters in Press and political circles, for days before the announcement, had tipped Churchill as favourite for Minister of Supply. There was some dismay and disappointment when Burgin, Minister of Transport, was nominated.

It was six months, all but a day, since Hore-Belisha in a speech at Cardiff had said: "Under our present system nothing can guarantee appreciable acceleration of our armament programme, nor can there be appreciable enlargement of it in the given time." The scale of planning for the Army had, however, in the six months been vastly expanded and the "given time" had been dangerously diminished.

CHAPTER XXII

Preparation for War

PARLIAMENT, both Lords and Commons, on the 27th April 1939, debated the Government's decision to introduce conscription. Ambassadors, representatives of the Commonwealth, and Military Attachés of foreign Powers filled the Diplomatic and Distinguished Strangers galleries. All were stirred by the importance of the occasion. Britain, while still at peace, was for the first time in her history to have the compulsory enrolment of men for military service.

The Prime Minister faced a crowded House of Commons when he introduced the motion, explaining the reasons which had impelled the Government to depart from their former pledges and their traditional policy. The new liabilities in Europe, he said, could not be discharged without effective means and the voluntary system of military service no longer sufficed to carry them out. Britain's acceptance of what was the universal rule on the Continent would be the most convincing earnest of her wholehearted co-operation in resisting domination. Legislation would be introduced forthwith to call up for six months' training all men between the ages of twenty and twenty-one ; and the procedure of mobilisation would be simplified in order to meet the continuous state of emergency in which the country lived.

Further steps, he added, would also be taken to limit the profits of firms engaged on the rearmament programme and there would be special penalties on profiteering, should war break out. Finally, he pleaded with the Opposition to show a united front, not only in their avowals to oppose aggression, but in their readiness to make any sacrifice to ensure the success of the cause that was common to both sides of the House.

But it was of no avail. Trade Union leaders, whom he had seen in the morning, had made plain to him their firm opposition to any form of compulsory military service. Attlee, on behalf of the Parliamentary Labour Party, took the same stand in the debate. "We are opposed," he said, "to the introduction of conscription because we believe that, so far from strengthening this country, it will weaken and divide it. . . . This country provides the greatest fleet in the world. It has a rapidly growing Air Force. It has to provide munitions for them . . . for its allies, and it cannot, in addition to that, provide a Continental Army." The leader of the Liberal Opposition was also unwilling to take the "awkward fence" of conscription.

Hore-Belisha wound up the debate. He twitted the Opposition on their embarrassment in trying to reconcile their protestations against aggression with their unwillingness to supply the means to resist it. "Let those," he said, "whose slogan is ' Stand up to the Dictators' give us the trained men with whom we can stand up. What infringement is it of our freedom to take steps to secure it ? "

He analysed the military needs arising out of the Government's increased obligations. The scheme would place at the disposal of the Army a trained reserve and enable the anti-aircraft forces to be permanently manned—both objectives would be achieved with all speed.

Every man at twenty years of age would do six months' intensive training, either with a Regular or with an anti-aircraft unit. He would then pass to the Territorial Army or to a Special Reserve. Magnificent though voluntary recruiting had been—since the 1st April two thousand men had enlisted every day in the Regular and Territorial Army—" if we cannot," Hore-Belisha went on, "properly discharge our commitments to the full extent that we should, either with the Regular or Territorial Army, it is plain that there is a gap in our organisation. It is this gap we will close by this scheme."

On practical grounds, he said, it would achieve the maximum advantage to the nation with the minimum of hardship to the individual.

"All will serve alike under this scheme, rich and poor, skilled and unskilled, professional and lay, and all will serve together.

This is as democratic a proposal as has ever been made to this House. There may be two systems of education, and there may be varying degrees of wealth, but there is an identity of service. Far from dividing the nation, it should do much to bring the younger generation together and unite it by a common experience."

His speech was acknowledged as a brilliant performance. Members were worked up into a pitch of excitement and there was tense expectancy as they trooped through the division lobbies. The motion was carried by a large majority. France hailed conscription in Britain as a momentous step.

M. Blum, leader of the French Socialists, in the *Populaire* trounced British Labour leaders for their inexplicable and contradictory attitude in denying the Government the means to resist the dictators. Walter Lippman, in the *New York Herald Tribune*, interpreted it for the United States. " These revolutionary changes inside Great Britain," he wrote, " are not mere gestures for an immediate effect. . . . What the British are undertaking to do looks far beyond the immediate moment. These measures are not something improvised for an emergency. They are the organisation for a long pull."

They were indeed historic changes. To the British people voluntary military service in peacetime had been almost an article of faith. They had been slow to realise that Hitler had upset the balance of power in Europe and had kicked the bottom out of the pleasant theories of limited-liability warfare on which they had been fed for the past twenty years. It had needed the Munich crisis to alert them to the new military technique, which could administer a swift knock-out blow without allowing time for mobilisation. Just as Britain was confronted with new perils, so also was the Commonwealth. Axis diplomacy had placed it in an unprecedented position, never before experienced. It was faced in 1939 with a potential menace in three vital areas simultaneously—in Europe, in the Near East and in the Far East, as well as on the narrow seas on which the Empire's maritime communications ran.

Speed was essential to implement the Government's purpose. Legislation had to be practical, effective and just. Prolonged discussions continued in the Cabinet and Inter-Service Committees until the texts of the two Bills necessary for the purpose were settled and published on the evening of the 1st May.

Under the Military Training Bill 200,000 men would be trained in the first year and 800,000 at the end of three years. Every man entering on his militia service would start level with his fellows, his progress thereafter being determined solely by his own merits.

The Reserve and Auxiliary Forces Bill would provide, from the moment it was passed, for the permanent manning of the anti-aircraft defences of the Territorial Army, without the declaration of a state of emergency. Its general effect would be to reproduce in Britain the state of partial mobilisation which prevailed in most European countries.

These two measures together would enable the Field Army to operate more quickly, in stronger force and with more abundant means. Britain was harnessing the machinery to meet the situation of war in advance of the actual outbreak.

The only exceptions to the principle of liability for military service were physical unfitness and conscientious objection, and in this latter respect the Government endeavoured to profit by the lessons of the 1914-18 war and to avoid the illegalities and cat-and-mouse procedure of the Conscription Act of 1916. " The human conscience," Hore-Belisha stated on the Committee Stage of the Military Training Bill, " obeyed no tribunal but the tribunal of its own conscience," and it was to do justice to the genuine feelings of conscientious objectors, and at the same time to avoid a means of escape for the shirker, that the regulations were framed. Unlike the procedure in the 1914-18 war, the Ministry of Labour and not the Army was put in charge. The tribunals before whom conscientious objectors appeared were of a civilian character and were presided over by a County Court Judge. They were required to do six months' service on work of national importance, provided or approved by the Ministry of Labour, with rates of pay and allowances corresponding as nearly as possible with those of the militiamen.

Heavy pressure of work was the lot of the War Office before the call-up of the militiamen. The Army Council sat daily until late. Hore-Belisha mentioned in his diary that " there was no time for lunch, so beer and sandwiches were brought in."

The complete readjustment and expansion of the normal machine was an unprecedented strain on Army resources. The business of turning the new Army into a competent force depended on the swift provision of uniforms, equipment, accommodation, training facilities, and thousands of officers and non-commissioned officers were required as instructors.

The Opposition showed, on the Second Reading of the Military Training Bill on the 8th May, that they were determined to resist it line by line—in less than four months the country was to find itself at war. The Government were just as resolved not to allow endless delaying tactics but to have the two Bills passed into law by Whitsun, in three weeks' time. A guillotine was therefore imposed. Day after day, sometimes until the small hours of the morning, amid barracking and stormy scenes, clauses were debated and regulations, including the governing of the civil liabilities of the militiamen and their reinstatement in their former employment, were approved. The purpose was to ensure that those called up would, as far as possible, be no worse off than if they had remained in civilian life, and an assurance was given by Hore-Belisha that, if experience revealed a need for improvement in the regulations, such improvement would be made. The House was informed of the educational facilities, technical classes and social amenities, including games and cinemas, which would be provided, in addition to the military training. Just as it was a new experiment for the militiamen, so it was for the War Office and the Commands. They intended to make the period of military training as profitable and as agreeable as possible.

By the end of May the Military Training Bill and the Royal Auxiliary Forces Bill were on the Statute book and on 3rd June 200,000 militiamen registered at Ministry of Labour offices throughout the country. Each man received a booklet, entitled *A Welcome to the Militiaman*, which in simple and homely language described Army life. In a foreword Hore-Belisha wrote :

"It is in the most friendly spirit that you will be received into the ranks of a great profession. You will learn much of permanent value from the Regular Army and you will form many enduring associations.

"You will also bring much to the Regular Army and your coming will forge a fresh link between the civilian population and the forces of the Crown ; while the sharing of the same experience by men drawn from all walks of life will tend to unify and strengthen our militiamen in mutual understanding.

" On the threshold of a new adventure in which the whole Army wishes you success, the War Office bids you welcome."

Medical examinations began on the 8th June and some remarkable results were shown. No fewer than 84.5 per cent of a cross-section of the first 20,000 men examined were classed as completely fit and only 2.3 per cent were found definitely unfit for military service. The remainder were graded fit, except for some minor disabilities. The level of fitness disclosed varied little in different parts of the country. The results were a striking tribute to the improvement in public health services during the preceding twenty years.

To provide the uniforms, the complete kit and the tents for the new Army, and to have everything ready for the call-up, was no easy problem. The doubling of the Territorial Army to 340,000 at the end of April and the intake of the first batch of 30,000 militiamen by the middle of July, involved the Supply and Contracts Department of the War Office in an operation quite beyond its power to perform in time. The organisation of the Ministry of Supply was only just being set up. There was no lack of foresight on anyone's part at the War Office, nor was there any unwillingness among those concerned to undertake the job. But the size and the suddenness of the orders, " involving money running into millions of pounds,"[1] was overwhelming, and it required the immediate and intensive co-operation of industry throughout the country, if the new Army was to be clothed in time. Far from the Prime Minister being unaware of the "unpreparedness of the Army"[1] in this respect, he was in fact in the closest touch with the Secretary of State for War and was fully informed of it. Sir Frederick Marquis, later the Earl of Woolton, because of his experience in the First World War and his position as managing director of Lewis & Co. of Liverpool, was asked if he was prepared to help and accepted the appointment of Honorary Adviser of Clothing and Textiles to the Army.

Early on a Friday morning in June, Woolton telephoned to ask

[1] *Memoirs* by Rt. Hon. the Earl of Woolton, P.C.,C.H. (Cassell 1959).

if he could see the Secretary of State. The message was put through to Hore-Belisha at Stafford Place and he at once rang up Woolton. When he heard of the administrative difficulties Woolton was encountering, he cancelled his visit to the Command at Aldershot and spent the best part of the day with Woolton at the War Office, seeing officials of the Treasury and the War Office over the financial and supply needs, in order to facilitate Woolton's work.

In his book Woolton speaks of his " horror " when " Hore-Belisha told me that he hoped I would consider getting a new walking-out dress for the Army—he thought it would be a great encouragement to recruiting." Yet in his letter to Hore-Belisha, dated the 12th July Woolton wrote : " I think the position regarding cloth has now reached the stage when we can begin to think about your ideas of a better dressed Army. From inquiries and experiments I have made I have no doubt about it that we can supply bracken serge at a price that is little, if any, more than the khaki cloth we are now using, and I am, therefore, proposing to build up a reserve of this cloth sufficient to provide ceremonial dress for the whole of the Regular Army. We could do this within the Treasury grant that has already been obtained."

In his letter of the 2nd September Woolton wrote : " I'm glad we did what we set out to do and it was a pleasure to work with you. And now I wish you all the strength you need in these grave times. If ever you need my help again, I'll gladly join you."[1]

The first contingent of 30,000 militiamen reported for duty on 15th July. Queen Mary took part in the welcome at Shorncliffe, and members of the Army Council and the Commanders-in-Chief received the new arrivals at various camps throughout the country. Hore-Belisha spent the day visiting depots round London and he

[1] Lord Woolton, asked for his permission to quote from these letters, stated that since the quotations seemed to be in contradiction of comments made by him in his book, some explanation was necessary. With regard to the new walking-out dress " it was my business to carry out the Minister's policy . . . I have no recollection of the second letter, but from its date I suspect that it followed an incident in which Mr Hore-Belisha had sought to secure some recognition of my services but which, in fact, did not interest me. That, I suspect, accounts for the statement that it was a pleasure to work with him. I got to know him very well, and over the years we always maintained a good relationship, although he was a difficult man with whom to work. It was entirely true that if he had ever wanted my help again whilst he was Secretary of State for War, I would gladly have joined with him again; that would have been a matter of duty and not of choice."

made a minute inspection of all the arrangements that had been made. " One of the outstanding features," he said, " was the great variety of militiamen to whom I spoke. Among them were public schoolmen, clerks, lorry drivers, gardeners and shop assistants." From all parts of Britain came reports of the enthusiasm and eagerness of the nation's young men and of the friendliness shown them by the Regular Army.

On the 26th May a telephone message came from Cowley, Oxford, to the War Office asking if Lord Nuffield could see Hore-Belisha, if possible that afternoon. An appointment was made for 6 o'clock at Hore-Belisha's house on Wimbledon Common. Hore-Belisha had known Lord Nuffield for some years and in the preceding October had received from him a gift, to be kept anonymous, of £50,000 for the encouragement of outdoor sport in the Territorial Army.

26th May 1939

We walked round the garden and Nuffield told me how tremendously impressed he was by the fine spirit of the nation in the way it had accepted conscription and that he wanted to make a contribution, as a recognition. In the most modest and casual way he said he was prepared to give £1,500,000. He might have been giving away a sixpence.

He said he had told no one else of his intention and that he wished it to be kept secret until the announcement was made.

He stayed to dinner and we discussed how the money should be spent. Finally we agreed that it should be devoted to sport and recreational facilities for the armed forces.

Nuffield was eager to have all the financial arrangements put in train at once and telephone calls were made to his solicitors and trustees. He would brook no delay or obstacle. After long discussions headway was made and he left for Huntercombe about 3 a.m. I never saw a man happier than he was.

On the completion of his arrangements next day, Lord Nuffield returned to the farm for lunch. It was decided that an announcement should be made to the Press, to be published the next morning, Whit Sunday, and that it should take the form of letters passed between Lord Nuffield and Hore-Belisha.

Lord Nuffield to Hore-Belisha :

" My dear Secretary of State—I have been greatly impressed and encouraged by the wonderful response to the national appeal for voluntary recruiting and by the willing acceptance by all of the principle of universal service, calling for equal sacrifice by all.

" I, of course, assume that everything necessary to the health and happiness of the troops will be provided by the Government. At the same time I am anxious to make some personal contribution towards the comfort and well-being of those who are giving up, however temporarily, the ordinary course of their civil occupations and their home surroundings in the service of our country.

" For this purpose I intend to place in the hands of trustees one million shares in Morris Motors of a present value of approximately £1,500,000, yielding to-day an annual income of some £105,000, to be devoted towards improving the facilities for recreation and enjoyment of the Militia, Territorials and other Forces, at the discretion of the Trustees.

" I intend this gift to be a permanent memorial to the spirit which animates us to-day.—Yours very sincerely, Nuffield."

Hore-Belisha to Lord Nuffield :

" My dear Nuffield—Your letter is characteristic of you. It is overwhelmingly generous and signalises in a most striking manner the willingness on all sides to meet the present situation.

" This gift, coming as it does from one who is a great employer of labour and who is closely in touch with everyday problems and needs of the ordinary man, is a fitting testimony to the national spirit and to the obligation which rests on every one of us to serve our country.

" Your great contribution will powerfully help to bind us together in understanding the significance of this common effort.

" May I, on behalf of those who are serving and who will in the future serve, express what will be their enduring gratitude.— Yours very sincerely, Leslie Hore-Belisha."

With the great expansion of the Field armies and of the defence forces at home, reorganisation of the Higher Command was plainly necessary. Two pre-war posts were revived. For one of them,

Inspector-General of Overseas Forces, General Sir Edmund Ironside was selected on the 31st May 1939. Soon after the Army Council changes in December 1937, Ironside, at Gort's suggestion, was appointed Governor and Commander-in-Chief at Gibraltar. It was Gort's contention that in view of the possibility of menacing developments in the Mediterranean, a strong man was needed there. But others argued that the Governorship of Gibraltar generally went to distinguished generals on the eve of their retirement and that it was Gort's desire to get Ironside out of the way as he had been a serious contender for the office of C.I.G.S. Ironside's new responsibilities as Inspector-General of Overseas Forces included the higher training of the Regular and Territorial Field Armies, inspection of garrisons abroad, consultation with the Indian Government on major military matters, liaison with foreign staffs, and the co-ordination of all training preparations for the despatch of an expeditionary force to the Continent.

The other pre-war post that was revived was Inspector-General of the Home Forces. To this General Sir Walter Kirke was appointed. It made him responsible for the basic training of the multiplied masses of men, Regular, Territorial and Militia, together with the co-ordination of military and civil defence.

General Sir Clive Liddell, who had been Adjutant-General since Hore-Belisha's major Army Council changes in December 1937, succeeded General Ironside as Governor and Commander-in-Chief, Gibraltar, and Lieutenant-General Sir Gordon Finlayson, who had commanded British troops in Egypt, became the new Adjutant-General.

Owing to the great increase of work in the War Office, Hore-Belisha felt the need for a " follow-up " department, closely associated with himself, to ensure that decisions were carried out with all speed. After consultation with the Prime Minister and on the recommendation of Sir George Beharrell,[1] he selected Mr. H. A. Fortington, who had been Director of the Department of Munitions and Raw Materials during the 1914-18 war and who had subsequently had considerable business experience on both sides of the Atlantic, to be Director-General of Progress and Statistics. His task was to

[1] Chairman, Dunlop Rubber Company, and a member of the Prime Minister's Advisory Panel of Industrialists.

organise a complete system of records, forecasts and returns, so as to enable the Secretary of State and the Army Council to obtain a comprehensive view of the main present and future trends of requirements. His daily reports to Hore-Belisha were most helpful in anticipating and breaking down bottle-necks and delays. He gave his services free as his contribution to the national effort.

Further important appointments were made towards the end of July. The Middle East, where three continents, Europe, Asia and Africa, meet, was vital to the security of the British Commonwealth, and as Hore-Belisha had disclosed in his Army Estimates speech, an additional Strategic Reserve was being built up in that area. Lieutenant-General Sir Archibald Wavell was appointed Supreme Commander. His functions were, in peace to supervise the preparations of the defence plans of the land forces in the Middle East, and to co-ordinate their action in the event of war.

Fresh scope was given to Lieutenant-General A. F. Brooke, who succeeded Wavell as General Officer Commanding-in-Chief, Southern Command, and to Major-General Sir Frederick Pile, who, on Hore-Belisha's insistence after some opposition, succeeded General Brooke as General Officer Commanding-in-Chief, Anti-Aircraft Command.

The purpose of all these changes, Hore-Belisha stated, was " to forward the military preparations of the Army."

Life under canvas for the first time for thousands of young men, in what was recorded as the wettest summer for over a decade, presented day to day problems, and Hore-Belisha devoted all the time he could spare to inspecting Territorial and Militia camps throughout the country in order to see how the training of the new Army was progressing and the conditions under which the men lived. Wherever there were complaints and shortcomings, the War Office made every effort to rectify them. Speaking on the 18th July at the inaugural dinner of the London Welsh Regiment, he described the strategic change which had come over Britain. " Flying, as I have been, over the country, I have been moved by those military groups which I have seen everywhere congregated to defend us against the potential invader. Guns and searchlights are spread in a wide chequerboard over the land, by lonely copses, alongside farm buildings, in the hills, in the Fen country, keeping an increasing watch over our homes day and night."

On the 4th July Hore-Belisha went to Paris as chief guest at the banquet of the Franco-British Association and later attended a ball at the Polish Embassy, to show, he said, by his presence, the new bond between Britain and Poland. André Maurois has recalled[1] the tragic memory of that occasion. " It was a beautiful summer night," he wrote, " the white marble sphinxes gleamed beneath the stars, an orchestra was playing Chopin waltzes and pots of red fire threw on the scene the glow of a conflagration. On the lawn beautiful women in crinolines were dancing with Polish and French officers. We all thought the war was near, that Poland would be the first to be attacked and that this ball resembled the one given by Wellington in Brussels on the eve of Waterloo."

Ten days later as the guest of the French Government Hore-Belisha was present at the celebrations of the Quatorze Juillet. It was the 150th anniversary of the fall of the Bastille. The annual parade along the Champs-Élysées, the march past before the President of the Republic, the French Prime Minister, the British Secretary of State for War and the British Chiefs of Staffs of the three services, was more impressive and more memorable than it had been before. Again and again through the long and troubled years of the war that followed so closely on its heels, it was recalled and re-lived, with a slightly misted nostalgia : The crowds pressing forward in a tight surging pack that the police could hardly hold back. The swinging arms of the soldiers and their glittering bayonets as they went by, on and on for two and a half hours without ceasing. The grey skies, the steady drizzle shot through suddenly by the flashing planes overhead. The gasps of admiration as the British squadrons were identified, Wellesleys and Blenheims, monstrously large for that time, the fighters, breathtakingly fast. And then the swelling cheers in the distance, gathering impetus as it came closer and the shouts of " *Voici les Anglais!* " as with the band of the Royal Marines in front, first the British bluejackets and then to an echoing, joyous shout of " *Les Gardes!* ", a detachment of the Brigade of Guards, in all their glory of scarlet, their band and pipers ahead, came into view. Enthusiasm rose to fever pitch. The precision of their marching, the magnificence of their uniforms stirred every Gallic heart. French troops, thirty thousand in

[1] *What Happened in France* by André Maurois.

number, had been drawn from every part of the French Empire—
Zouaves in their red fez-like chéchias, tirailleurs from Algeria,
Morocco and Tunis in their baggy blue trousers, the Foreign Legion
in their white-topped kepis, three hundred and fifty tanks, more than
a hundred motor-drawn guns.

To mark the occasion, the most striking since the Victory March
after the 1914-18 war, and as evidence of the spirit of military
fraternity between the two allies, the British Chief of the Imperial
General Staff, Lord Gort, was accorded the exceptional honour of
taking the salute jointly with General Gamelin, Commander-in-Chief
of the French Forces. In a message to King George VI, President
Lebrun paid tribute to the magnificent bearing of British troops.
" It is with emotion that twenty years after their passage under the
Arc de Triomphe, Paris once more salutes these companions in glory,
whose presence symbolises the solidarity and community of ideals
of our two countries."

This was the last occasion on which Haydon accompanied the
Secretary of State as his Military Assistant. On the 15th July Haydon,
promoted Lieut.-Colonel, was appointed to command the re-formed
battalion of the Irish Guards. Hore-Belisha was very much attached
to him and put on record his regret " to be deprived of his assistance
which I have really valued."

In a letter of the 18th July on his leave-taking, Haydon wrote :
" It has been an unforgettable experience which should for all my
life provide a background of thought and action. I have seen the
character and the scope of the Army change under just one and a
half years and I was so happy to feel that my last days with you
should have brought the fulfilment of what I always sensed had been
one of your dreams since September last—the actual birth of the
Militia scheme.

" It has indeed been a memorable phase in my life. At times
it has been hectic, but that has only made it all the more absorb-
ing.

" I think you know how sad and sorry I am that it should have
come to an end. But to command one's own battalion is a very
proud, and, I believe, a very essential part of a soldier's life, and I
shall always be more than grateful to you for your immediate and
complete recognition of this."

In a tribute[1] after Hore-Belisha's death, Haydon wrote : " H.-B. was a great patriot. England and all it stood for in the world always shone as a beacon before him. He was, too, a great friend, and those who knew him best, loved him best. That surely is a tribute few can earn."

When Parliament rose early in August negotiations with Russia were still dragging on. War was barely four weeks away.

[1] *The Tablet*, 9th March 1957.

CHAPTER XXIII

War

ON THE evening of Sunday, the 20th August 1939, Hore-Belisha, in Cannes on a brief visit, learned that a trade agreement had been signed between Germany and Russia. Negotiations had been in progress for some time and doubts had been expressed that an agreement would ever be reached.

The news seemed to him ominous and he left at once by the Blue Train for London. He stayed in Paris for a few hours in order to talk to Gamelin and Daladier.

21st August, 1939

Gamelin called on me at the Embassy. Campbell, our Chargé d'Affaires, and Major de Linde, Assistant Military Attaché, were also present.

Gamelin took a very serious view of the situation, which he considered far worse than in September last year, because the Germans had mobilised reserve divisions and were therefore more prepared to embark on war. He had learned that four German divisions had moved towards the Polish frontier.

France, he said, had taken immediate measures. They had recalled men on leave; units in camp were ordered back to garrisons; about 55,000 men were called up.

The General complained strongly of the Polish attitude towards Franco-British military discussions with Russia, and said that they were playing for disaster. He was sending a French General to Poland immediately to see the Polish C.-in-C., Marshal Smigly-Ridz. He said the French had put pressure on the Poles not to take the offensive against Danzig, but had heard strong rumours that they intended to attack Danzig if it declared itself a German city. Gamelin's view was that the Poles would be within their rights, but stood a better chance of evoking formidable world opinion if they accepted a *fait accompli* of Danzig, but prevented the Germans from using the Corridor. It was Gamelin's view that Hitler would not take the offensive, but would try to provoke the Poles to do so instead.

I called on Daladier at the Ministry of War. He reaffirmed the view expressed by Gamelin and described the Poles as fools governed by the outworn opinions of Pilsudski.[1]

He was quite emphatic that the situation was really serious, and that it appeared as if hostilities would be inevitable.

He envisaged the position of France and Britain with some confidence, but thought that Italy should be compelled to come in against us if she was not prepared to come in with us. This would give us a chance of an initial military success. He also thought that we had superior resources and that the German material was very poor.

He was confident that the Russians would support the Poles and that, if war broke out, in his opinion, the Poles would be only too pleased to accept Russian troops to assist them.

He thought that in the event of war we should derive great help from those hostile to the régime in Germany and attached importance to assistance by German émigrés, who were extremely anxious to disrupt the régime.

Hore-Belisha had lunch with Reynaud, Minister of Finance, and then left by air for London. Reports kept pouring in from Paris of troop concentrations on Germany's eastern as well as her western frontier.

Late in the evening Hillman rang. He told me that an announcement had just been made in Berlin that the German and Soviet Governments had come to an understanding with regard to the conclusion of a non-aggression pact. A complete bombshell. Ribbentrop is to go to Moscow immediately to bring negotiations to conclusion. Germany has two million men under arms.

[1] Former ruler of Poland, died 1935.

The Prime Minister, who had been in Scotland, hurried to London and a Cabinet meeting was called for 3 p.m. on the 23rd August. This statement was issued to the Press after the meeting :

" The Cabinet at their meeting to-day considered the international situation in all its bearings. In addition to a report that had been received as to military movements in Germany, the Cabinet took note of the report that a non-aggression pact between the German and Soviet Governments was about to be concluded. They had no hesitation in deciding that such an event would in no way affect their obligations to Poland, which they had repeatedly stated in public and which they are determined to fulfil. . . . But if, in spite of all their efforts, others insist on the use of force, they are prepared and determined to resist it to the utmost."

It was broadcast by the B.B.C. in French, German, Italian, Portuguese and Spanish.
Parliament was summoned to meet the next day.

23rd August 1939
Immediately after the Cabinet meeting I sent an urgent letter to P.M. asking for general mobilisation :
" I have just heard from Chatfield that you do not think it desirable to call out so many men as 110,000 at the present time in addition to those already authorised for A.D.G.B.
" I can appreciate your reluctance to allow any step to be taken which would be alleged to be a general mobilisation, and I would therefore ask you urgently if you would agree to enough reservists being called out to secure the Aldershot Corps, the Base and the Lines of Communications, and the Advanced Air Striking Force. This will involve about 60,000 men.
" Chatfield, no doubt, put the case to you very forcibly for the calling up of the 110,000 for which we ask, but I would like you to be aware of certain facts which, in the judgment of my advisers, make some immediate steps necessary.
" In the absence of a proclamation for general mobilisation, it takes up to a week to bring any particular unit up to war strength and this, of course, is an exceedingly long time to have before one at a moment like the present. By delaying the

necessary action for calling up the reservists we run the risk of increasing congestion should we be confronted by an air raid or by the evacuation of the civil population or both. Therefore there is a great advantage in getting the machine in working order while we still have the opportunity to do so without friction.

" For these and other reasons we would prefer to call up the full 110,000, but I do not wish to press you against your judgment to go so far as this and I am asking you whether you would agree to the modified number of 60,000 which will, at any rate, get us over the first fence.

" I am reinforced in making this request because the C.I.G.S. has just received a personal message from General Gamelin in the following terms :

' On account of the military measures taken by Germany I should be very grateful to General Gort if he would hasten all measures for the organization of the Field Force.'

" Naturally, it would not make a good impression if we returned a completely negative answer and I hope you will be able to agree, particularly because of the degree of readiness which has been authorised in the case of the other two Services. . . ."

I sent a copy to Chatfield. The P.M.'s view is we should not take any such step at present.

Soviet-German non-aggression Pact signed in Moscow to-night by Ribbentrop and Molotov.

The first and chief article of the Pact was that " the two contracting Powers undertake to refrain from any act of force, any aggressive act and any attacks against each other or in conjunction with any other power."

Nevile Henderson flew from Berlin to Berchtesgaden to see Hitler and gave him a note from the Prime Minister, containing the statement of policy issued by the Cabinet. A German communiqué was promptly issued declaring that " The Führer left no doubt in the British Ambassador's mind that the obligations undertaken by the British Government could not move Germany to renounce her national vital interests."

24th August 1939

This morning I wrote to P.M. again, saying :

" Following upon my letter last night and in view of the development announced this morning I would ask you if we might now call out the whole of the Regular Army Reserve and also embody the Territorial Field Army.

" The Commanders are sitting in the War Office now and it would greatly facilitate our discussions and arrangements if I could give them definite instructions before they leave for their Commands again.

" The case for the calling up of the Regular Army Reserve, I think, is obvious. As regards the Territorial Field Army, we are being obliged to take the whole of the Militia which is not engaged in anti-aircraft training to guard vulnerable points. This is not their proper duty as it interferes with essential training, and I am anxious to relieve them by Territorials in accordance with their pre-arranged war plans. We shall be losing 50,000 Territorials on the comb-out for reserved occupations and we shall want the best part of 50,000 for guarding vulnerable points. It is more likely to cause chaos if we wait for something to happen before these necessary steps.

" I should be so grateful to you if you could let me have your decision, if possible, while the Commanders are still sitting this morning."

I sent a copy to Chatfield.

12.45 p.m. Cabinet met, not to take decisions, but to be informed of latest developments regarding :

(i) P.M.'s letter to Hitler and Hitler's reply. P.M. said he felt it would be necessary to give gist to Parliament that afternoon and that the text would probably be published later. Henderson has reported Hitler as saying that if Britain took further mobilisation measures, he would order general mobilisation in Germany "as a protection and not a threat."

(ii) Letter from Seeds, our Ambassador in Moscow, saying that our military mission proposed to return home.

I informed the Cabinet that I had issued instructions to call up " key " parties of all Coast Defence and A.A. units immediately after the last Cabinet meeting. Instructions to call up the remainder of Coast Defence and A.A. units were now being issued and most of the personnel would be on duty that evening.

Parliament met that afternoon. The Emergency Powers Bill, which authorised the Government to make regulations by Order in Council, was passed rapidly and without opposition, through all its stages in both the Commons and the Lords, and received the Royal assent at 10.15 the same evening.

Hore-Belisha had a letter from Chatfield the next morning on the question of general mobilisation:

" I saw P.M. Some of the Committee[1] were there to reinforce what I said, which was all to the good. The P.M. said that Henderson had been summoned to see Hitler at 1.30 to-day and this would probably be decisive. He would wait till he heard the result before seeing you."

25th August 1939

At Hitler's request Nevile Henderson had half an hour's conversation with him. Then Henderson left by plane for London.

Anglo-Polish (Mutual Assistance) Treaty signed by Halifax and Count Raczyinski, Polish Ambassador.

Germans in Britain ordered to return home. German Merchant Navy recalled.

Saturday, 26th August 1939

10.30 a.m. Defence Plans Policy meeting at War Office.

6.30 p.m. Cabinet met to consider British Government's reply to Hitler. Nevile Henderson present.

I thought the draft reply prepared was fulsome, obsequious and deferential. I urged that our only effective reply was to show strength and determination, that in no circumstances should we give the impression that we would weaken in our undertaking to Poland. Kingsley Wood supported me.

P.M. did not take our suggestions in any unfriendly spirit. Having been up most of the night drafting reply, he perhaps did not see it as objectively as those of us who came to it with a fresh mind.

[1] Committee of Imperial Defence.

I had a word with Halifax before the meeting and impressed on him the importance of calling up the Territorial Field Army. Mentioned it to P.M. and I urged at the meeting that certain precautionary measures should be taken. Kingsley asked how many men would be involved by calling up the Territorial Field Army. I replied about 300,000.

P.M. authorised me to call up a further 35,000 Territorials to relieve militia on vulnerable points and man further points.

I asked Henderson what Hitler's reaction would be to our mobilisation of the Territorial Field Army. He replied that it might make the difference between Peace and War !

Sunday, 27th August 1939

Cabinet sat from 10.30 a.m. to 12 noon.

Lunched with John Simon and Nevile Henderson, who apparently thought, as I was at the lunch, that my outlook *vis-à-vis* Germany was the same as his ! Went through the new draft of our reply with Simon and Henderson. My object was to stiffen the reply.

The 3 p.m. Cabinet meeting was delayed because P.M. was engaged.

I returned to the War Office, wrote to Simon setting out my comments to draft reply to Hitler :

" Generally speaking, my comments and alterations are based on a desire to leave in the reply, if unfortunately the present conversations do not achieve their object, nothing that will prejudice our position *vis-à-vis* Poland or *vis-à-vis* our own people. I think that my amendments will clear the draft of any suggestion that we are qualifying our guarantee to the Poles or bringing pressure to bear on them, and this attitude should be rigorously maintained.

" Further, I think you will observe that I have endeavoured to remove any suggestion that we have received with pleasure and relief the proposal that Germany should guarantee a somewhat diminished British Empire."

This referred to the supplementary communication from Hitler which he had handed to the British Ambassador two days before, on the 25th August, in the course of which he said :

" The Führer declared that the *German-Polish problem* must be solved and will be solved. He is, however, prepared and determined after the solution of this problem to approach England once more with a large comprehensive offer. He is a man of great decisions, and in this case also he will be capable of being great in his action. He accepts the British Empire and is ready to pledge himself personally for its continued existence and to place the power of the German Reich at its disposal if—(1) His colonial demands which are limited and can be negotiated by peaceful methods are fulfilled and in this case he is prepared to fix the longest time limit. . . ."[1]

Hore-Belisha's letter to Simon added :

" My point about an international guarantee to Poland is as follows :

" At present the Eastern Front is essential for our strategy. If an international guarantee is given to Poland, and she becomes dependent upon that for her security, rather than upon our guarantee and that of France, she is no longer in a position to afford us any reciprocal help. We should thus lose our hold on the East, and an attack upon us in the West by Germany would be facilitated."

The diary continues :

Made rough notes for speech I intended to deliver at Cabinet meeting. Is he bluffing ? We did not resist Rearmament—Rhineland—Austria—Sudetenland—Czechoslovakia. What is the moment to resist ? No negotiations in present atmosphere.

Not necessary to deliver speech, as I was quite satisfied with stiffened attitude in the second draft.

Communiqué is to be sent to the Press explaining that Hitler's communication was being carefully considered and it is expected that Nevile Henderson will return to Germany to-morrow with our reply.

28th August 1939

12 noon. Cabinet. Final draft reply expressed in much stiffer terms. Quite satisfied. Nevile Henderson flew to Germany with it.

Churchill lunched with me.

[1] *White Paper* CMD. 6102, pp. 6 and 7.

4 p.m. A.R.P. practice War Office.

5 p.m. Audience H.M., Buckingham Palace. The King expressed a desire to see the War Board Room (maps) at War Office. I immediately had arrangements made for his visit to-morrow.

Still urging at every opportunity that, if no general mobilisation, the T.A. Field Army should be called out. We do not want to regret the things we have left undone.

30th August 1939

11.30 a.m. Cabinet. Hitler's reply, which arrived at midnight, was discussed. He accepted discussion with Polish Government, but discussion must start at once in Berlin. He wanted Polish emissary to arrive with full powers. I said I thought it was important to make it clear we were not going to yield on this point. A suggestion was made that the P.M. should send a personal message to Hitler !

I said we had received information that Germany had 46 divisions on the Eastern front and 15 on the Western Front.

3 p.m. The King, Duke of Gloucester and Alexander Hardinge came to War Office. Stayed an hour.

4.30 Greenwood[1] called to see me. Yesterday he had pressed in the House for the immediate evacuation of children and women invalids. He said his party were in favour of mobilisation at once and all necessary steps being expedited.

Halifax telephoned, said he was in favour of expediting mobilisation : that we should progressively do about 20,000 every day. He said he would support me with P.M. I asked to see P.M. in the evening.

Wrote letter to Halifax :

" I hope we are going to avoid drifting into what I think is a dangerous strategical position. In our reply to Hitler's message we spoke of ' the securing of the settlement by an international guarantee.' Hitler, in his answer conveyed to-day, states that ' The British Government attach importance to two considerations : (1) That the existing danger of an imminent explosion should be eliminated as quickly as possible by direct negotiation, and that (2) the existence of the Polish State, in the

---

[1] Arthur Greenwood, Acting Leader of the Opposition.

form which it would then continue to exist, should be adequately safeguarded in the economic and political sphere by means of international guarantees.' This, in my judgment, shows that Germany is not unappreciative of the blessing which may fall on her as the result of a diminished Poland being internationally guaranteed and therefore presumably neutralised.

" Our Eastern front will have gone at once, for not only will the power of Poland to give us reciprocal assistance have disappeared, but Rumania and Turkey would probably feel themselves unable, without the support of Poland, to be actively on our side. In this way the balance of power in Europe would be finally tilted against us, and we should be left in any dispute with Germany to rely solely upon the French.

" While I am sure you will be conscious of these considerations I would like to take this opportunity, before we send the next telegram to Hitler, to stress that, in my view, we should do everything to avoid the present negotiations having this result. As long as the Nazi régime exists, and possibly even afterwards, it is essential strategically to strengthen and not to weaken the Eastern front, carrying with it as it does, not only the direct military advantage, but the possibility of making a blockade successful.

" I noticed at the Cabinet that one or two of our colleagues seemed anxious that the venue of the discussions between Poland and Germany should be Italy. To present to Mussolini this opportunity of appearing as the *tertius gaudens* at the end of all this sorry business would be to strengthen Fascism by increasing its prestige quite unnecessarily at a moment when it seems to be more than a little uncertain of itself."

31st August 1939

Chatfield telephoned to say he had seen the P.M. and we met at once : decided to call up Army Reserve, about 140,000 men. Decided also to start evacuating women and children.

4 p.m. Meeting of Cabinet Committee on Recruiting.

At midnight Germany's Sixteen Points were broadcast.

1st September 1939

5.30 a.m. Gort telephoned : " Germans are through." He said

information was from reliable source. Got on to D.D.M.I.[1] (Beaumont Nesbitt) who gave me information that Germans were reported to have invaded Poland at three points.

Left the farm for London. Some routes closed because of evacuation of children.

10.15 a.m. at D.P.P. Committee,[2] decided to mobilise Fleet and whole Army and Air Force.

11.30 a.m. Cabinet met.

Lunch with Horace Wilson put off. Lunched at War Office with Gort and Grigg.[3]

6 p.m. House of Commons.

Saturday, 2nd September 1939

Cabinet met at 4.30.

A proposal had been made by Italy for a Five Power Conference (G.B., France, Germany, Italy, Russia). Our attitude was that withdrawal of German troops from Polish soil should take place before Conference could be held.

Re ultimatum: desire of French to postpone it for another 48 hours. Chief of Air Staff opposed delay. So did Admiralty: I said War Office was also opposed. I added that personally I was strongly opposed to further delay, which I thought might result in breaking the unity of the country. Public opinion was against yielding an inch. If Germany were prepared to consider a standstill, it showed that she was weakening, and we should show the greatest possible strength. I thought we should stand firmly on the statement previously sent to Germany and insist on the immediate withdrawal of German troops from Poland.

I also thought it likely Italy was acting in collusion with Germany and I instanced various troop movements that lent support to this view. I therefore favoured giving Germany until midnight 2-3 Sept. to accept the proposal to withdraw her troops. Otherwise we should regard ourselves at war. Hitler had made demand after demand and, if we were to hesitate now, we might well find ourselves faced with war in a year's time, but in the meantime we should have lost ground by hesitation.

[1] Deputy Director, Military Intelligence.   [2] Defence Policy Plans Committee.
[3] Sir James Grigg; he succeeded Sir Herbert Creedy as Permanent Under-Secretary War Office, on the 25th October 1939.

Unanimous decision was taken that ultimatum should end at midnight 2-3 Sept.

The Prime Minister was due to make a statement in the House of Commons at six o'clock that evening. Every seat was occupied and many members had to stand. All the galleries were packed. There was an anxious wait of two hours. The Prime Minister was delayed and did not come in until 8 o'clock. He had been engaged in discussions with the French over the Italian proposal and the timing of the two ultimatums.

His statement was not what the House had expected. He said : " His Majesty's Government will . . . be bound to take action unless the German forces are withdrawn from Polish territory. They are in communication with the French Government as to the time limit within which it would be necessary for the British and French Governments to know whether the German Government are prepared to effect such a withdrawal."

Arthur Greenwood, speaking with great emotion, said : " I am gravely disturbed. An act of aggression took place thirty-eight hours ago. The moment that act of aggression took place one of the most important treaties of modern times automatically came into operation. . . . I wonder how long we are prepared to vacillate at a time when Britain and all that Britain stands for, and human civilisation, are in peril."

The diary continues :

P.M.'s statement gave the impression that we are weakening on our undertaking to Poland and that the French were ratting. The House was completely taken aback. Greenwood acted with great patriotism and statesmanship. Had he turned on the Government, he would have had Tory support, and it might have meant the fall of the Government.

In view of the Cabinet decision at 4.30 p.m. we were completely aghast. We met in Simon's room (Elliot, de la Warr, Euan Wallace, Anderson, Stanley, Colville, Burgin, Dorman-Smith). We pressed that Cabinet should meet again at once and deputed Simon to see P.M.

P.M. saw us in his room at the House. (Kingsley Wood was with him). Simon put the case very forcibly. He said P.M.'s announcement had taken us completely by surprise, that the Cabinet in the afternoon had decided that ultimatum expired at midnight, whether French came in or not. P.M. said he had not seen any means of consulting the Cabinet in the interval, that there had been no means of making the French agree to synchronise their ultimatum with ours. The French had earlier in the day said they wanted a further 48 hours to complete evacuation and mobilisation.

The P.M. said he wanted at once to retrieve the impression he had made in the House. We urged that a statement should be made forthwith, irrespective of French.

P.M. went over to Downing Street. We again met in Simon's room and sent P.M. a letter rehearsing our points.

Dined with Simon, Kingsley Wood, Colville and Dorman-Smith.

10 p.m. met again in Simon's room. Simon then went over with Anderson to No. 10 to see what was happening. I urged we all ought to go too, but others disagreed.

Rang War Office. Heard Chief of Staff had been sent for to get new instructions. Rang Ismay[1] who confirmed this. Heard from Simon that the P.M.'s statement was incubating. Got message to say Anderson was on his way over to see us.

Anderson told us announcement was to be made that ultimatum was to be given in the morning at 8 a.m. to expire at 12 noon. I said the interval was too long.

Cabinet assembled at once. I said that the ultimatum should be given at 2 a.m. to expire at 6 a.m.—less time involved the better. P.M. said he had spoken to Daladier and Halifax had spoken to Bonnet, but they refused to alter their decision. If an ultimatum went at 8 a.m. to expire at noon, they would deliver theirs at 12 noon to expire at 9 p.m. Sunday. Bonnet said he was under obligation to Ciano to consider Italian proposal about Five Power Conference.

[1] Major-General Sir Hastings Ismay, Deputy Secretary (Military) to the War Cabinet; later Lord Ismay.

Ultimately it was agreed that the ultimatum should expire at
11 a.m. the next morning.

Sunday, 3rd September 1939

Was at War Office early. Air raid alarm. We all went down to
W.O. shelter.

There was a small room underground for the Secretary of State,
with a telephone and a bed if he wanted to sleep there.

Fifteen minutes after the ultimatum expired the Prime Minister
broadcast to the nation from No. 10 Downing Street. In a sad, soft
voice he informed the nation that Britain was now at war. " You
can imagine what a bitter blow it is to me that all my long struggle
to win peace has failed."

At noon, when the House met—it was the first meeting of Parliament on a Sunday for nearly a hundred and twenty years—he made
a similar announcement. " Everything that I have worked for,
everything that I have hoped for, everything that I have believed in
during my public life has crashed in ruins. . . . I trust I may live to
see the day when Hitlerism has been destroyed, and a liberated
Europe has been re-established."

The National Service (Armed Forces) Bill was passed through
all its stages before lunch. Hore-Belisha explained that the Government had selected the range of years from eighteen to forty-one as
representing the most vigorous manhood of the nation.

The diary continues :

Lunched with Simon at the House. Came over to W.O. 3 p.m.
for D.P.P., now called War Committee. Winston told me
yesterday that the P.M. had asked him to serve on this committee.

That was on the 2nd September. On the following day, shortly
after Chamberlain's broadcast to the nation on the declaration of
war, Churchill was appointed First Lord of the Admiralty in
place of Lord Stanhope. The diary entry for the 3rd September
continues:

P.M. telephoned me. He said he was forming a small War
Cabinet and he invited me to be a member of it.

The War Cabinet was limited to nine members. In addition to the

Prime Minister and his three associates in " The Big Four " (Halifax, Simon and Hoare), there were the Ministers in charge of the three Defence Services—Hore-Belisha, Kingsley Wood (Air), and now Churchill. The other two were Chatfield (Minister for Co-ordination of Defence) and Lord Hankey (Minister without Portfolio). Hore-Belisha was the youngest of them by a dozen years.

The appointment of Commander-in-Chief of the British Expeditionary Force and of any adjustments in the higher military commands that this might involve were dealt with next. On the outbreak of the First World War General Sir John French was Inspector-General of the Forces. His selection as Commander-in-Chief of the B.E.F. led to the belief that the office, which had been abolished after the First World War and was not revived until 1939, was in effect that of the Commander-in-Chief designate. Ironside himself seemed to be of this view, for he went down to the Expeditionary Force, which had been assembled between Camberley and Aldershot, and many felt that he had come to assume the role of Commander-in-Chief; on the other hand, it may well be that he was there as Inspector-General of Overseas Forces.

The diary adds :

I told the P.M. I would like to have a further word with him about the C.-in-C. and the proposed new appointments. Went across to No. 10.

P.M. told me he left the new appointments to me, but suggested that I discuss the matter with Kingsley and Winston.

Telephoned Kingsley, who came over from Air Ministry to see me. Left message at the Palace, where Winston had gone to receive the seals of office, asking him to come too.

Hore-Belisha informed them that the proposal was to appoint Gort Commander-in-Chief of the British Expeditionary Force and to bring Ironside in to succeed him as Chief of the Imperial General Staff. Over Gort's appointment there was complete agreement. The diary goes on :

Discussed Ironside's appointment as C.I.G.S. with them. Winston was favourable, but Kingsley was not.

5 p.m. first meeting of War Cabinet. There was some opposition

to Ironside's appointment, but Winston came down on my side and strongly supported it ; and that settled it.

Saw Gort on my return to the W.O. and told him of his selection as C.-in-C.

Audience with H.M. at 7.30 p.m. Was told by the Palace I need not change into morning clothes. I put before H.M. the Cabinet's recommendations—Gort (C.-in-C.), Ironside (C.I.G.S.) and Kirke to be C.-in-C. Home Forces.

Saw Gort again on my return to the W.O. and told him he was now definitely appointed C.-in-C. He was very pleased.

Ironside's appointment is not popular in W.O. To my repeated question on what grounds of merit as a soldier should Ironside's claims be disregarded I could get no answer. If he had the disqualifications attributed to him—indiscreet, intriguer, not liked in the Army—he had that dynamic strength which was essential in the present crisis.

I saw Ironside and told him of his appointment as C.I.G.S. At first I think he was a little disappointed, as he had expectations of being C.-in-C., but he warmed to it during our talk. I said I was going to be quite frank about what his critics had said. When he spoke up for himself, I told him he need not put up any defence. The decision had been made and I would stand by him. I urged him to be frank with me always, and that, if he had any criticism to make, to say it to me and not outside.

I also saw Kirke and told him he was now C.-in-C. Home Forces. I rang Brownrigg up at 11.30 p.m. and told him he had been made Adjutant-General of the Forces to go to France.

The outbreak of war swept back into various positions of trust and responsibility senior officers who had been by-passed by the promotion of younger men, once their juniors in rank and length of service. They bitterly resented being at a far lower level than they regarded was their right. On Hore-Belisha, as the man responsible, all their hostility centred. And war brought them their opportunity to settle the score, since civilian interference was easier to attack in wartime, no matter how exalted the position of the civilian. Their denunciation of Hore-Belisha, freely expressed in the intervening years, was now more vocal and concentrated, especially at the headquarters of the British Expeditionary Force where many of these officers were now serving.

Gort, the Commander-in-Chief, who owed so much to Hore-Belisha, did not at this stage share their feelings. They were determined, however, by one means or another, to win him over, as they felt that, with his support, it would not be difficult to get Hore-Belisha out.

CHAPTER XXIV

Despatch of the B.E.F.

DE GUINGAND, who succeeded Haydon as Hore-Belisha's Military Secretary, has set down his impressions of the man and his methods:[1]

" Hore-Belisha I found a most colourful character. Initially I did not take to him very much, but later I developed a great affection and regard for my new master. One was made to work very hard indeed, and those first few weeks were a nightmare. Gradually, however, I managed to get my head above water. . . .

" He was undoubtedly an ambitious man, and when discussing this subject with me one day he said : ' Well, surely a carpenter wishes to be successful at his own particular job ! ' . . . He possessed great drive, and when convinced that he was right, would fight whatever the opposition. Most of the top soldiers in the War Office were frightened of him, although they would not admit it. On one occasion a certain distinguished soldier had asked me to get the Secretary of State to agree to some proposal for sending divisions out with the Expeditionary Force with a modified scale of equipment. I knew his views on this matter and said I had little hope of success. I returned with the answer I had expected. ' Good God, man,' said the soldier, ' give me the paper, I'll see he does,' and off he rushed. Being interested to see how he could succeed where I had failed, I shortly followed him into the office, and was amused to hear, ' Yes, sir ' and ' No, sir ' and ' I quite agree, sir.' There was no change in Hore-Belisha's decision ! . . .

[1] *Operation Victory*, by Major-General Sir Francis de Guingand (Hodder and Stoughton 1947).

"I had a very full day. At 7 a.m. would arrive the night's telegrams, and any Cabinet papers that were still outstanding. These I would have to scan through whilst dressing and breakfasting. By 8.15 I had to be at Hore-Belisha's house, where I would spend an hour or so giving him a verbal synopsis of the various papers and telegrams. Like Montgomery he disliked reading such things. I would sometimes start in the bedroom, move on to the bathroom, and then to the breakfast table."

Hore-Belisha's diary supplements this daily routine.

4th September 1939
    I arrive War Office at 9 a.m., see D.M.O. and I., who explains with map the strategic position of combatants. Discuss any points I may need for War Cabinet with Army Councillors or others.
    War Cabinet meets every day at 11.30 a.m.

It was the practice for the C.I.G.S., or in his absence his Deputy, and the Chiefs of the other Services to be in attendance at these War Cabinet meetings in order to explain the military situation. They then retired. They were not present at Cabinet discussions. The diary continues :

    Lunched at Stafford Place with Winston, Hankey and Ironside.
    3 p.m. War Cabinet met again. Winston's view was that we were allocating to the Field Force too generous a scale of ammunition and thus delaying their departure to France. I insisted that the Force should not go until it was fully equipped. I said the General Staff disagreed with Winston's view. They had worked out precisely the amount per day per gun of the ammunition to be used.
    Winston asked for an inquiry. He wanted all the calculations on which our view was based. This involved the General Staff in heavy additional work. D.C.I.G.S. and others had to work on it far into the night.
    Meeting called at 10 p.m. Burgin present to discuss supply position.
6th September 1939
    Lunch Stafford Place : Chatfield, Ironside, Hankey.

Hore-Belisha at this time used to have Cabinet colleagues and advisers to lunch with him at his home, which was conveniently near Whitehall, so that they could have informal discussions, following and often also preceding, War Cabinet meetings.

Working closely with Ironside from day to day, Hore-Belisha in time began to realise that his appointment as C.I.G.S. was not the ideal one. He was fully co-operative ; in his manner deferential[1] and even obsequious[2]—he would certainly not have dared to thump the table when he spoke to the Secretary of State, as has been said since Hore-Belisha's death[3] ; but he was in his sixtieth year and was found to be quite inadequate in his dealings with the other services on the Chiefs of Staff Committee in overall planning. Churchill, who supported Hore-Belisha over Ironside's appointment as C.I.G.S., removed him from that office soon after becoming Prime Minister in May 1940.

The diary for the 6th September continues :

6.30 p.m. War Cabinet. My view is that the size of the Land Forces on which planning is to be based should be laid down at an early date. We should assume the war would be a long one, at least five years, and that our efforts should be a maximum one. The personnel of 32 divisions existed and it was vitally important to accelerate supply for these divisions. It was only in March we decided on the 32 divisions and then only on paper. The expansion should be to 60 divisions for France and the planning should be based on this size for our Land Forces. We have to make a greater effort than in the last war. We are in less advantageous circumstances.

Our present supply plans would only admit of 16 divisions being sent in the first year. To provide for forces on the 60 division scale, we would have to take a number of important steps —to mobilise our industrial resources, to safeguard the raw material position and to make the best use of labour available. Priority control would be needed for tonnage exchange (particularly dollar exchange) and raw materials. Steps would have to be taken to accumulate stocks.

[1] Sir David Roseway's statement to the author.
[2] Maj.-Gen. Sir Francis de Guingand's statement to the author.
[3] In *The Business of War* by Maj.-Gen. Sir John Kennedy.

Increase in divisions would mean large expansion in factory space, particularly for cordite explosives. Above all, it was essential to take steps to accelerate the production of guns and tanks.

The whole problem is to be examined by a committee of Ministers.

A Land Forces Committee is to be set up (Sam Hoare, Chatfield, Winston, myself, Burgin—with power to co-opt Board of Trade and Min. of Labour) to report to the Cabinet as quickly as possible on the size of the Land Forces at which we should aim and the date of completion of equipment for the various contingents as a basis for the production arrangements to be made by the Ministry of Supply.

10 p.m. Another late meeting at W.O. to prepare paper on Supply to put before Land Forces Committee.

7th September 1939

Eden and Newall[1] lunched with me.

Letter from Hardinge saying the King excused me from accompanying him to Aldershot.

4 p.m. Land Forces Committee met.

Another 10 p.m. meeting at W.O. on supply needs.

8th September 1939

Land Forces Committee are to recommend to War Cabinet that supply on the full British Army scale of 55 Divisions should be the objective by the end of the second year of war.

9th September 1939

Oliver Stanley and Ismay lunched with me. Oliver remarked apropos of Winston that he regretted his expenditure on *The World Crisis*, as Winston in his speeches to the Cabinet recited his (own) chapters verbatim.

War Cabinet. No decision is to be taken on ultimate size of the Land Forces until the requirements of all 3 Services have been reviewed. Ministry of Supply is to start preliminary planning for the supply on the full British Army scale of 55 divisions by the end of the second year of the war.

11th September 1939

6 p.m. War Cabinet met. P.M. is going with Chatfield to

---

[1] Air Chief Marshal Sir Cyril Newall, Chief of Air Staff.

France to-morrow for the first meeting of Supreme War Council.

After the meeting I went to Simon's room at the Treasury and drafted with him a suggestion which we sent to the P.M. for his announcement on the Anglo-French attitude towards enemy propaganda that we would desert Poland.

13th September 1939

Lunched with Winston at Morpeth Mansions.

Informed War Cabinet that disembarkation of the B.E.F. is proceeding according to plan. The P.M. told me that Gamelin had stated yesterday that no hitch of any kind had occurred re B.E.F.

14th September 1939

Nuffield lunched with me at Stafford Place. He seemed eager to give more money away.

On the 19th November Hore-Belisha informed the House of Commons that Lord Nuffield had presented £50,000 for "amenities for men of the three Fighting Services." The following month, on the 12th December, Hore-Belisha announced at the Mansion House the inauguration of a welfare organisation for the Army, co-ordinating Lord Nuffield's gift with the funds of regimental societies and of other organisations to help and advise the soldiers. Welfare officers were being appointed to each Command to " form the link," he said, " between the kindliness of the community and the human requirements of the troops. They need not only tangible gifts but mental and moral refreshment and sympathy. Let the men engaged in fighting this war for our security feel that they are being cared for."

15th September 1939

This morning at the Cabinet the Duke of Windsor's appointment came up. He arrived back in England with the Duchess two days ago.

Hore-Belisha had earlier received a letter from the Palace to say that the Duke of Windsor had been to see the King and had expressed a desire to offer his services " in any capacity." His Majesty thought that the Duke would be most suitably employed as a member of the Military Mission to France, of which General Howard Vyse was the head. The Duke, who was a Field-Marshal in the British Army, was prepared to revert, the letter stated, to the rank of Major-General for the duration of the war. The King had discussed the proposal informally with the Duke, who was giving the matter his immediate consideration.

Hore-Belisha, who had been at Oxford with the Duke, had often called to see him as Minister of Transport. The Duke was King at the time and took a keen interest in Hore-Belisha's campaign to reduce road accidents. After the abdication, Hore-Belisha paid an informal courtesy call on the Duke in Paris in September 1937. He was the first British Cabinet Minister to do so.

The diary continues :

At the Cabinet the P.M. passed this note to me : " I understand from the King that H.R.H. has agreed to this proposal. It is very desirable that he should. I am also inquiring whether H.R.H. could pass what time he spends here (say a fortnight) with one of the military Commands."

At 4 p.m. the Duke of Windsor called at the War Office and was received in the hall by the Military Secretary, who escorted him to my room.

The call was made in complete secrecy. The Press was unaware of it. He attracted no attention as he alighted from his car wearing a dark double-breasted lounge suit and carrying his gas-mask.

The diary continues :

H.R.H. started by saying that he did not want to give up his baton. I said it was unique for a Field-Marshal to take the rank of a Major-General.

H.R.H. then said that before he went to France, he would like to be attached to the different Commands in England so that he could be in contact with the soldiers again. He added that he wished to take the Duchess with him.

I began to see difficulties, so I said I would see what could be done. He then referred to the Duchess's desire to give her villa in the South of France as a convalescent home for British officers.

237

THE PRIVATE PAPERS OF HORE-BELISHA

I said I thought she wanted to run a hospital on the south coast of England, but he replied " No," he wanted her to be with him in Paris.

I called in General MacArthur[1] and I told H.R.H. I would send an appropriate officer to discuss the matter with the Duchess.

The Duke stayed over an hour and saw C.I.G.S.

Hore-Belisha accompanied the Duke to the door of the War Office, where they parted with a warm handshake.

16th September 1939

The King sent for me at 11 a.m. He was in a distressed state. He thought that if the Duchess went to the Commands, she might have a hostile reception, particularly in Scotland. He did not want the Duke to go to the Commands in England. He seemed very disturbed and walked up and down the room. He said the Duke had never had any discipline in his life.

I suggested that I would see the Duke and arrange matters so that he need not come into it at all. I had to take leave of H.M. to go to the War Cabinet. The King asked me to return at 2.30 p.m.

During the Cabinet meeting the Duke, who was with Horace Wilson, asked to see me. I saw the difficulty of doing so before my further audience with H.M., so I arranged to see him at 3 that afternoon at the War Office.

2.30 p.m. I went to Buckingham Palace with Ironside. H.M. remarked that all his ancestors had succeeded to the throne after their predecessors had died. " Mine is not only alive, but very much so." He thought it better for the Duke to proceed to Paris at once.

3 p.m. The Duke came to the War Office. He expressed his pleasure at going to the Commands in England and making contact with the soldiers. I pointed out that when a soldier was given an appointment, he invariably took it up without delay. I explained that the troops were moving about, the secrecy involved, and that the Duke's presence would attract attention. It would create an excellent impression with the public, I said, if the Duke showed readiness to take up his appointment at once ;

[1] Director-General Army Medical Services.

238

that Howard Vyse was impatiently waiting for him in Paris. The Duke appreciated all the arguments and expressed agreement. That difficulty, therefore, of his going to the Commands was solved.

He then asked if his brother, the Duke of Gloucester, was being paid.[1] I rang at once for the Military Secretary. The Duke said that he had come back to offer his services and he did not want to be paid, and that he would like this to be announced in the Press. The Military Secretary said the Duke of Gloucester was not being paid and that no members of the Royal family ever accepted payment for services in the Army.

He asked for Metcalfe[2] as his Equerry. I said that everything would be done to make things easy and pleasant for him and that his chauffeur would be enlisted as a soldier. I then said I would take him to Ironside, who would give him his instructions. These were subsequently given to him in writing.

Hore-Belisha was very moved, he records, when " I had to take him in to get his instructions."

The Duke returned later to my room, said he had seen the Military Secretary and was coming back on Monday to see him again.

He then raised the question of his Hon. Colonelcy in the Welsh Guards. He had ascertained that they wanted him back again, and said he would like this. I told him I did not appoint Honorary Colonels of Regiments and asked if he had spoken to the King about it.

I then said that if the Duke was asking my advice, the best advice I could give him was to get back into the Army as a Major-General. He asked if he could wear his decorations on his battle-dress and I replied " Yes."

The Duke left after about an hour. A small crowd had collected outside the War Office. They gathered round his car and cheered him as he drove away. He seemed very pleased, smiled and raised his hat.

[1] The Duke of Gloucester had been appointed Chief Liaison Officer with the B.E.F.
[2] Major E. D. Metcalfe, with whom the Duke and Duchess were staying in Sussex.

I telephoned Hardinge to reassure the King that the interview had been satisfactory.

The diary for the 16th September continues:

Burgin put in a paper on Supply following the approval of the Land Forces Committee re 55 divisions. I wrote on the top of Burgin's paper: " Why we should *not* have an Army! by the Ministry of Supply! " I am convinced we shall have to make our Land Forces preparations without delay and on the maximum scale. I had been in touch with Walter Layton,[1] who was at the Min. of Munitions during last war. I had asked him to draft a paper for me on the Gun and Ammunition Programme in the 1914-1918 war ; on the employment position at that time (Burgin's thesis was that we would not have the personnel available to carry out the Army programme I asked for) ; and on the development of our War potential.

Layton dined with me at the farm. He came on a bicycle in spite of the blackout. He told me it was the first time he had ridden one for 20 years. Till the early hours of the morning we discussed the paper and the urgency of planning on the most extensive scale. I decided to put in a Memorandum on the size of the Army at once to the Cabinet, asking for the objective of 100 divisions. My purpose was to set out what the Army objective should be on the assumption that we are now engaged in a war of total effort. Our aim should not be less than to prepare production capacity for 100 divisions.

Sunday, 17th September 1939

I was reinforced in my resolve by the news this morning that Russia has invaded Poland.

Max Beaverbrook came to tea. He was depressed. He said he would refuse any offer to become adviser to the Minister of Information, but he thought that Camrose would accept. I think Beaverbrook would make an excellent Minister of Information. We need a man of his calibre to outmatch Goebbels.

Monday, 18th September 1939

The Empire is faced with a situation of great peril. I urged at this morning's meeting that the country should be roused to

[1] Later Lord Layton.

make far greater efforts and far greater sacrifices than are at present contemplated. There must be greater efforts in production, particularly in land armaments.

Had Anthony[1] and Hankey to lunch and did some propaganda on my objective for 100 divisions. Spent some time drafting my memo. Lobbied several Ministers, Sam Hoare, etc., to gain their support. Just before dinner went over to Admiralty to see Winston.

Tuesday, 19th September 1939

Events favoured me this day. The Cabinet was disquieted about Gamelin's fear of the nature and timing of Germany's attack on the Western Front.

I passed a note over to the P.M. suggesting I should go to France and see Daladier and Gamelin. P.M. agreed, so did Halifax. The P.M. passed me a note :

" I think you would find it very helpful if you took another member of the Cabinet with you. Would Hankey be agreeable?"

To which I replied : " Delighted."

It was decided that I should go to France to-morrow to see Daladier and Gamelin and obtain an urgent decision on the disposition of the B.E.F.

Wednesday, 20th September 1939

9.30 a.m. Flew to France from Hendon with Hankey and Major-General Dewing, D.M.O.

I first saw Gort and discussed with him the subjects we intended to take up with the French. Gort was anxious to know what sector of the Franco-Belgian frontier the B.E.F. was to be allotted so that he could begin the digging of the defences.

I am more than ever concerned that there is no Maginot Line from the other side of Givet to the coast ;[2] only continuous anti-tank obstacles and a number of forts and pillboxes.

Hankey and I had discussions alone with Daladier at the War Ministry in the afternoon, then Dewing joined us.

Daladier indicated the French position on Franco-Belgian frontier, and said work there was being helped out by Spanish

[1] Anthony Eden, Secretary of State for Dominion Affairs. He was not in the War Cabinet.
[2] The Maginot Line ended between Longuyon and Montmédy and that stretch, facing the Ardennes, was the weakest in defences.

workers. Any assistance the British could give in the way of labour battalions, Territorial units or mechanised diggers would be of great value. Operations in Poland had shown the importance of fighting on prepared positions.

I explained it was essential that the B.E.F. should know on what sector of the frontier they were to be employed.

Gamelin joined us half an hour later. He said he feared a sweep through the Low Countries, but, without previous conversations with the Belgians, it would not be possible to employ French forces in co-operation with the Belgian defence on their line of Albert Canal-Meuse. He was determined to avoid an encounter battle in the centre of Belgium.[1] He emphasised that B.E.F. would be supplemented by French garrisons holding the permanent works. He saw no difficulty in agreeing with Gort's desire that B.E.F. be allotted a sector south of Lille. (Gort had said, if attacked, B.E.F. would have strong French positions in the Lille and Valenciennes areas on their left and right.) Gamelin also saw no difficulty in our transferring our base to Le Havre after concentration of our 4 divisions had been completed. He emphasised his need for more British fighter aircraft in France and asked for the largest possible land effort.

I promised to communicate his request to the Cabinet re fighter aircraft, though unable to make any promise on this point ; and added that, while I could not speak in terms of numbers of British divisions in France, or of proportion between the three services, the effort made by Britain would be the maximum possible and that it would not be less than it was in 1918.

Stayed night at the Embassy.

Thursday, 21st September 1939

It had been my intention to fly this morning to G.H.Q. (Le Mans), but weather too bad, so we went by car. On the way Hankey told me that L.G.[2] on such journeys would suddenly start singing Welsh hymns, then in the middle of them he would break off and say he had to write a note to President Wilson.

Saw Gort at G.H.Q. and told him of my conversations with

---

[1] This is what Gamelin actually invited and produced by his subsequent D Plan of advancing into Belgium.

[2] Hankey, Secretary to the War Cabinet in 1916 and the Imperial War Cabinet in 1917, worked closely with Lloyd George during the First World War.

Daladier and Gamelin. Gort was thoroughly satisfied with the progress made. Discussed with him the great importance of having a strong R.A.F. component with the B.E.F.

Returned by air 7 p.m. Hendon. Went straight to Downing Street and saw the P.M.

Friday, 22nd September 1939

I reported on my visit to the Cabinet. More A.A. guns and fighter aircraft are to be sent to France.

During the morning I received a message from Gamelin that the sector to be held by the Field Force would have to be changed. The new sector would have to be between Lys and the Scheldt. There has not been time to examine this change, but it appears satisfactory from the British point of view.

Simon is disturbed about the total expenditure of the war. It is already higher than in 1918. He says the implementation of the full programme of supply for the 55 divisions, plus Aircraft and Navy programmes, will involve us in very serious difficulties *vis-à-vis* dollar exchange by the end of the second year of war.

I am convinced that our aim for the Land Forces should be the maximum, even though it entails the exhaustion of our dollar resources in two years. Gort told me that the war could be lost in France, even if it could not be won there, and we cannot afford to take that risk. If you start with a strategical conception of what is necessary, you can't reduce it except in terms of defeat. Suppose you lose the war, all the most careful expenditure will have gone down the drain. If you start a 3-years war with the idea that you can only be on the defensive, then you might as well not start at all.

Mechanical diggers are being sent to France with special crews attached to them.

Saturday, 23rd September 1939

I informed Cabinet of the measures being taken for an early increase in the strength of the B.E.F.

Monday, 25th September 1939

At the Cabinet I urged that the fullest advantage should be taken of the lull on the Western Front to construct the strongest possible defence line on the B.E.F. sector. I said with this object in view I had arranged for consultations between the War Office and civilian contractors. In addition it might also be possible to give valuable assistance to the French in further improving their defence lines.

During the next three months, following his visit to the B.E.F., the need uppermost in Hore-Belisha's mind was to strengthen the defences on the B.E.F. line.

Tuesday, 26th September 1939
I informed the Cabinet that Phase II, which completed the 1st Corps, sailed yesterday. Up to date 98,000 men and 16,000 vehicles have been shipped, in addition to 20,000 tons of stores during the first week.

I saw representatives of MacAlpines and arranged for one of their engineers to accompany a senior R.E. officer to examine the construction of a defensive line on the B.E.F. sector.

In all 10 Field Cos. of R.E.s with mechanical diggers will shortly be dispatched. These will be over and above anything the Field Force already has.

It was through MacAlpines that Lieut.-Colonel John French, a Territorial officer and a senior member of the firm of W. C. French, of Buckhurst Hill, Essex, well-known civil engineers and building contractors, was called in. He left for France at once, together with Major S. A. Westrop[1] who was on the Regular Army Reserve, and Colonel Minnis of the Royal Engineers. They had been told that the Maginot Line was to be extended right up to the sea, on the French side of the Belgian frontier. After inspecting the terrain they returned to England and French set about raising a construction force and collecting its equipment—concrete mixers, compressors, vibrators, etc. The force he assembled, known as X Force, was essentially a civilian force drawn from the construction industry and included specialists in reinforced concrete construction; French had his headquarters at Douai, but he and Minnis, who was in charge of these operations, worked directly under the supervision and control of the War Office in London. "From the start," says Westrop,[2] " there was trouble between them and G.H.Q., who did not like an irregular unit working independently of them and not

[1] Later Brigadier.   [2] In a statement to the author.

244

responsible to G.H.Q. Although the man in charge of the force there was Minnis, who was a Regular sapper, French, and the others under him, were regarded as 'civilians in uniform' with what appeared to be special privileges not fitting into the Army administrative pattern.

" Things did not go smoothly. Difficulties were greatly accentuated by delay in deciding just what type of pill-box to build and the fact that each Corps Commander in France had his own Chief Engineer, each of whom had his own idea how his section of the line should be sited. *They* got on with their work, drew on the available resources and labour, and French and Minnis were unable to get on with their original plans."

After the Cabinet meeting on the 26th, Hore-Belisha wrote to Gort:

" I hope you are pleased with the additional measures that we have taken to supplement the Field Force as a result of my visit. I was so glad to have your views at first hand and you will see from what we have done how much we are out to help you.

" I feel that the great thing is to get a very strong defence on the whole frontier line before the spring, and with this in view we are sending out to you a sapper and a contractor. They will be followed by the necessary labour and instruments.

" What I would like to be sure of is that the French are going to do exactly the same. If they are not, we would consider giving them help. It would be a pity if some part of the line were left weak.

" When I got back I received a severe shock. In the first paper put in front of me was a memorandum by the Chancellor suggesting that the provision of anything in excess of 20 divisions would reduce the country to bankruptcy. It looked as if the weary fight would have to start all over again. I felt, and the C.I.G.S. agreed, that we could not bear our responsibilities at the commencement of the war if the aim of 55 divisions in two years was not accepted.

"We have now got our proposals through the Cabinet for a productive capacity for 55 divisions.

" I am pressing hard to see that the Army gets an adequate

share of aircraft, and we are preparing a paper advocating a special type of machine in large quantities for close support, to be under your command."

The German intervention in the Spanish Civil War had impressed Hore-Belisha of the need for the close co-operation of the Army and the Air Force. The German attack on Poland had shown the devastating effect of the tactical support of troops by dive-bombers. He felt it was essential that aircraft must be recognised as an integral part of the Army, just as it had already come to be recognised as an integral part of the Navy. Again and again he pressed for this. He insisted that there should be a separate Army Air Arm with its own land-based aircraft, comprising reconnaissance planes, low-flying fighters, dive-bombers, transport planes and so on, and that it should be under the direct control of the Commander-in-Chief. But the Air Ministry were firmly opposed to any kind of independent air arm for the Army.

Gort replied on the 1st October :

"I am afraid I have been some days in answering your letter, which had to go to the place you came to and then on back here to the hotel where Gamelin gave us luncheon before the unveiling of the memorial last year. To-morrow we move forward again and we will have a good château to entertain you in when next you can find the time to come out for a short visit.

"I am indeed most grateful for all you have done for us to supplement our present resources. With the wide fronts we will have to hold, the additional reinforcements are more than welcome.

"Dill[1] is busy going into the line now and, as you know, we assume responsibility for our sector on 4th. Personally, I will be glad when it happens as it will do much for the troops to have real soldiering to do instead of being in back areas or on the road. I have seen some of the M.T. columns on the move and they were keeping distances well and maintaining good discipline. They looked to me a fine lot of men and cheerful.

"So far I have not had a chance to see the infantry as they have been moving up by rail, but I will see them during the next few days. They will all be busy from now on digging in, but I

---

[1] Commander of the 1st Army Corps.

have warned them to be a little careful about their concealment with a neutral frontier so close. I think we must take it as a foregone conclusion that the Germans know the site of every blockhouse and armoured O.P. in the area we take over. Round about 25,000 workmen go backwards and forwards across the frontier daily. That is inevitable. When the labour and material come out we should then get so highly organised as to make leakage of information about defence works of secondary importance.

" It seems almost inconceivable what you say was contained in the memorandum from the Chancellor, as I had hoped those wearying arguments were over for good and all while the war lasted. The French will certainly expect us to pull more and more weight on land as the war proceeds. Your aim in divisions will certainly keep them happy when the time comes for the Government to disclose it to them.

" It is indeed cheering news to hear you are pressing hard to get us more aircraft for our use, as we must aim at effecting paralysis in their rear areas. They will undoubtedly give us a rotten time until we have more A.A. guns and fighters, but I do feel even our small arms fire will make low-flying attacks more hazardous than they proved to be in Poland.

" I gave your message to His Royal Highness[1] saying how sorry you were not to be able to say good-bye and he thoroughly understood the reason. We will hope to see you again before long if you have a moment to come and stay. It will be an easy journey now."

Wednesday, 27th September 1939

I reported to Cabinet that units of the 2nd Corps were starting to land in France. Phipps[2] had pressed a few days before, for French morale purposes, that a public announcement be made to the effect that the transportation of the B.E.F. was a record achievement, particularly of a mechanised Army. No statement is to be made at present.

Press reports of large German forces arriving on Western Front from Poland. Gamelin is very apprehensive of German attack

[1] The Duke of Gloucester.   [2] Sir Eric Phipps, British Ambassador in Paris.

through Belgium. I pointed out that both I and Hankey had made it quite clear to Daladier and Gamelin in Paris that in no circumstances would the British Government agree to the B.E.F. leaving their prepared positions and advancing into Belgium.[1]

Thursday, 28th September 1939

I told the Cabinet of all that was being done to secure a strongly fortified line for the B.E.F.

Wednesday, 4th October 1939

An excavator unit has arrived in France to work on the defences.

Thursday, 5th October 1939

The 2nd Corps has arrived in France. The transportation of all the troops has been carried out without a single casualty or hitch of any kind.

Behind that brief report lay the recurrent anxiety : Have they arrived safely ? A few days later[2] he informed the House of Commons : " We have fulfilled—and more than fulfilled—our undertaking recently given to France to despatch to that country in the event of war a British Expeditionary Force of a specified dimension within a specified time. Nor are the contingents at present across the Channel the last that will arrive." Then he gave figures :

" Within six weeks of the outbreak of war in 1914 we had transported to France 148,000 men. Within five weeks of the outbreak of this war we had transported to France 158,000 men. . . . Night by night we have waited at the War Office for tidings of the convoys. These have averaged three a night."

In 1914, he added, the men marched on to the ships, the horses were led and a light derrick could lift what the soldier could not carry. " In those days there were only 800 mechanised vehicles and

[1] The British troops did in fact in May 1940 leave their prepared positions and advance into Belgium. Commenting on this, in *The Second World War*, Vol. ii, Winston Churchill posed the question "whether we would not have been wiser to stand and fight on the French frontier, and amid these strong defences invite the Belgian Army to fall back upon them, rather than make the hazardous and hurried forward leap to the Dyle or the Albert Canal." He added: " The British General Staff and our headquarters in the field had long been anxious about the gap between the northern end of the Maginot Line and the beginning of the British fortified front along the Franco-Belgian frontier. Mr. Hore-Belisha, the Secretary of State for War, raised the point in the War Cabinet on several occasions."

[2] House of Commons debates, 11th October 1939.

it was a rare load that exceeded two tons. We have on this occasion transported to France more than 25,000 vehicles, including tanks, some of them of enormous dimensions and weighing 15 tons apiece and more. Normal shore cranes could not raise them, special ships were required to carry them and highly trained stevedores to manipulate them." And the voyages were longer, as more remote landing places had now to be selected in France.

The growth of the Army, he pointed out, had been rapid. " When I first introduced Army Estimates to the House in March 1938, we were preparing out of our strategic reserve 5 divisions—none of them upon a Continental scale. By the time of the next Army Estimates in March this year, the Government had decided, in view of menacing developments, to prepare 19 divisions—all upon a Continental scale. Subsequently the European tension increased and in April the plan for 19 Divisions became a plan for 32. This will not be the limit of our effort."

Then, quoting the tributes of American observers who had visited the B.E.F., Hore-Belisha added :

" I would prefer to give that rather than my own opinion. It is generally felt that they are equipped in the finest possible manner, which could not be excelled. Of course no army is ever fully equipped ; there can always be more of everything, there can always be new developments, and I do not pretend that everything is absolutely perfect down to the last gaiter button or that there are not certain deficiencies. I think that on the whole, however, it is as well if not better equipped than any similar army."

This was endorsed by Winston Churchill at the time of Dunkirk :[1] " The best of all we had to give had gone to the British Expeditionary Force, and although they had not the numbers of tanks and some articles of equipment which were desirable, they were a very well and fully equipped Army."

[1] House of Commons debates 4th June 1940.

CHAPTER XXV

The " Pill-Box " Controversy

GAMELIN, who expected an early enemy attack in the West, kept changing his mind from day to day as to exactly where it would come. He pressed constantly for still more British troops to be sent, suggesting that this could be done if the standard of equipment was lowered.

Friday, 20th October 1939
I said I was against sending any divisions overseas until they were properly equipped. We were keeping up our flow of troops to France and were ahead of our programme, which had been settled with the French before the war. Winston took the French point of view.[1]
On Saturday the 21st October, Hore-Belisha broadcast to the nation after the 9 o'clock news. In the course of it he said :

" There is something more, something greater in this war than a combat between opposing armies ; something more eternal than a grapple in the skies between the Spitfires of Britain and the Heinkels of Nazi Germany ; something more desperate than a death struggle between the U-boats and the destroyers. There is a conflict between the forces of good and the forces of evil, and what has to be determined is which shall possess the soul of countries and of men.

" We did not enter the fight merely to reconstitute Czecho-slovakia. Nor do we fight merely to reconstitute a Polish State. Our aims are not defined by geographical frontiers. We are concerned with the frontiers of the human spirit. This is no war

---

[1] Three partially equipped divisions were sent to France in the course of May 1940. They suffered heavily and contributed little.

250

about a map. It is a war to re-establish the conditions in which nations and individuals—including, may I say, the German nations and individuals—can live or live again.

" There can be no question of our wavering in any degree. This tyranny, whose challenge we have accepted, must and will be abased. . . . Only the defeat of Nazi Germany can lighten the darkness which now shrouds our cities and lighten the horizon for all Europe and the world."

After the broadcast he was sent by a listener a bronze plaque depicting the conflict between the forces of good and evil. The design showed an armed knight battling with a dragon. Hore-Belisha hung the plaque in his dressing-room.

Tuesday, 24th October 1939

We have assured Gamelin that Britain will create at earliest possible date the largest B.E.F. which can be effectively maintained. The only limiting factor is the speed with which industry can produce the equipment required.

On the 28th October, Gort wrote to him :

" Everything here is fast becoming quite waterlogged and unfit for any attack. For an army which depends for success on tanks and low flying, I can imagine no worse combination than Flanders mud and low cloud. Even our aerodromes up here are soggy and the one at Merville was yesterday temporarily out of action. The troops, however, remain in grand fettle and they are learning fast how to dig, revet and drain trenches. Their health is extraordinarily good and better than in peace stations at home, the result of ample food and exercise. I am shortly going to do some training in back areas as many of them badly want to put in some field work. As you know, for reasons outside our control, training has been very difficult during the past year or two. Palestine, for instance, made very heavy demands on signal and R.A.S C. personnel.

" The administrative machine is getting run in well and Lindsell[1] has got a very good liaison with the French authorities.

[1] Major-General W. G. Lindsell, Q.M.G., B.E.F., later Lieutenant-General Sir Wilfred Lindsell.

When one recalls that the distance from our Western bases is the same as Edinburgh to Newhaven it gives some idea of the maintenance problem. Every day we consume 450 tons of petrol, which equals 108,000 gallons. In other words, if your car goes 20 miles to the gallon you could travel 2,160,000 miles on our daily consumption.

" I believe the King is contemplating a visit to the troops and I sent a suggestion that if he does so he would probably find it most convenient to do so in December. . . . I do not know whether the Prime Minister would like to visit the troops some time when he is over in France, but I am thinking of sending him an invitation to do so. Paris is only 3 hours away by car and if he stayed two nights with me he could spend one whole day going round. I am leaving yours an open invitation as I will naturally be delighted to put you up at any time."

Hore-Belisha replied on the 31st October :

" As you know, I read the main parts of your letter of the 28th October to the War Cabinet, because I thought it would interest them very much. It was indeed a most vivid letter, particularly the manner in which you illustrate the distance to the Base.

" I spoke to the King some time ago and suggested he should pay a visit to the Front, and I have no doubt that he will do so later. I suggested to him that the nearer Christmas the better.

" The Prime Minister tells me that he will be very glad to come and see you and I will let you know as soon as he feels like coming. I would like him to get the local atmosphere. . . .

" The Air Ministry is stone-walling again about our requirements of direct support machines to be under your control, but we are plodding along and the matter will now come before the War Cabinet. I can only hope that I can get good support. . . .

" We have nearly had all our plans jiggered up by the reports of an intended 'invasion ! ' I will write you more fully about this later, as it will interest you. Winston took it very seriously."

He followed this up on the next day, the 1st November :

" On Friday night last, at W.C.'s request, a committee of Service Ministers was assembled, with military advisers. A telegram to which the General Staff did not attach credence was the basis of the meeting.

" In this telegram the French Military Attaché in Yugoslavia had reported his receipt of information to the effect that an enormous invasion was being planned on this country by sea, land and air, and would take place at any moment.

" W.C. felt that the Fleet could not get advance information of the project and that the invasion would be upon us before we knew where we were, and he felt that the Navy could not stave it off. The Air Force felt equally uncomfortable and it was to be assumed that the Army would have to deal with a formidable foe. We tried to riddle the arguments, but nevertheless we were instructed to prepare plans for meeting the invasion and even for bringing back divisions, if necessary, from France.

" In the next day or so the same rumour came from various other 'reliable resources' and I pleaded throughout that our main strategy should not be deflected.

" I thought you would like to know about all this. We are preparing a statement to make to the War Cabinet on Saturday, showing what dispositions we can make, and I hope that my colleagues will all agree that we need not do anything which would upset our training or programme."

Hore-Belisha was strongly opposed to any divisions of the British Expeditionary Force being brought back from France at this juncture. He felt it might well be no more than a ruse of the Germans in order to disrupt our plans and disorganise the B.E.F.

On the next day, the 2nd November, Hore-Belisha delivered an address to representatives from the Dominions, in the course of which he said :

" We started the war with plans for 32 divisions and on the assumption that if Z was not earlier than October 1940, the whole of the 32 divisions were to be sent over in one year. But unfortunately Z was not in October 1940, but in September 1939. Therefore we had to make a revised plan and, as far as I can at present say, subject to correction, the dates are—5 divisions over-seas now ; 1 division ready to proceed overseas on 1st January

1940 and 4 divisions on 1st February 1940—a total of 3 Army Corps.

" Thereafter accurate forecasts of dates of despatch are difficult, but it is hoped that a 4th Army Corps of 4 divisions will be equipped and ready to proceed overseas in the spring. This Corps will, it is hoped, contain a Canadian division. We are doing our best by pressing on with the supply output to accelerate these dates. . . .

" We will supply you with all our forecasts of production and assist you to the best of our ability to equip your divisions."

Saturday, 4th November 1939

Submitted Memo to Cabinet on Defence of G.B. against invasion.

I told the Cabinet that further divisions would be sent to France in the middle of December.

During the month of October aerial reconnaissance photographs had revealed that a number of additional bridges were being constructed by the Germans across the Rhine.

Belgium had, ever since 1936, adopted an attitude of strict neutrality and was at the utmost pains not to engage in any Staff conversations that might be misconstrued by the Germans. But it was agreed by the Belgians that, if their country were attacked, they would not hesitate to appeal to Britain for immediate assistance. We indicated, however, that without Staff talks and the other necessary preliminaries, we could hold out little hope that any such immediate assistance could be effective.

Gamelin, however, was more and more inclined, in the event of a German attack coming through Belgium, to move the troops forward.

By the 7th November rumours of an imminent attack by the Germans alarmed the Belgians and on the 11th November they agreed to accept any information we were able to pass on. But they imposed many restrictions.

De Guingand, who was present at many of the discussions at the War Office, records :[1]

[1] *Operation Victory.*

" November 12th was an exciting day. We expected at any moment that the Belgians would co-operate, and Gamelin was waiting ready to carry out his plan.

" Hore-Belisha was somewhat apprehensive regarding the hazards of advancing into Belgium to the chosen line, and wishing to satisfy himself that we could attain our object without major German ground and air interference, asked the Air Ministry for an exposé of our air plan for delaying a German move from the east.

" In answer to his request two or three R.A.F. officers arrived with an enormous map. After some trouble this was hoisted up against the wall in the Secretary of State's office, and then we gathered round to hear the plan.

" The map embraced the various routes by which the enemy could advance, and it was covered with a great number of black spots—some large, some small. It was explained that these represented potential targets which when hit would interfere with the enemy's advance, or prevent supplies reaching his forces. The targets selected were bridges, cross-roads and defiles which constituted bottle-necks along the various routes. . . .

" In theory it was all very nice, but there appeared to be many major snags in practice. The targets had to be hit accurately, and even then it was questionable whether much harm would have been done. To achieve any prolonged effect, sustained attacks would have been necessary. How were we going to fulfil these heavy commitments ? Had we the right type of aircraft for both day and night attacks, and had we enough of them ? Would they survive the enemy's fighters and A.A. defence ? These were some of the questions which I am sure those who were watching turned over in their minds.

" The exposé came to an end, and silence descended upon the room. After a pause Hore-Belisha asked : ' In view of our shortage of medium bombers, what do you propose to use against those numerous targets by day ? ' There was no satisfactory answer.

" The large map was rolled up again, the R.A.F. Staff Officers departed, and we were left with an uneasy foreboding as to the dangers of a policy which dictated a move of our forces into Belgium."

That same day Hore-Belisha sent a further letter to Gort about the Army Air Arm:

" Whatever you may have been doing in France, we have been having a hell of a battle here on the Army Air Arm question. . . . I think the Prime Minister's statement meets us, at any rate for the present, but unfortunately they went and put down the wrong conclusions, which I had to dispute on the ground that they did not carry out the Prime Minister's statement. So I am having another battle to get this right. I think that Chatfield will definitely cause to be allocated to us a bombing force and, if once we can get this under your control, we shall have broken the ice. I feel myself that in the end we shall have to have an Army Air Arm because there are other aspects of our use of the air, such as transport, parachutists, etc., which have not been studied or provided, and I cannot for the life of me see why the services of an army should at all times be on the ground.

" You very kindly said that you would welcome me whenever I could come over and I am proposing to leave here with Kennedy,[1] and de Guingand on Friday afternoon, the 17th. I would like to dine with you and stay the night wherever it may be convenient to you, if I may. During my visit I am most anxious to have a talk with you, to see the conditions, and to be able to help you in every possible way on my return. I would like to see as much as possible in the time and to come in contact with sample formations down to a battalion. Perhaps all this could be done on the Saturday morning. If also I could see, as last time, your principal Staff Officers and the Corps Commanders, I should be most grateful. Towards the evening I could perhaps move into the French area and see something of their positions the next morning, sleeping at some place like Cambrai. The Mission are, I believe, putting this *en train*. I would then go on to reach Paris on the Sunday evening and perhaps meet Daladier and Gamelin, returning to England on Monday morning."

[1] Brigadier John Kennedy, Deputy Director of Military Operations; later Major-General Sir John Kennedy.

Hore-Belisha talking to Lord Gort, C-in-C, B.E.F.

Hore-Belisha attending the French Army manœuvres in 1937
with Sir Cyril Deverell, C.I.G.S.

Hore-Belisha with C.-in-C Lord Gort and Lieutenant-General
Alan Brooke (later Lord Alanbrooke) in France, November 1939

This was followed, on the 15th, by this brief note :

" The Prime Minister has now revised the Draft Air Conclusions. . . . You will see that they are much more favourable to
us.

" Chatfield is mediating, and Massy[1] is seeing him, I hope,
to-day. In the meanwhile, Massy has been to Manchester to see
about the prototypes of the new close-support machine, so you
see matters are progressing.

" I am very much looking forward to seeing you on Friday?'

He left Hendon in the afternoon. It was foggy, so Hore-Belisha,
with Kennedy and de Guingand, went on to Paris, landing at Le
Bourget at 4 p.m. They drove straight to the Embassy where they
had tea. Then they took a train to Arras, arriving late.

Hore-Belisha's previous visit, in September, had been but briefly
recorded by the Press. On this occasion, with newspaper correspondents at G.H.Q., vivid accounts were published, together with
pictures of him, in raincoat and muffler, taking long strides through
the squelching mud, with Gort and other senior officers, British and
French, beside him. Among them were General Dill and Lieut.-
General A. F. Brooke. The correspondents described him and the
" top brass " having a picnic lunch out of paper bags in a country
lane. In one of the sectors he visited, a Guards colonel had set up
improvised Belisha beacons at crossing points along the road.

Saturday, 18th November 1939

Went along practically the whole front of the British sector.
Gort's command includes a French division, which has been
strengthened by a British brigade, British machine-gun battalions
and an artillery regiment—an illustration of the permeation of
English and French forces.

The permanent fortifications of the line include blockhouses
about 1000 yards apart and a continuous anti-tank obstacle in the
form of a trench which has been strengthened and reveted.

Two lines of defences are being constructed behind the main
line.

A great deal of digging is in progress along the front, but I was

[1] Lieut.-General Hugh Massy, Deputy Chief of the Imperial General Staff.

surprised to see only two new pill-boxes being constructed. I mentioned this to Gort. He informed me there is some difference of opinion with the French as to the best form of pill-box. Our people do not agree that the French type of pill-box is the best that can be devised.

A bigger conception will have to be taken of the defences. It looks now as though the Germans may not attack until the spring. What the Germans did in a few months on the Siegfried Line, we should be able to accomplish with equal speed.

Sunday, 19th November 1939

9 a.m. Met Press correspondents and visited 51s: French Division under Gort.

In the afternoon by car to Paris. Dined and slept at the Embassy.

Monday, 20th November 1939

I saw Gamelin at his G.H.Q. at Vincennes.

He said we were more liberally equipped than the French. The Germans, he said, would have 30 more divisions, making 160 in all, between now and the spring. It was very important to add to our numbers. I asked him for his equipment tables which he is going to let me have.

He said their own production of tanks weighing 35 tons was good. They had a tank being made of 125 tons weight as an experiment.

We discussed the making of pill-boxes. He said that the French had found a method of constructing pill-boxes within 3 days. He offered to send an officer, if required, to Gort to explain the method, but he thought it more important that Gort should send engineers down to see how they did it.

He said our bombers, both heavy and medium, should be used in support of the Army and to create as much havoc as possible among advancing Germans. He stated that he did not believe in an independent Air Force.

Gamelin also spoke to me about 2 inventions, which he asked me to keep particularly secret, but in the development of which he required our help.

Lunched with Daladier, Guy de la Chambre (Air), Campinchi (Marine), Dautry (Supply), etc. ; Gamelin, Darlan and Viullemin.

My conversation with Daladier followed the same lines as

with Gamelin. He expressed himself as dissatisfied with the air liaison.

In the afternoon returned by air to London.

Hore-Belisha was very disquieted about the British defences. De Guingand, who was with him in France and attended some of the conferences, states in his report that Hore-Belisha was anxious to accelerate the building of concrete pill-boxes and wanted to procure more labour and machines to achieve this.

Hore-Belisha called a meeting of the Army Council the moment he returned to the War Office. It took place at 6 p.m.

I reported my main impressions during my visit to the B.E.F.

I discussed various questions of policy and dealt at some length with the question of pill-boxes. I emphasised that far more concrete pill-boxes were essential.

Tuesday, 21st November 1939

I reported to the War Cabinet on my visit to France.

Meanwhile the Dominions representatives had been to G.H.Q. with Mr. Anthony Eden, the Secretary of State for Dominion Affairs. On their return their impressions were conveyed to Hore-Belisha.

Writing to Gort on the 22nd November, he said :

" This is to thank you for your wonderful hospitality, which extended not only to food and shelter, but to a personal attention which went to my heart. By accompanying me personally and by arranging so complete a programme you enabled me to profit by every instant of time.

" The impression that is deepest in my mind is of the great knowledge which you show of every detail. Your interest in the task and in the men is most inspiring. . . .

" I am seeing the engineers to-morrow. I really think the pill-boxes should spring up everywhere. The Dominions' representatives and Anthony Eden commented on their absence. I thought you would like to know this.

" Gamelin told me in Paris that they could make them in three days apiece. He also said they were lining and flooring their trenches with cement and that you could have cement works in the area. He hoped you would send down some officers to study their methods."

On the same afternoon he made his second statement in the House on the B.E.F. and said that, to the 158,000 mentioned in his last statement, some thousands were being added every week. Territorial units, he said, had been sent across the Channel at a much earlier stage and in greater numbers than in 1914.

He then guardedly referred to the gap in the Maginot Line :

" The major system of the Maginot Line—with its subterranean railways, its underground accommodation and its ingeniously emplaced batteries—extends along the frontier which divides France from our enemy. That frontier is 200 miles in extent.

" But the low esteem in which the given word of Germany is held, illustrated, as it has repeatedly been, by the world-wide credence that so spontaneously attaches to the slightest rumour of designs upon a neutral country, has necessitated that the defences of France should extend beyond these limits. Indeed, whereas Germany has to defend 200 miles of frontier against possible attack by the Allies, France has had to envisage the possibility of aggression by Germany along 800 miles, from the North Sea to the Alps.

" We now share the task with them. There are French troops in the British part of the line and British troops in the French part of the line. The understanding and good relations are complete. The sector at present allotted to the British Army, while not comparable with the major system of the Maginot Line, was thus fortunately provided in advance with field works. The task which fell to our soldiers on arrival was to add to and improve upon these, and this task they are undertaking with a will.

" This is a fortress war. The House can see in its mind's eye the busy work of our soldiers, digging and building. Under their hands blockhouses and pill-boxes take shape, and with digging machines and with squelching spades they throw up breastworks or carve out entrenchments. . . ."

It showed how much in his mind was the need for strengthening the fortifications and extending them all the way to the coast. The soldiers were digging and building, the excavators were active—but was enough being achieved ?

Friday, 24th November 1939

I saw the Prime Minister in the morning and he mentioned to me the recent visit of the Dominion ministers to G.H.Q. He said it was the opinion of some of them that a great increase of concrete pill-boxes was required.

During the afternoon I was told privately by a friend who had sat next to Colonel French at a luncheon at the Ritz—he had come over from France with the Chief Engineer—that he had said he wanted to see me, but he was being put off. I saw him for a few minutes. He left an impression on me that it was not being made too easy for him as " an outsider."

Brigadier Westrop, who was supervising the digging of anti-tank trenches in France and was in frequent touch with French though his unit worked under G.H.Q., says : " Brigadier W. C. H. Pritchard at the War Office, who was Deputy Director of Works in charge of Supplies, was doing all he could to help French. The difficulties were out at the Front. Some of the officers at G.H.Q. were not only critical of Hore-Belisha's interference, but were distinctly hostile to him. The atmosphere was unpleasant. French met with many frustrations. There was a common pool of supplies and equipment and the Army Corps engineers took what they wanted. French, who was a keen, efficient and extremely capable engineer, could not get the co-operation to plan or carry out the job and was consequently fed up. The pill-boxes were certainly not being built fast enough."

This " civilian interference," as they called it, presented the many scheming officers at the Front with the chance they had been looking for. It might well be the means of alienating Gort from Hore-Belisha.

The diary continues :

I had called an Army Council meeting for 5.30 p.m. in order to have another conference about the pill-boxes.

I felt bound to inform them of my talk with the P.M. and the comments of the Dominion representatives. I added that my own impressions coincided with what they had said and that a great increase of concrete pill-boxes was essential if the position was to withstand a German onslaught with real confidence.

Pakenham-Walsh,[1] who had returned from France for this discussion, stated that General Billotte planned to have six pill-boxes per kilometre and had asked for the necessary labour to construct them to this scale on his front. He hoped we would do the same. The pill-boxes should be sited in depth. I asked Pakenham-Walsh how many pill-boxes would be required on the B.E.F. front, and he replied 240 and they would take until April to build. Design for standard pill-boxes had been approved two weeks ago. Enough steel and concrete were available in France for some time. Difficulty was anticipated in obtaining all the stone required. Also provision of labour was difficult as about eight new-type Engineer companies would be needed.

A. G.[2] suggested that the best method of obtaining skilled concrete workers would be to get Colonel French to enlist them, in view of his contacts with the industry.

I asked how the construction of these pill-boxes could be speeded up, as I wished to do everything possible to help the C.-in-C. in the strengthening of the defences in France. I summed up by saying that there were two reasons why we should do all in our power to hasten this work, namely in order to give our soldiers the best possible defences and so that no one could say we had not done our very best.

Before Pakenham-Walsh left the meeting I said that my remarks about the shortage of pill-boxes were in no way meant as a criticism of the C.-in-C. All I wanted was to give him all possible help.

De Guingand states : " Several times during the next few days S. of S. mentioned the pill-box question to me. His whole attitude was one of endeavouring to help rather than one of criticism."[3]

Five days after the Army Council meeting, on the 29th November, the C.I.G.S. left for France. A telegram had been sent in advance by his Personal Assistant to Gort's Military Assistant,

[1] Major-General R. P. Pakenham-Walsh, Engineer-in-Chief, B.E.F.
[2] General Sir Robert Gordon-Finlayson, Adjutant-General to the Forces.
[3] Operation Victory.

stating that the object of the visit was " to inspect defences in B.E.F. area on War Cabinet instructions." Hore-Belisha was not aware at the time that such a telegram was being sent, nor had any such instructions been given by either the War Cabinet or by him. It proved to be most unfortunate that the telegram should have been so worded.

Saturday, 2nd December 1939

Ironside, after his visit to B.E.F., came to see me and with great emphasis told me that the officers were most upset at the criticisms made about lack of defences and that everyone was talking about it. I told him I was amazed that the matter had been so widely spread.

He said that Gort greatly resents it. Instead of Ironside explaining the misunderstanding, it is clear that he has not put the matter right. He said Gort was threatening to resign.

I at once wrote to Gort :

" I have received from the C.I.G.S. a most encouraging report of the progress of your defences in France. I think the speed of the achievement is quite remarkable, as we can see from the map I was shown. I will see that an account is given to my colleagues in the War Cabinet of what you have done.

" C.I.G.S. has shown me a *procès-verbal* of a message given you by Pakenham-Walsh on his return to France and I can quite understand your being disturbed at this, as I was. He seems to have got the facts slightly wrong. The P.M. did not say anything at the Cabinet. It was to me that he gave an account of what the Dominions representatives had said. This was just before an Army Council meeting at which we were due to discuss how we could help. P.W. came to the meeting for the purpose of explaining his needs and we spent at least an hour discussing ways and means of giving you everything in the way of help in view of the urgency. Although we discussed pill-boxes at great length, it was made quite clear to P.W. that no criticism was intended and that our sole desire was to give you everything you could possibly want. This is made perfectly plain in the Minutes. As to the need for pill-boxes, I know that you and we are in complete agreement.

" What has been done, and what will be told to the War Cabinet is a complete answer to anything the Dominion representatives have said and this is what I have in view in going into the matter so fully.

" It is understandable that being so far away you may have got a wrong impression. I can assure you that while I will always be frank with both you and my colleagues, you will get all the support in my power in any difficulty with which you may be confronted. We shall have some hard times to go through and we can afford to put the pill-boxes in perspective. The incident is closed.

" On the Army Air question, in which Pownall gave such valuable evidence, you will be glad to know that Massy and Pierce have reached an agreement. I will send you a copy of this and of Chatfield's report, as soon as it is printed."

To this letter there was no reply. It is obvious that Gort was extremely annoyed by what had been told him, and this pleased those around him who had been seeking for a means of getting Hore-Belisha out. In the friction between these two men they saw their chance. Events began to move swiftly to a climax.

Thursday, 7th December 1939

At 5.30 p.m. I saw the P.M. to discuss my letter to Chatfield on air co-operation with the Army. In a very friendly way he said he thought the phrasing of my letter was peremptory. I remarked that I thought my relations with Chatfield were too good to have this effect on him.

Did this introduce a new note in the Prime Minister's relations with Hore-Belisha? Was it a sign that he was losing the Prime Minister's confidence and support? The diary continues:

The P.M. said if I did not pursue my idea of a separate Army Air Arm, my proposals would commend themselves to my colleagues. I said I would be prepared to concede this if my proposals were conceded.

Afterwards I saw Chatfield and said I hoped he had not thought my letter peremptory. He said it had not occurred to him—our relations were too good for that. I admitted that I erred on the

side of emphasis when I attached importance to anything, just as
he did in the opposite direction, so we ought to reach a good
balance.

Exactly a month later, in a letter dated the 7th January 1940,
Chatfield, writing to Hore-Belisha on his resignation, said : " I am
glad to think that during our time together we have *never* had a
discordant note, even though we have sat elbow to elbow daily."

CHAPTER XXVI

Resignation

Thursday, 14th December 1939

I had a telephone message from the P.M. and saw him at 3.30 p.m. He said the King had asked him to see Ironside, but he did not know really what it was all about.

He put the question at once to me whether I had confidence in Gort. I had only to tell him if I wanted a change. He was most friendly.

I told him I had complete confidence in Gort. The idea of making a change had never entered my head.

He then asked me whether I had instructed Ironside to go out to G.H.Q. I said " No." I added that I thought it was most unfortunate a misconception should have arisen from the telegram sent on behalf of Ironside to Gort, stating that it was on War Cabinet instructions that he was going out to inspect B.E.F. defences. This, I felt, had upset Gort. I only knew about this telegram after Ironside's return from France.

I then explained to him step by step the action I had taken about the pill-boxes immediately after I returned from my visit to the B.E.F., including an account of the two Army Council meetings I had called for this purpose.

I referred lightly to Gort's sensitiveness and said that, as soon as I was aware that Gort was under some misunderstanding about the pill-boxes, I wrote to him in order to put the whole matter in the right perspective. My sole concern throughout was to see that Gort got everything he wanted, and, above all, to give him the maximum support possible in strengthening the defences.

The P.M. then asked me if I had confidence in Ironside, to which I replied " Yes."

He remarked that Ironside was a tactless man, but I replied that he had great qualities. No man was without defects.

It is manifest from the phrasing of the Prime Minister's questions about Gort and Ironside and the indication set down in the diary " I had only to tell him if I wanted to make a change," that the replacement of these two men would have been supported by Chamberlain. By not availing himself of this offer Hore-Belisha undoubtedly misjudged their attitude towards him and had to pay dearly for his misplaced trust. But at that moment the thought uppermost in his mind, as he revealed a few weeks later,[1] was the unsettling effect such changes at the very summit of Army control would have on public morale. He could not, he felt, weigh any personal advantages against the vital interests of the country. His concern was that the military skill and judgment, which he was convinced these two men possessed, should continue to be used for the direction and control of the Army at this critical moment in our history. How gravely this might affect his own position he did not pause to consider.

The Prime Minister spent the next few days in France, visiting G.H.Q. and going to Paris for a meeting of the Supreme War Council.

Wednesday, 20th December 1939

I saw the P.M. for a few minutes after the Cabinet meeting. He told me the French were pressing for more troops to be sent to France, that they were again suggesting that our scale of equipment was unnecessarily lavish and that, if we reduced the scale, we should be able to put a great many more men into the field. It was arranged I should see him again after lunch when he would tell me about his visit to G.H.Q.

3 p.m. The P.M. said he had gone into the matter of the pill-boxes. They were all talking about it at G.H.Q. They had even discussed it with his own staff. The feeling was strong and he wanted to let me know exactly what was going on.

He said Gort's story was that he had been told that the P.M. and the Cabinet were very disturbed by my report to them about

[1] In a statement to the author in January 1940.

the defences after my recent visit. He added that they were resentful at what they regarded as my criticism of them. The P.M. said that he had told Gort that he could speak from his own knowledge that what I had said about the pill-boxes at the Cabinet meeting was not in any carping spirit, nor in criticism of Gort, but that I had emphasised the need for more defences and had urged that everything possible should be done without delay to ensure that they were greatly strengthened. He said that he had not minimised my anxiety to Gort, but he had assured him that the impression I had left on him and his colleagues was that my one object was to see that he had all the assistance the War Office could send out.

He said he had also assured Gort of my complete confidence in him and that anything he might have heard to the contrary was quite unfounded.

He had the impression, with all the gossip going about—it was just like an officers' club—that there were people who were out to make trouble and he advised me to be careful. He had appointed me Secretary of State for War and he did not want me to be tripped up by this kind of thing.

I asked him what he meant by all this. I said he had always talked to me with great frankness. I knew he spoke to me not only as Prime Minister, but in a fatherly way because I was a much younger man. Several times I had interrupted him and had asked him to say exactly what was in his mind and not to mince his words.

He replied : " I will give you an instance. During your visits to G.H.Q. they say you took little notice of the officers and were only interested in the men." He said he did not want to identify himself with all this in any way.

" Well," I said, " the facts speak for themselves. I have been to G.H.Q. twice. On the first occasion with Hankey to fix Gort's sector of the line and then my time was mainly taken up with officers. During my second visit I toured the whole line and of course I talked to the men. But officers and men are all part of the Army to me."

I said I would show him all the correspondence I had had with Gort since he went to France and he could see from it how I had kept in the closest touch with Gort and my anxiety to send out everything we could to assist him with the defences. I had informed him of every step in my fight for air co-operation with the Army.

The P.M. was extremely nice throughout and ended by saying that he had complete confidence in me, adding, " You have great courage and you do not mind being criticised."

It is surprising that the hostile atmosphere at G.H.Q., to which the Prime Minister referred and of which men like Westrop and others were fully aware, should not have been sensed by Hore-Belisha during either of his two visits to France, for he made no note of it in his diary.

During the fortnight that followed, Hore-Belisha saw the Prime Minister constantly at the War Cabinet and other meetings and had no consciousness of any change in Chamberlain's attitude or manner towards him. Did he once again fail to sense that something was amiss, that possibly the Prime Minister might be contemplating moving Hore-Belisha to another Ministry so that the tension at the Front might be eased ?

Thursday, 4th January 1940

At the Cabinet meeting a note was brought in to me from the War Office to say that there was a telephone message from No. 10 that the P.M. wished to see me at 2.45 p.m.

The meeting finished at 12.50, rather earlier than usual. I asked the P.M. whether he wished me to be documented in any way. He replied : " Not at all. I have merely a proposal to make to you."

I then walked home across the Park. Grigg lunched with me.

I arrived five minutes early. The P.M. was smoking a cigar. He started by saying that what he had to say to me might be disappointing to me. He spoke of the very high opinion he had of my work and then said there was prejudice against me. Because of it he thought it was in my interest to leave the War Office now.

I then asked : " Can you give me some details of the prejudice you refer to ? " He said : " No, but it exists." I asked, " Where does the pressure come from ? " He made no reply. I then asked him what was behind the pressure. He said, " There is feeling," and he used the word " resentment."

He then said : " I want to offer you the Board of Trade—it's very important."

He seemed to assume that I would accept.

I said to him : " You were prepared for this interview but I was not. I am completely taken aback. Therefore I would like time to reflect."

He expressed the utmost surprise and observed : " You surely cannot hesitate. You are an ambitious man. You surely do not want to go out into the wilderness." At which point I interjected : " There are more ways of serving the country than in the Board of Trade."

His surprise seemed to increase and he reiterated that I was an ambitious man and that if I stayed in the Government I might have a great career. He had been thrown out by Lloyd George— " and look where I am now," he said.

It was true, I said, that I was ambitious. But I did not spend my time thinking of Downing Street. My mind was centred on the War Office. My heart was there also. I had a job of work to do there and it occupied all my time and all my thoughts, and I had hoped to see it through. My idea of ambition was fulfilling oneself and not just holding an office in a Government. After my mother died I had lost ambition in the ordinary sense and I had hesitated at that time whether to continue in politics or to occupy myself more spiritually.

He said he understood this and was aware of the change that had taken place in me, but he wanted me to do as he advised, that it was important in my best interests. He went on urging me to accept the Board of Trade and pressed me to give him an immediate answer.

I said I could not understand why he would not give me a little time to think it over, and I repeated that I was completely taken aback.

He said he feared that it might leak out.

I assumed, I said, that he and I were the only two to know, and I asked him : " Is that so ? " and he said : " Yes." To which I replied : " Then how can it leak out ? "

He continued to press me. I said I could give him an answer at once and it would probably be the same answer as I would give him to-morrow, but the reason he had given me for making this sudden change was such that I felt I ought to reflect before giving him my decision. If he were offering me the Admiralty, the Foreign Office, the Chancellor of the Exchequer, because of prejudice against me at the War Office, I would still beg him not to press me for an answer. If that were my attitude towards a promotion, was it not reasonable that I should have time to consider the proposal he was making me?

He asked me how long I wanted. I told him that the C.I.G.S. and members of the General Staff were waiting for me to deliberate about Finland,[1] that after my meeting with them I had to attend the Cabinet Co-ordinating Committee at 4 p.m. At 5.30 I had an Army Council. I wanted to put the matter completely out of my mind so as to finish my day's work. To-night I would have time to reflect.

It was agreed that I should give him my answer at 10 the next morning.

At 6.30 p.m. a letter came by messenger to me from the P.M. written in his own hand:

" My dear Leslie—I feel so much distress myself at the thought of the trial through which you are passing that I cannot refrain from sending you this note.

" I do not know what decision you will come to about the Board of Trade and I don't propose to say anything more about that. But whether you accept my offer or not, I realise that what has happened must seem to have laid your life in ruins and it is to that point that I want to address myself.

" There is a very wise saying, which I have heard attributed to the Duke of Wellington, that ' Nothing is ever so good or so bad as it seems at first.' I have often reminded myself of that saying at good and bad moments.

" Secondly, I want to observe that this is wartime when no one can feel satisfied unless he has made some sacrifice. Do you remember an incident related in Spears' book about a French

---

[1] Russia had attacked Finland on the 29th November 1939, and Hore-Belisha was anxious to send ambulances to Finland in answer to an appeal.

General who passed a soldier being taken out by an execution squad, and said to him ' This is your sacrifice for the country ' ? I am not sure if I have got the words right but that was the sense and the General recorded that the man held up his head again and felt that he had recovered his self-respect. You are not being led out to execution, but you will perhaps feel that the story has its application.

" It is above all in a time of adversity that a man shows the best or the worst of himself and that is what I had in mind when I said that this was a testing time for you.

" Since we have now been associated for some time in various offices I have got to see perhaps deeper into you than most. What I have seen has not only won my affection, but it gives me confidence that you will emerge from your ordeal stronger and not less spiritually minded than before.

" One last word. Don't let this keep you awake to-night.— Ever yours, Neville Chamberlain."

Hore-Belisha was busy at the War Office until 9.30 p.m. He returned home with de Guingand and they dined together.

After dinner Lord Beaverbrook and Brendan Bracken,[1] who was at the time P.P.S. to Winston Churchill at the Admiralty, came to see him. Much earlier that day, before Hore-Belisha saw Chamberlain, Churchill had left for France on a visit to the Commander-in-Chief and the B.E.F.

Beaverbrook, despite the severing of the link between them when Hore-Belisha ceased to write for his newspapers, maintained a friendly regard for him and held a high opinion of his ability. They met from time to time during the intervening years. On occasion his newspapers were sharply critical, as over the shortage of A.A. guns, but in the main he admired what Hore-Belisha was trying to do for the Army and was well aware of the difficulties he had to overcome. Talking on the phone earlier that day, he was told by Hore-Belisha : " It is by no means certain I shall be staying on at the War Office." Beaverbrook had urged him to do nothing until they had a word together.[2]

That evening Beaverbrook, sensing the possibility of a dramatic

[1] Later Viscount Bracken.   [2] Statement by Lord Beaverbrook to the author.

Personal & Private

10, Downing Street,
Whitehall,

Jan 4 . 1920 .

My dear Leslie,

I feel so much distress myself at the thought of the trial through which you are passing that I cannot refrain from sending you this note.

I do not know what decision you will come to about the Board of Trade and I don't propose to say anything more about that. But whether you accept my offer or not I realise that what has happened must seem to have laid your life in ruins and it is to that point that I want to address myself.

There is a very wise saying, which

Page from Neville Chamberlain's letter to Hore-Belisha,
4 January 1940

Newspaper headlines at the time of
Hore-Belisha's resignation

RESIGNATION

intervention by him, went to the Admiralty to see Bracken. " Try
and contact Churchill on the phone," he said. " You might get him
at our Embassy in Paris. If he isn't there, leave a message asking
him to phone this number. Say it's urgent." The number he gave
was Hore-Belisha's.

They waited some time at Hore-Belisha's house. It was quite
late before Churchill got through. Beaverbrook took the call.
Churchill told him he already knew what had happened. Hore-
Belisha was astonished and thereupon took the phone. Churchill
sounded very detached, but revealed that the Prime Minister had
informed him earlier of what he proposed to do—that was before
saying anything about it to Hore-Belisha and assuring Hore-Belisha
that nobody else knew. Churchill strongly advised Hore-Belisha to
accept the Board of Trade, of which, too, he had been told.

Churchill's own record of this advance knowledge appears in his
History of the Second World War.[1] He writes :

" In the morning, before I left, the Prime Minister sent for me
and told me he had decided to make a change at the War Office
and that Mr. Hore-Belisha would give place to Mr. Oliver
Stanley.[2] Late that night Mr. Hore-Belisha called me on the
telephone at our Embassy in Paris and told me what I knew
already. I pressed him, but without success, to take one of the
other offices which were open to him."

It is difficult to understand why Churchill was singled out by the
Prime Minister and was the only one in the War Cabinet to be given
this confidence. Was it because Churchill was going to France and
would be seeing Gort ? Did the Prime Minister feel that Gort ought
to be reassured that a change was being made ?

Late that night, when he was alone, Hore-Belisha wrote the
following reply to the Prime Minister's letter :

" My dear Neville—Your letter reached me earlier this evening
and your personal references, which are very kind, make it all
the more regretful that I cannot do what you ask and go to the
Board of Trade.

" It is not the proposed transfer, but the circumstances of it
which cause me so much disquiet. It was only on Dec. 20th last,

[1] Vol. i " The Gathering Storm."   [2] Then President of the Board of Trade.

when the controversy about the defences in France was at its height, that you assured me of your complete support and of your desire that I should remain at the War Office to see the job through.

" This afternoon you told me that you continued to have the highest approval of my work, but that pressure had been put upon you to replace me and you offered me the Board of Trade.

" In such circumstances, whether I went to the Board of Trade or to any other Department, I would have the feeling that my tenure did not depend on the merits of my work. Unless a Minister is to be judged on this standard how can he render good service to the State and fearlessly execute his policy ?

" From the moment when you asked me to go to the War Office, at a time when the Army was falling out from the bottom owing to the shortage of recruits and the failure of prospective officers to come forward, I have had to take many hard decisions and my programme of reforms, alike in mechanisation, in anti-aircraft protection, in the struggle for an Army Air Arm, and particularly in the improvement of conditions and prospects known as the democratisation of the Army, has been at every stage made harder by resistances of which you know the strength and character.

" Through all this period it has only been possible for me to continue because I had your support.

" Since the outbreak of war I have realised, of course, that my conception of the work we should undertake in France did not meet with the approval of some of my military advisers—and you have been categorically assured that there is no reason whatever for anxiety about a German break-through.

" Yet my visits to France have convinced me that unless we utilise the time that is still available to us with far more vision and energy, the Germans will attack us on our weak spot somewhere in the gap between the Maginot Line and the sea.

" If the Maginot Line policy is the correct one—and I fail to see what alternative is open to a country whose population is half that of Germany—how dangerous is it to leave the Line incomplete !

" I am ready to recognise that since my last visit to the B.E.F.

274

much has been done in the way of making an anti-tank ditch and pill-boxes, but still I do not feel that the conception is great enough in relation to what may have to be faced.

"In view of the recency of the decision only a few months ago, to create a Continental Army, with its consequences of conscription and a Ministry of Supply, it must inevitably be some time before its strength can be built up to a European standard.

"Therefore both France and ourselves must rely on the perfection of our defences while we are developing and deploying our superior potential resources.

"These views have been resented as an interference by a civilian Minister in military matters and are, as you tell me, the immediate cause of the pressure to which you feel bound to yield.

"I do not pretend that my departure from the War Office is anything but a wrench. I had wanted to do so much more for the Army.

"The dilemma I am in is that if I explain, as is usual with retiring Ministers, the reason for my departure, I shall be giving to the enemy information about the weakness of our defences and, if I do not, I lay the reason open to conjecture and perhaps to misrepresentation.

"Should I decide to take the latter course, this will be the real measure of the sacrifice which I am called on to make.

"With my good wishes to you and my deep regard for the friendship you have given me.—Yours ever, Leslie Hore-Belisha."

Friday, 5th January 1940

10 a.m. I arrived five minutes before time again. I opened : "In the short time available to me, I have given my best thought to the matter and I think I am entitled to know what is the prejudice of which you spoke and which you feel disinclined to resist."

He replied that it was prejudice in the Command in France, and then, after hesitation, as though he felt he had not said enough, in the War Office too.

I asked him what form the prejudice took ? He hesitated and then said : "They say you are brusque with seniors in front of subordinates : that you don't interest yourself in their problems."

I answered simply : " What else ? "

I tried to ascertain from him who was responsible for all these things being said against me, but he said he would prefer not to say.

Then I said : " Surely the prejudice was as strong a fortnight ago as it is to-day."

" Yes," he answered.

" A fortnight ago," I said, " you were telling me how highly you thought of my work, and you gave me no impression that you had any idea of making a change."

" That is true," he said, " but I have thought the matter over since and I have come to the conclusion that it would be in your best interests to change from the War Office."

I said : " Frankly, Neville, I am completely perplexed. On the one hand, I have had throughout every assurance of your confidence in me, and on the other, you are prepared to accede to prejudice against me. You are delivering me to my enemies. I have no ill-will, but logically I can only reach one conclusion. If you are not prepared to support me against prejudice in the office which I now hold, the same thing might happen to me in the next office. And if I accepted the other office, I should be in a less advantageous position to defend myself."

" That," he answered, " would depend on you." He then pressed me very strongly to reconsider my decision. I said I could not.

" Is it irrevocable ? " he asked. I answered, " Yes, and it only now remains for me to write you a letter of resignation."

I returned to the War Office, drafted the letter of my resignation, and attended the Cabinet meeting at 11.30 a.m.

I showed him my draft letter after the meeting. He read it and said, " This is a very nice letter," and asked if I would mind adding a sentence or two about there being no difference of policy between us. I said : " Certainly."

He then said : " Now I must write to you. But what am I to say ? " It struck me as very funny that having thrown me out of office, he should be asking me what he should say.

He said it was a difficult letter to write. I suggested that the best thing would be to say that he had reconstructed his Government and had offered me another office, which I had not accepted. He said he thought that was what he would say. I observed it had the merit of being true.

He then put his hand on my arm in an affectionate way, saying, " Leslie." I said : " Good-bye, Neville."

I then went to wash my hands and I noticed Chatfield leaving No. 10. Something important occurred to me about the letter I had written and I put my head in the Cabinet room to see if the P.M. was there. I noticed all the other members of the Cabinet were present, except Winston, who was in France, and I gathered that my resignation was being explained to them. I quickly shut the door.

Kingsley Wood dashed after me and said : " It is awful. It is quite a surprise to me. We none of us knew. What strikes me is if this can happen to you it can happen to me."

I replied : " Precisely, Kingsley, that is the right philosophy."

He asked : " Is there nothing that can undo this ? We have always been friends, there has never been a rift between us. I don't like to see you go and it will do harm to the Government."

I answered : " I wish it could have been avoided." I was as anxious, I said, to preserve the Government from any appearance of dissension as he was, but I could not take any other course than the one I had.

I returned to the War Office to write my letter of resignation in my own hand. After about a quarter of an hour Kingsley came over to the War Office and for about an hour pressed me to alter my mind and remain in the Government.

Hore-Belisha's official letter of resignation, dated 5th January, 1940, stated :

" My dear Prime Minister—I wish I had felt able to accept the important office which you have been good enough to offer me in your reconstructed Government, but for the reasons I gave to you verbally this morning, I regretfully cannot see my way to do so.

" I shall, however, naturally give all the support in my power to the firmest conduct of the war until it is brought to a successful issue. I am glad to think that there is no difference of policy between us.

" On the personal side, I recall the kindness you have shown to me in our relationship during the many years we have been together. In my work, particularly at the War Office, I have relied on your understanding co-operation in the inspiring task of reorganising and preparing the Army for war.—Yours very sincerely, Leslie Hore-Belisha."

The Prime Minister's reply bore the same date :

" My dear Leslie—It was with very great regret that I received your decision not to accept the office which I offered you in the course of the reconstruction of the Government which I have in hand. At the same time I fully understand and respect the reasons you gave me.

" I should like now to pay my sincere tribute to your work at the War Office and to the important reforms you have carried out. It is a great satisfaction to me that there is not now and never has been any difference between us on policy and in particular on the necessity for prosecuting the war with the utmost determination to a successful issue.

" I should like also to thank you for the loyal support you have always given me and for those pleasant personal relations which have characterised our association over so many years.—Yours ever, Neville Chamberlain."

For the rest of the day Hore-Belisha was busily engaged at the War Office. No one there had any idea of his impending resignation.

In the late afternoon he attended a Press Conference at which a large number of correspondents representing British and foreign newspapers were present. He showed no sign of strain or tension, but appeared unruffled, smiled and even jested. A very few hours later, when the news was sent to the Press for publication in the next morning's papers, their surprise was all the greater and many commented on his composure throughout the conference.

When he left the War Office at 10 o'clock that night, there were reporters waiting for him outside, for the news had by now been received in Fleet Street. Cheerfully he told them that he had nothing to say.

Star, 8 January 1940

Two years before, almost to the day, Sir Fabian Ware had given him this remarkably prophetic warning : " Nothing will happen at once, but you will find in the months ahead attacks on you from various quarters. There will be whispering in drawing-rooms and words will be dropped in influential ears. They will get you out." And when Hore-Belisha had inquired how long it would take before they got him out, Fabian Ware had replied : " Eighteen months to two years."

Thus, with the coming together of the scattered hostile elements, the remarkable prophecy of Fabian Ware was fulfilled. Some had been opposed to the changes Hore-Belisha had made in the Army, others were angry at having to give way to younger men, while many had been appalled by his energetic intervention in order to get

279

things done, instead of allowing the military members of the Army Council to make the decisions.

The next morning, Saturday the 6th January, the newspapers published the news of his resignation under bold dramatic headlines. "Brass Hats Have Won "—" Generals Get Their Own Way." "Belisha resigns after clash with Generals "—" Generals Resented his Drastic Reforms "—" Pushed out by the Old Gang : " so the

GAD, GENTLEMEN, HERE'S TO OUR GREATEST VICTORY OF THE WAR

Evening Standard, 10 January 1940

headlines ran. Some of them were in letters two inches deep. "The Cabinet has lost its go-getter. Why has he gone ? " asked the Press and the public, seeking for facts, since it was apparent that the facts had been withheld from the official letters exchanged between him and the Prime Minister. It was a shock to the nation—" a bombshell " many called it : in the buses, the trains and in the streets people talked about it. Day after day it was kept up. All over the world the headlines flashed. In the United States it was described as the outcome of a " feud." The Nazis hailed it with delight. While many wondered as to the causes of his going, many hints appeared in the Press indicating that the facts, when revealed, would prove sensational.

There were many callers at the War Office. Letters and telegrams poured in and were delivered in sacks at Hore-Belisha's home by the Post Office van.

Tuesday, 9th January 1940

In the afternoon I went to Buckingham Palace to hand back my seals of office to the King. I looked at the seals in Hardinge's office, then tied them up again, badly.

I entered the presence and handed the red box to H.M. He said at once : " This is a sad moment."

I said : " Not at all, sir. It has been a privilege to serve you and I have tried to do what I could for the Army."

H.M. said : " You have indeed and how quickly you have done it. No man could have done more."

By this time we were sitting by the fire. H.M. said : " You wanted to introduce conscription earlier—before you doubled the Territorial Army ? "

I said that was so.

He spoke of his camp for boys. I said universal service brought all classes together, in the same way as his camp was intended to do. It made the nation far more solid. It also gave every man a sense of order and discipline which was invaluable to the nation. The people had shown a marvellous spirit. Although in the past there had been much unemployment, Bolshevism had never spread. Unemployment should never be tolerated. We ought not to let men waste.

During the half-hour interview H.M. expressed his regret at my departure and his last words were : " I hope very much, and I have no doubt, that I shall be handing you back seals again."

During the course of the interview I asked H.M. about his visit to G.H.Q. France. He pulled himself up and said : " My goodness, I meant to see you immediately on my return. I sent you a message, but was told you could not come, as you had a meeting." He said he had been meaning to see me since, but he had had so many engagements and it had gone out of his head.

I was very surprised at this. I told him that I had received no

281

message from him after his return from France and did not know how it could have happened that I did not receive it.

Who was responsible for the King being side-tracked when he wanted to see Hore-Belisha ? Why was the message not passed on ? His personal staff at the War Office had no knowledge of any such message having been received, and, not being any longer there himself, Hore-Belisha was never able to fit together the pieces of this mosaic. Hore-Belisha knew that the King had asked the Prime Minister to see Ironside on the 14th December and that almost immediately after this Chamberlain paid a personal visit to G.H.Q. in France.

That night Louis Greig rang up and said that Eric Mieville had telephoned and told him that H.M. was very impressed by the way I had taken my departure from the Government and my talk with him.

On the 11th January an Admiralty messenger, arriving on a motor cycle at 1.30 in the morning, brought him a letter from Churchill :

" My dear Leslie—I much regret that our brief association as colleagues has ended. In the last war I went through the same experience as you have suffered, and I know how bitter and painful it is to anyone with his heart in the job.

" I was not consulted in the changes that were proposed. I was only informed after they had been decided. At the same time, I should fail in candour if I did not let you know that I thought it would have been better if you had gone to the Board of Trade or possibly to the Ministry of Information, and I am very sorry that you did not see your way to accept the first of these important offices.

" The outstanding achievement of your tenure of the War Office was the carrying of Conscription in time of peace. You may rest with confidence upon this. I feel sure that this temporary set-back will prove no serious obstacle to your opportunities of serving the country, and I hope that I may yet survive the various perils of office in wartime long enough for us to be colleagues again.—Believe me, Yours very sincerely, Winston S. Churchill."

To this Hore-Belisha replied on the same day:

" My dear Winston—My first instinct after hearing from Neville was to get in touch with you. I rang you up but you had gone. As you know, I subsequently spoke to you in Paris. The fact that you had, unjustly, undergone the same experience was not the only reason why I had a natural recourse to you. I never had any doubt as to the course I should take.

" I know you will do much to win the war and that is the only thing that matters. Thank you for writing—Yours sincerely, Leslie."

Lord Winterton, father of the House of Commons for many years and a close friend of Hore-Belisha's, was among the many people who wrote to him :

" I am staggered by the news of to-day. I shall always remember when we sat together in the Cabinet how you like others of us pressed again and again for financial authority to proceed with essential schemes and how you, like us, consistently met with the same reply. It is astonishing that the real story of the Treasury's attitude is still unknown to Parliament, and to the people. . . . I remain, ever since we became colleagues, your very sincere friend and well-wisher."

Every day the farm was besieged by the Press urging him to speak out. There were many forecasts that he would do so. Pressure was also exerted by other callers, Beaverbrook among them, to induce him to tell the truth in the resignation speech he was to make when Parliament reassembled the following week. Separately Kingsley Wood and John Simon came to see him to ascertain the line he would take. But he gave no clue to them. In his mind his dilemma was sharply defined. Should he tell the nation quite bluntly of the weakness of the B.E.F. defences and the opposition he had encountered while striving to strengthen them ? If he did so, it might well rouse, in the light of the general feeling over his departure, a formidable wave of public opinion, leading to immediate action to strengthen them. On the other hand, the disclosure would reveal to the enemy the weakness of the line.

On the morning before the reassembling of Parliament he retired

THE PRIVATE PAPERS OF HORE-BELISHA

to his study and gave instructions that he was to be left undisturbed and that no telephone calls were to be put through. After about an hour he came down. He seemed at ease. He handed his speech to his secretary, saying, " Here is the speech. There will be no alteration." Then he went for a long walk in the woods. Before dinner he rang Kingsley Wood and asked him to give a message to the Prime Minister. " Tell Neville from me he has nothing to worry about."

Snow fell on the afternoon of the 16th January as he drove along Birdcage Walk to the House. The Chamber was full. Members stood below the gangway. Ambassadors and military attachés occupied the Distinguished Strangers Gallery. Hore-Belisha said :

" I would have preferred at this stage to have left the matter of my departure from the Government upon the published correspondence and upon the message which I gave to my constituents, that I had no thought at the moment but that of winning the war. I am guided, as we must all be guided, by that overriding consideration."

With a brief reference to the reforms during his administration, he went on :

" I have always looked upon it as an ideal that the Army should be a part of the nation, and not apart from the nation ; that it should be a career which every young man could enter with the knowledge that he could rise according to his character and ability, regardless of his status or his means ; and I have hoped that in some way we might thus gradually bind all the members of the nation more closely in mutual understanding. At any rate, I worked for that, and those with whom I was associated worked with me."

Then with the only trace of emotion he showed in his speech, he added :

" It did not occur to me to consider that we were making the Army too democratic to fight for democracy."

He went on :

284

" I hope it has been realised that a Secretary of State cannot divest himself of accountability to Parliament for all matters, both great and small, concerning the Army and this is so whether the question be the provision of defences, their adequacy and speed of construction, or the well-being of the soldier, the conditions of his service and the matter of his equipment.

" One of the traditions—and indeed the regulations—of the Army for which I have always had the greatest respect, and which has seemed to me to furnish the securest safeguard against the abuse of position or rank, is the requirement that any complaint or grievance can be directed to a superior officer, if desired for transmission to the highest authority ; and this is none the less so if the superior officer is the Secretary of State. I mention this because I desire to clear those who have worked with me of an aspersion. I am reluctant to believe that any of the high officers with whom I have been associated would have been so unfaithful to the code, which imbues the whole Army, as to make any representation irregularly, or that, if he had done so, it would have been countenanced."

The Prime Minister concluded his speech on this personal note :

" I would only like to say that I deeply appreciate the note and spirit of what was said by my Right Hon. Friend. He has put before all personal considerations the one object which should be the object of every one of us, the service of the country for the purpose of winning the war. I know that he is anxious to make his contribution towards that object and I trust that it may not be long before he finds the opportunity of doing so."

The diary records :

After it was over Kingsley Wood said he was awfully glad I spoke in the way I did. He left me saying he wanted another talk with me. During the preceding week he and Simon had come down to the farm, really to ascertain what line I was taking, as they were worried about my speech.

Winston said to me that I had delivered my speech " with masterly dignity, it was absolutely right ; it would have been wrong to make an attacking speech during the war." I told him

I had been reading his own account of what he felt like when he was dismissed from the Admiralty in the last war.

In the Lobby the P.M. came up to me and took me by the arm. "Leslie," he said, "I think you made a remarkable speech. I know how hard it must have been. I want to thank you. You heard my concluding passage and you know I meant it—and even more."

I ran into Ironside on his way to a Co-ordinating Committee. He said he had not heard my speech but would read it. I told him he would find he had nothing to be uneasy about.

L.G. asked me to go to his room in the House and have a chat. He said he thought I was well out of the Government, that it could not last.

That evening he dined with Charles Haydon, his former military assistant, and his wife Chicha. They were joined by de Guingand, and one or two of his closest friends who had worked with him at the War Office.

CHAPTER XXVII

Epilogue

I

During the week-end after Hore-Belisha's resignation, *Truth*, a weekly journal, sent a copy of its issue of the 12th January to every Member of the Lords and Commons, addressing them to the Houses of Parliament. Members were seen to have a copy of *Truth* with them in the Chamber when Hore-Belisha made his speech. This issue contained an article attacking Hore-Belisha and certain companies, of which he was either chairman or a director for a short period nearly ten years before. Finding that the work entailed, particularly of the companies of which he was chairman, absorbed too much time, he resigned from three of them in February and March 1929. On taking office in the National Government in 1931, he automatically resigned from the remaining four.

It was only after making his resignation speech that Hore-Belisha read the article and he at once took advice of eminent counsel, including Sir John Simon and Sir William Jowitt. The advice he was given throughout this time was that it would not be in the national interest for him to take an action against *Truth*, with all the publicity it would involve.

The articles—a second appeared in the following issue of 19th January—were blatantly anti-Semitic and would give comfort, they said, to Hitler. If he were to take action, it would undoubtedly be asked in the courts why the journal had waited for ten years to launch such an attack on him and had chosen the momentous week-end before his resignation speech, when his prestige was so high, for its attempt to discredit him. Questions would be asked why he resigned—which was precisely what he had refrained from disclosing

287

THE PRIVATE PAPERS OF HORE-BELISHA

in his resignation speech. What better answer to *Truth* could there be than that the Prime Minister had offered him the important office of the Board of Trade ? His reputation could rest on that. " I confess," Hore-Belisha said later, "that in the light of subsequent events, had I been guided alone by my own personal feeling, I would have taken action."

On 29th October 1954 *Truth* published the following :

" *Truth* is glad to publish the opinions[1] of so distinguished a man upon this subject. But this paper is happy for a more particular reason that Lord Hore-Belisha has felt able to accept our invitation to write this review. In January 1940, as Secretary of State for War, he resigned from the Government for reasons connected with his views about the defences in France, which he could not, in the national interest, openly discuss at the time. It was then that *Truth* published two articles containing unfair and baseless attacks upon him, motivated by racial prejudice. The present owner and the present editor wish to take this opportunity of repudiating a policy which could permit such examples of racial discrimination to disfigure its pages. It is impossible to apologise for the actions of a previous editor. But we hope that a rejection of his policies at this time may make it clear that as far as may be possible that part of *Truth's* past is now buried and forgotten."

2

Hore-Belisha's speeches in the House during the war were often critical. The first of these, delivered within a few weeks of his resignation, while Neville Chamberlain was still Prime Minister, he prefaced with the words : " There is a distinction to be drawn between the desire to criticise and the intention to analyse what has occurred. The first is a barren pursuit, the latter a helpful process."[2] Nevertheless into these analyses there crept such phrases as " Hesitation is permissible in the formulation of policies, but not, surely, in their execution."

On the 22nd May 1940, soon after Winston Churchill became Prime Minister, Hore-Belisha, indicating that Hitler never undertook

[1] A review of Lord Templewood's *Nine Troubled Years*.　　[2] 19th March 1940.

an operation unless he had adequately and completely prepared for it, stated :

" If we have made errors in the past, they have been errors of inadequate preparation. We have waited until a calamity came upon us before realising its full magnitude. When Norway was invaded we completely underestimated the situation. We sent a small number of troops to meet a large number of troops. Hitler despatched to that country a far greater army than was necessary to achieve his purpose. He sent 100,000 men or more. But our conception was that we could discharge the task, if we could discharge it at all, with about 4,000 men. That was an under-estimate. Then we heard that Hitler was landing troops by parachute, and everywhere we read, ' This new device, this stunt, is a complete failure.' But it was not a failure, and a small detach-ment at Narvik is still holding out against superior British forces, and presumably being nourished to some extent by parachute."

When on the 20th August 1940, Churchill declared " Almost a year has passed since the war began, and it is natural for us, I think, to pause on our journey at this milestone and survey the dark, wide field," Hore-Belisha was most laudatory.

" In all the great succession of speeches which my Right Hon. Friend the Prime Minister has made, I feel that he has made none greater than that which he delivered this afternoon. He expressed our cause and our purpose in fitting language, and we may be proud to have a leader of that stamp at this time. It is, however, not only for my Right Hon. Friend's speech that we need be grateful this afternoon. We can depart for this brief Recess enheartened by the knowledge that in one important respect the fortunes of war have been decisively turned in our favour. No more formidable challenge has been offered to us, in this or any other war, than that which we are now meeting. By repelling, so frequently and so intrepidly, superior numbers, our fighter pilots have indeed placed us in their gratitude. They have definitely checked the unbroken sequence of Hitlerian victories, and have disproved the legend of Hitler's invincibility."

The Battle of Britain continued for a further four weeks, but the reference to victory was by no means premature. Hore-Belisha, however, was not content merely to pay a tribute. He went on to stress, as he had done so often as Secretary of State for War, the urgent need for a much wider harnessing of the country's resources.

" The creation of an army depends upon supply. We cannot hope to defeat the authoritarian powers, who are waging total war and who have the whole of their populations mobilised, unless we rapidly mobilise ourselves. They have great armies, they have great air forces, and they have expanding fleets. In addition, they have kept their industrial organisation concentrated on the war effort. We are not doing that. There is no time to lose. You cannot win a war with 800,000 unemployed. The winning of a war is a conscious process. You must reduce the manufacture of goods which are not necessary, and turn over your production to the war effort. It is no use relying on appeals. You have to do that as a deliberate act. People speak as if you could maintain an export trade in an unlimited manner. Surely, your export trade must be kept at as low a level as is compatible—in addition to your other resources—with paying for the goods you must import. The whole of your industrial machine must be concentrated primarily on the war effort."

Again and again he reiterated this. On the 6th May 1941, following upon a series of reverses in Greece and North Africa, Hore-Belisha said :

" The Army must have more mobility and more armour. If there are 10 Bren-gun carriers in a battalion there should be 30. Speed and protection are being shown to be everything. We should henceforward devote as much attention to the production of tanks as we have to aeroplanes. The necessary priorities should be given. The Germans conquered Cyrenaica without air superiority. They conquered with tanks. At least the armoured divisions of our Army, and preferably all divisions, should have air support as an integral part of their establishment. The Army must have dive-bombers and specialised ground straffing machines

such as the Germans have. The Army must have its own transport
planes to carry troops, guns, light tanks, food, water and oil over
long distances, just as the Germans have. The Germans in Libya
have flying workshops and flying garages."

In this one hears the echo of what he had been clamouring for
while at the War Office and of the battles he waged to secure air support for the Army. Churchill, however, always quickly roused by any
note of criticism, hit back vigorously on the following day in the
House. After rebuking Hore-Belisha for his " temerity yesterday
to raise the subject of our admitted shortage of tanks," he added :
" My Right Hon. Friend played a worthy part in bringing in compulsory service. I should not have referred to this matter if he had
not endeavoured to give the House a sort of idea of his super-
prevision and super-efficiency and shown himself so aggressive
when, I think, with all good will, he sometimes stands in need of
some humility in regard to the past."
Hore-Belisha rose instantly and said :

" I think that what the Right Hon. Gentleman is doing in
indulging in petty recriminations is quite unworthy of the great
purpose that we have in common. I made no reproach whatever
against the Government for any lack of tanks. I suggested,
and I think the House concurred with me, that the same priority
that has been given to aircraft should now be given to tanks,
because the Germans achieved their victory in Libya without air
superiority. If I am responsible for the present tank position, I
will willingly accept, although I could never claim some part in
the credit of the advances of General Wavell. I have never
claimed that at all. The point is that my Right Hon. Friend has
been in office for 20 months. I have been out of office for 16
months. During that period he has enjoyed unprecedented
powers. With the abrogation of trade union regulations, with the
full support of every party, which I never enjoyed, and indeed
some of those supporting him now were opposing me, in my
own proposals, and to reproach one who has been out of office
16 months is irrelevant."

Churchill replied : " My Right Hon. Friend must restrain himself.

Let me tell my Right Hon. Friend that we are now making every month as many heavy tanks as there existed in the whole British Army at the time he left the War Office—and we should very soon, before the end of this year, be producing nearly double that number. . . . I only say this to him by way of reassuring him that the good work which he did, the foundations which he laid, have not been left to stand where they were when he went out of office. He must learn to ' forgive us our trespasses as we forgive them that trespass against us.' "

On the 10th June, following the loss of Crete, Hore-Belisha returned to his analysis of the course of the war with a further series of searching questions :

" It would be helpful for the future if we were to ask ourselves whether at Dakar, in Cyrenaica, in Greece, and now in Crete the forfeits which we have incurred have not been at least in part due to an imperfect assessment of possibilities, and indeed of probabilities, and consequently to ineffective preparation. Except in the case of Greece, these are all areas in which the initial advantage and the opportunity of exploiting them have been with us. In Greece there was a period of six months to prepare before the arrival of the Germans. . . .

" Summarising the position then, before the invasion of Crete was launched, it must have been obvious to the responsible authorities, firstly, that the Army had been driven out of Greece because of a lack of aeroplanes or because operational use of aerodromes could not be made ; secondly, that experience had shown that the Army, despite its valour, could not hold its ground without such support ; and thirdly, that the preliminaries to an airborne attack on Crete were in train. Every one of these lessons was discarded. No adequate measures for defending aerodromes were instituted in an island of which we had been in occupation for seven months. . . .

" Aircraft must be recognised to be as integral a part of a Navy or Army as any other weapon. We have gone part of the way in the Navy by establishing the Fleet Air Arm, which has amply justified itself. Why should not the process be carried as far as this in the Army and to its logical conclusion in the Navy ?

Should we not give to the commander in the field or a commander conducting operations at sea, control over the land-based aircraft which are shown once again by the events to be essential to his task ? "

All these arguments had been used by him when he was Secretary of State for War. He did not achieve his purpose because there was not a ready recognition of the need for such an adjustment. Churchill, nevertheless, was stung to return to his earlier mood of anger. He said :

" The Right Hon. Member for Devonport has made to-day a very cogent and moderate, well-informed and thoughtful contribution to the Debate, but he used a different mood and tone in a speech which he recently delivered in the country,[1] and that at any rate makes it necessary for me to say that the state in which our Army was left when the Right Hon. Gentleman had ended his two years and seven months' tenure of the War Office, during the greater part of which he was responsible for production and supply, was lamentable. We were short of every essential supply, but most particularly of those modern weapons, the anti-aircraft gun, the anti-tank gun and the tank itself, which have proved themselves the vital necessities of modern war, a fact which he is now prepared to suggest we are so purblind and outdated as not to be able to comprehend."

Hore-Belisha instantly retorted that Churchill's remark was

" quite out of accord with what he himself said after the retreat from Dunkirk, that we had lost the finest lot of equipment that had ever left these shores, and that the Army had been fully equipped in almost every particular. The French Ambassador stated that we had fully discharged our obligations to the French. Perhaps my Right Hon. Friend will be good enough to recall that up till very recently before the war the whole House and indeed the country were opposed to the creation of a Continental Army, which nevertheless I proceeded to try and create. I do not seek to be judged by my achievements, but by what I tried to do, and

[1] At Edinburgh on the 6th June 1941.

THE PRIVATE PAPERS OF HORE-BELISHA

my Right Hon. Friend will realise that my obstacles were greater

my Right Hon. Friend will realise that my obstacles were greater than his to-day."

Churchill replied :

" I thought I had misquoted my Right Hon. Friend in some way, but it appears he wished to continue the argument. I am dealing not with the particular equipment of the troops who went to France, who naturally drained the rest of our Forces, but the fact remains that the equipment of our Army at that time, and at the outbreak of war, was of the most meagre and deficient character, and that the deficiencies made themselves most marked—and still make themselves most marked—in the very type of weapons for which there is the greatest possible demand. . . . I am not throwing all the blame for this upon my Right Hon. Friend at all—certainly not—but I think it is only fair, when he himself comes forward and sets himself up as an arbiter and judge, and speaks so scornfully of the efforts of some others who have inherited his dismal legacy, I think when he speaks in this way—he has a great responsibility in the matter—it is only fair to point out to him that he is one of the last people in this country entitled to take that line."

At the end of the debate, when Hore-Belisha left the Chamber, he heard heavy padding footsteps behind him which he recognised as the footsteps of the Prime Minister. Presently he heard the Prime Minister's voice call him by name " Leslie." He stopped and Churchill caught up with him. " Come in here," Churchill said, gesturing towards the Smoking Room.

They walked together to it in silence. As they entered Churchill pointed to one of the benches and said sharply, rather like a head-master, " Sit down." Hore-Belisha sat, but Churchill remained standing ; then, wagging a warning finger at him, Churchill said : " If you fight me I shall fight you back. And remember this : You are using a 4.5-inch howitzer, and I am using a 12-inch gun." Having said this, Churchill turned and walked out of the room.[1] It is interesting to observe that the gun he assigned to Hore-Belisha was one of the lighter Army field pieces, whereas he retained for

[1] As stated by Hore-Belisha to the author later on that same day, the 10th June 1941.

his own use, as was only natural for a former First Lord of the Admiralty, the heaviest gun mounted on the original dreadnoughts.

Hore-Belisha was in no way deterred by the warning. He continued to watch events with a vigilant eye. A fortnight later, on the 24th June, following the German attack on Russia, he said in the House:

" This is not the occasion to dwell upon our defects, but they are numerous and conspicuous, if we are to profit by the lapse of time which must occur before the Germans can achieve a success in Russia, even if they can achieve it in the end."

The debates during the succeeding years are strewn with criticisms, like " the usual self-confident statements, indicative of our under-estimation of the skill and resources of the enemy, statements which have proved to be the invariable preludes to disaster."[1] On the question of production, Churchill, who had himself been so critical in the late thirties, confessed more than once in the House that delays had to be faced, accepted and eventually overcome. " It takes three or four years," he said,[2] " to put the industries of a country on to a war basis."

When the tide eventually began to show signs of turning in our favour, Hore-Belisha fixed his gaze upon the post-war world. In a debate on Foreign Affairs on the 15th December 1943, he condemned any fragmentation of Europe. " The true vision of Europe is one of unity." Germany could be kept down for a time in a military sense by punitive measures, by encirclement, but none of these means would be necessary if the productive resources of Germany could be knit together with those of her neighbours in such a way that she would lose control of the very instruments with which she makes war. France, bound to us by comradeship in the Great War of 1914 and, he thought, in the present one, was united inescapably with Britain by the facts of geography and would play her part in resurrecting Europe. The one international organisation that has survived two wars is the British Empire. It is the strongest force in the world. " We have to show by the living example of the British

---

[1] House of Commons Debates 29th January, 1942, following Pearl Harbour and the entry of the United States of America into the war.
[2] House of Commons, 19th December 1940.

295

Empire that it is possible for many races and many religions on that Continent to combine for one great purpose."

Hore-Belisha, now in his fifty-first year and regarded by his friends as a confirmed bachelor because of his undimmed devotion to his mother, surprised them by announcing his intention to marry. Before the war he had met Miss Cynthia Elliot, the daughter of Mr. Gilbert Compton Elliot, a kinsman of the Earl of Minto. She was tall, dark, attractive and vivacious. In May 1940, together with two friends, she had formed the first British Women's Mobile Canteen unit, which was attached to the French Army. The following month, while they were in a wood near Nancy, the Germans broke through and they were taken prisoner. Cynthia, in captivity for three and a half years, served as nurse and ward sister in British prisoner-of-war camps. She was repatriated with other British women in November 1943 and was awarded the B.E.M. in March 1944 " for devotion to duty and untiring services in a prisoner-of-war hospital in Germany." Hore-Belisha met her again shortly after her return and they were married in June, 1944.

3

As the war was ending de Guingand, a Major-General by now and Chief of Staff to Field-Marshal Montgomery, whose forces were advancing into Germany, thought of the Secretary of State he had served at the outbreak of war.

27th March 1945

While we were dining, Freddie de Guingand came through on the telephone from main H.Q. in Belgium. His voice was clear as though we were in the same room. Our forces had just crossed the Rhine. He said : " I don't think it will last much longer now. You were in at the beginning, I would like you to see the end."

He added that he would send his aeroplane for me to Northolt on Friday.

Friday, 30th March 1945

Freddie's A.D.C., Major Culver, U.S. Army, rang me up from Northolt. I motored there and left in de Guingand's private

Dakota, which had just brought General Fortune back home from captivity.

Arrived Moelbroeke aerodrome, near Brussels, 4.30 p.m., said to be the biggest aerodrome in Europe, built by the Germans. Motored to de Guingand's house in the Boulevard Nationale. It had been occupied previously by a German General. The concierge and his wife had been there the whole time and the linen, silver, etc., was in good condition. Tea and very good pastry with de Guingand.

Then we went to main H.Q. where he explained the position of our forces to me on maps. I met several of the Staff Officers.

We then went to a farewell cocktail party given by General Galloway. Dinner in de Guingand's house. Other Generals there.

31st March 1945

Attended conference of Generals and Staff Officers at main H.Q. This was formerly the German H.Q., occupied by von Falkenhausen. He had left relics here including a picture of Frederick the Great, a Belgian sword, and some maps.

Left Brussels by de Guingand's aeroplane at 10.20 a.m. with his A.D.C. Arrived Venlo on Dutch-German border 10.55 a.m. A.D.C. went off to the new main H.Q. into which de Guingand is moving on Tuesday. I motored with a Liaison Officer into Germany, through Rheinberg and across the Rhine at Wesel by way of the pontoon Bailey bridge, which now carries our line of communication. Wesel has been completely destroyed, not a house, not a building is intact.

I motored into the area where the 6th British Airborne and the 17th (U.S.) Airborne Divisions had landed, and lunched on sandwiches amid the crashed gliders. Tried to motor down through the Ruhr on the way back to the west bank of the Rhine, but the bridges were all broken, so we crossed back at Wesel and went to Krefeld, also completely destroyed, although here people were walking about the streets. The Germans seemed well fed and well dressed.

In the evening on my return I was shown at my request some of the welfare arrangements. The Montgomery Club is in a Royal Palace of very great size. When I put my head in the huge dining-room, I was immediately offered a glass of beer, brought by a good-looking waitress, who told me that it had been sent by a soldier at one of the tables, so I went over and sat down with him and his companions.

In another room the atmosphere of an English country public house was reproduced and everyone was drinking beer. I had a riotous reception here. Other rooms were confined respectively to reading and good music on gramophone records. One of the soldiers took me aside and said : " Your dreams have come true." It is indeed strange to recall how hotly welfare was opposed when I instituted it : it was said it was the duty of a C.O. to look after his men. No C.O. could do this, however. They have night clubs, which I also visited, where Belgian girls danced with our soldiers. The leave men are put up in the best hotels, with sheets and breakfast in bed brought in by chambermaids, and they have baths and haircutting facilities, and all sorts of other amenities. It is really wonderful.

1st April 1945

Saw some more of the welfare. Then to main H.Q. Said good-bye to de Guingand and left by air for Paris, arriving at Le Bourget. Duff Cooper's[1] car met me. Motored to the Embassy and lunched with Duff and Diana. She showed me round. Nothing changed in the Embassy—only the angle of the bed in Pauline Borghesi's room, in which I used to sleep.

4

Churchill, in his *History of the Second World War*,[2] recalling the letter he had sent to Hore-Belisha at the time of his resignation, when he expressed the hope " that this temporary set-back will prove no serious obstacle to your opportunities of serving the country," records : " It was not possible for me to realise my hope until, after the break-up of the National Coalition, I formed the so-called ' Caretaker Government ' in May 1945. Belisha then became Minister of National Insurance. In the interval he had been one of our severe critics ; but I was very glad to be able to bring so able a man back into the Administration." It is not quite clear why

[1] British Ambassador, Paris.　[2] Vol. i.

Churchill found it "not possible" to bring "so able a man back into the Administration" before, since Churchill was Prime Minister for almost the whole of the intervening period and one wonders if the fact that Hore-Belisha " had been one of our severe critics " had any influence on Churchill. Earlier, when they were in the War Cabinet together, there were recurrent clashes between the two, Churchill generally taking the opposite point of view to Hore-Belisha's, giving thus early an indication of his desire to have a hand in the management of all defence matters and to subordinate the War Office to an overall defence control, which, on becoming Prime Minister, he did.

At midday on the 23rd May 1945, Churchill handed his resignation to the King as head of the War Coalition Government he had formed five years before and was immediately asked to form a new Ministry. On the following day, as the diary records :

24th May 1945

At 6.50 p.m. a telephone call came through from Colville, asking me to go and see the Prime Minister.

Went to Storey's Gate entrance. The P.M. asked me to come in at once. He was lying in bed, wearing a blue flowered silk dressing-gown with a golden collar and smoking a big cigar. He had a breakfast tray in front of him and a sponge at either side on which to lean his elbows. He apologised for being in bed, but said he worked better there.

He then said he was engaged in the task of Cabinet making and invited me to be Minister of National Insurance. He said he attached great importance to this office, particularly from an electoral point of view. The scheme wanted humanising and purging of its present traces of Socialism. He felt that it was a matter of great urgency that I should go into the scheme forthwith and see him in a fortnight with proposals for its reform, which he might include in his Election programme. He said there was a great field here which wanted popularising, and that is why he had asked me to do the job.

He said that nothing was to be said on any account until Saturday, when he hoped to have all the offices filled, except perhaps two. He wanted me to go into the office on Saturday and take over from Jowitt,[1] or as soon as I can take the oath. Our talk lasted three-quarters of an hour.

Saturday, 26th May 1945

In the morning went to the Ministry of National Insurance and took over from Jowitt.

28th May onwards

During these days I have been installing myself in the Ministry office at 6 Carlton House Terrace with its opulent rococo interior, in which Pierpont Morgan lived. The furniture, strangely enough, is that which I had for my room at the Ministry of Transport.

I got my legislative programme agreed.

On Monday, 11th June, Hore-Belisha, on the Report stage of the Family Allowances Bill, introduced two new clauses as amendments. He said the Bill provided for an allowance to any family with two or more children without exception. Every family would benefit, whether the breadwinner was at work or not. He added :

" The Government take the view that the Forces are as much entitled to benefits as any other wage-earners. They are indeed wage-earners engaged in the most honourable, and at this moment indispensable, of all professions. It is on that footing therefore that they will receive this allowance in addition to any allowances which are paid to them by the respective departments."

He paid a generous tribute to the work done by his predecessor and also to the pioneer work of Miss Eleanor Rathbone, who began to campaign for family allowances as far back as 1912.

The Bill passed through all its remaining stages in the House of Commons that night and received the Royal assent four days later.

On the 13th June, two days before the dissolution of Parliament, Hore-Belisha presented the National Insurance (Industrial Injuries) Bill, which had been prepared by Jowitt. The new Bill embodied the scheme of workman's compensation laid down in the White

---

[1] Sir William Jowitt was the first Minister of National Insurance. Later Lord Chancellor and Earl Jowitt.

Paper of the previous September, but added substantially to the benefits proposed at that time.

Parliament was dissolved on the 15th June. The results of the Election, save for thirteen University seats, were declared on the 25th July. Labour won a resounding victory. The Conservatives lost 150 seats. The Liberals elected to the new House were reduced to only eleven. Among those defeated were Hore-Belisha, Duncan Sandys and Brendan Bracken. The Caretaker Government went out of office after barely nine weeks. Hore-Belisha lost his seat by 2,000 votes and was out of Parliament after a continuous representation of Devonport for twenty-two years.

5

It was not unnatural for Hore-Belisha, who was only forty-six years old when he left the War Office, to feel that he was still young enough to be able to render some further service to the country.

Obviously his first course now was to try to get back into Parliament. He joined the Conservative Party the day after Lord Woolton joined it, in 1945, after its defeat. Safe Conservative seats were found for Duncan Sandys at Streatham and for Brendan Bracken at Bournemouth, but Hore-Belisha was not given a like opportunity. This many deplored, feeling that his brilliance and skill as a debater would have been of considerable advantage to the Conservatives in harrying the Labour Government during its years of office.

It has often been asked why nothing worth while was offered him. The answers this elicits are varied. That there was, especially among people of influence, a vague but widespread hostility towards him, not always overt, is undeniable. One cannot be a reformer and put through an extensive programme of reforms without upsetting some people ; and if you upset people they dislike you. As against this his popularity among the general public was immense, but this was discounted by the others, who felt that it had been carefully cultivated by his consistent pursuit of personal publicity. Both his features, so beloved by caricaturists, and his unusual name proved to be assets. It was found quite often that the antipathy, where it existed, was in the main, though by no means always, most prevalent among those who had not come to know him. It had been built up or encouraged by gossip, not always founded on fact. For example, there was the ridiculous story that, when inspecting a Guards brigade, he had offered a cigarette to the Sergeant Major, on parade. Many wanted to believe this story, unlikely as it was : it served to belittle the man they happened not to like.

Brigadier-General Wallace Wright, V.C., and M.P. for the Tavistock division of Devonshire from 1928 to 1931, who was a member of His Majesty's Body Guard of the Honourable Corps of Gentlemen at Arms, had met Hore-Belisha and apparently liked him. He suggested to his fellow Gentlemen at Arms that they might invite him to dine with them one evening. Many demurred. They had heard things about him that were not very flattering. The General none the less persuaded them to send the invitation. At the end of the evening, they appeared to be won over completely, for they informed Wright that they had " no idea at all that he was such a charming and intelligent man."[1]

Mentally he was dynamic. At times peremptory, as Chamberlain had accused him of being to Chatfield, he was also often inconsiderate. In office he was always impatient, especially when things had to be done with urgency and did not appear to him to be accomplished fast enough. Routine and red tape maddened him and he was often sharp if short cuts were not taken to produce results. Yet invariably he was solicitous of subordinates, of clerks and typists, of servants, his own as well as those in the houses he visited. While out for a country walk, often not in his own constituency, he would stop to talk to miners or farm workers or fisherfolk, asking about their work, discussing their problems and their way of life. By temperament he was consistently cheerful, one very rarely saw him depressed. He took a rosy view of life and was inclined occasionally to be over-optimistic.

He was accused of being thoughtless. It was wrong, it was said, that one so relatively young should receive elderly generals while still in his pyjamas. This, according to his two Military Assistants, Haydon and de Guingand, was greatly exaggerated. He might have been shaving or in his bath when they arrived, and they had to wait,

[1] As told by Wallace Wright to Alexander Elliot, Hore-Belisha's brother-in-law.

but he was always dressed when he came down. Following the manœuvres of the French Army in Normandy soon after he became Secretary of State for War, the world was informed in bold headlines that Hore-Belisha had received Gamelin, the French Commander-in-Chief designate, while still in his pyjamas. Hore-Belisha laughed when he read this. " If only they knew the exact facts," he said.[1] " I actually received him without any clothes on at all. I was in my bath when Gamelin dropped in unexpectedly. He called from the outer room and asked if he could come in. I told him I was not dressed. He said he did not mind at all. He came in and sat by the tub and discussed the speech he was to make that night after dinner."

It is surprising that neither in his diary, nor in his talks with his most intimate friends, could one discern any note of bitterness against Chamberlain or Gort, Ironside or Churchill. Whatever he felt or suffered, he kept pent up within him.

6

Was it to free himself of some inner conflict that he turned to the monasteries ? Having to leave the War Office was a severe blow, and not long after it came the shock of Dunkirk, more acute to him than to most as in anguish he witnessed the tragic fate of the Army he had so painstakingly built up. He sought the peace and detachment that monastic seclusion offered. He was a near neighbour at Wimbledon of the Apostolic Delegate to Great Britain, Archbishop Godfrey, the Cardinal Archbishop of Westminster, and they used at times to walk together on the Common. A friendship grew between them. Hore-Belisha asked Archbishop Godfrey if he could suggest some place of seclusion. In September 1942, during the Parliamentary recess, he spent ten days at the Cistercian Abbey at Mount Saint Bernard in Charnwood Forest.

11th September 1942
I feel as though I were on Mount Ararat, safe from all the turmoil of the world.

When asked on his return to London why he had so withdrawn

---

[1] In a statement to the author.

himself, he answered: "It isn't an experience you want to advertise." But he allowed himself to say that "a politician, mixed up as he is all the time in affairs, ought to have an occasional period of retirement and reflection on the ultimate reasons behind existence. There is much to be said for the provision of such periods of quiet reflection for all those who burn up their brain cells." And he added, laughingly, that such an experience would do journalists no harm either.

From that time for the rest of his life he went at intervals— once for a period of nine weeks—to Mount Saint Bernard, and later to St. Michael's Abbey, Farnborough, where the Father Prior was the convert son of the late Heath Robinson, the famous cartoonist. He conformed to the simple life, spent his time reflecting and reading —the Old and New Testaments, theological and philosophical books, poetry—Gerard Manley Hopkins was a favourite. The Gregorian plain chant of the Liturgy appealed to him and he worked with the white-habited monks on the farm, helping to cut and shock corn. He watched them weave cloth, bake bread, bind manuscripts, work at sculpture and wood carving.

18th November 1946

There is in the world outside a misapprehension about monks. It is thought they are peculiar and unsociable men, who from their earliest years, having abstracted themselves from all contact with their fellows and lived only inwardly and mentally, are ignorant of all the ways and avocations of the world. Not at all. I have found here a greater diversity of experience in practical affairs. There are so many aptitudes, there is no monotony. I came here in all humility, scarcely knowing what to expect, and they received me with so much understanding.

The members of the community are drawn from greatly contrasted environments. All live together in goodwill, fellow-feeling and mutual service. Here is the true democracy. Has the world nothing to learn from the monastery?

The world has gone wrong by losing contact with nature. The world does not know where the food it eats comes from. Here they are not afraid to soil their hands in helping to raise it. Here is the secret of the balanced life.

If ever I were to become Minister of Education, I would consider applying the rule of Saint Benedict, who so consummately proportions the labour of the body to the labour of the mind, both kinds of labour deriving grace and illumination because they are a devotion to God. Instead of spending so much time on what is called exercise and is mostly concerned with chasing a ball, the same purpose might be served, less artificially and more sanely, if some part of the day were allotted to agriculture.

It was in a dark period of history that the need for monasteries was first felt. They kept alive the flickering flame of civilisation. Men, seeing their spires, directed their steps towards the monasteries. Poor men came for material help, the sick for care and cure, the mentally hungry for education. They developed music and cherished the arts. To-day the towers of their Abbeys have been overtopped by factory chimneys. The silhouette of their buildings has been blackened out by the smoke of industry and the blindness of men's eyes. But they still render service to the world by prayer and by example. They show men how they might live, if they appreciated the essentials of truth and happiness. Theirs is the good life.

It was not only by detachment and reflection that Hore-Belisha strove to equip himself for such further service as he might be called upon to render. He set out on a series of journeys, visiting many countries, studying political trends and technical developments, meeting people—politicians, scientists and others.

In September 1945, he went with his wife on a nine-months' tour of the American continent. At Ottawa he stayed with Malcolm MacDonald, the High Commissioner, his colleague in the Cabinet for many years. In New York he declined invitations to lecture and broadcast, saying " I want to draw in, not put out." In Washington, together with our Ambassador Lord Halifax, he went to the White House for a talk with President Truman.

During the four following months they visited by air all the countries of Central and South America, except Paraguay and Bolivia.

Arriving in the middle of February at Miami, he was present at a large luncheon at the Orange Bowl Stadium, when Winston

Churchill, for whom his admiration never wavered, was given the degree, *honoris causa*, of Doctor of Laws by Miami University.

26th February 1946

There were a number of brief speeches by representative men and a short very gracious one by Mrs. Churchill. Then the University Principal called on me. I said that Churchill was woven into the texture of our national life, as inseparably as Washington and Lincoln were woven into theirs. They had spoken of his past services, but there was a service for him still to render. . . . What was the great conception that he could and, I feel, did set before him? It was the reunion of the English-speaking people, the consolidation of Britain and the United States. This was an ideal, partly achieved as a by-product of the war, that Winston Churchill was fitted by blood and purpose to achieve. . . . Help him to achieve this, without which there could be no assurance of peace in the world.

Returning to Washington, he lunched on the 8th April with General Eisenhower at the Pentagon. In New York he called on Cardinal Spellman and had a long talk with John L. Lewis, leader of the American Federation of Labour.

Later in the year he flew to Germany, at the invitation of Marshal of the Royal Air Force, Sir Sholto Douglas,[1] Civil and Military Governor, British Zone of Germany, and from Berlin he went to the Nürnberg trials.

Further journeys took him to Spanish and French Morocco, and Central and South Africa, India, Pakistan, Ceylon, Burma, Singapore and Malaya, Hong Kong and Japan, Israel (three times) Cyprus, Turkey, Jordan, Lebanon, Persia (where he had a long interview with the Shah and later visited the oil fields), Abadan and Aden.

He stood for the Westminster City Council in March 1947 and was elected unopposed. At the General Election of 1950 he fought Coventry South, but was unsuccessful in his endeavour to return to Parliament. Four years later, in the New Year's Honours List of 1954, he was made a peer and took the title of Baron Hore-Belisha of Devonport.

[1] Later Lord Douglas of Kirtleside.

In his maiden speech in the Lords, on the 16th March, he suggested the need to free ourselves from dependence on the single artery, the Suez Canal, the most widely used international waterway in the world :

"Of the oil consumed in Western Europe, including this country," he said, " 95 per cent, if not more, comes from the Middle East, 75 per cent of it through the Suez Canal . . . the oil to sustain a future campaign. . . . Why not construct a pipe-line at moderate cost, in relation to our obligations, from the Gulf of Akaba to the Mediterranean ? In time this could lead to the construction of an alternative canal. . . . Military dispositions consist not only in placing men, but in placing material."

This suggestion was made more than two years before Nasser seized the Suez Canal.

Lord Swinton, Secretary of State for Commonwealth Relations, reminded their Lordships that, " remarkable " as Lord Hore-Belisha's maiden speech had been, it came from " a very experienced virgin." The *Manchester Guardian*[1] said : " Lord Hore-Belisha's contribution to the Debate shows what Parliament has lost during his nine years' absence."

In November 1955, he became Chairman of the House of Lords Foreign Affairs Committee.

7

While in Japan in 1956 Hore-Belisha had a slight heart attack. Little importance was attached to this at the time. He went on with his strenuous tour, which took him through India, Pakistan, to Cyprus and to Israel. On his return a careful course of treatment was adopted and he was said to have recovered.

On 13th February 1957, soon after returning from still another long and exhausting tour in Persia and the Near East, he set out for France as leader of a Parliamentary delegation, consisting of two Peers and eight M.P.s Conferences had been arranged on French, British and European unity and on Anglo-French commercial relations.

[1] 17th March 1954.

After a short stay in Paris they left early on the morning of Saturday the 16th for Rheims, where they were conducted by Prince Caraman-Chimay on a tour of the vaults of the Cliquot-Ponsardin. It took nearly two hours. Emerging up a long and very steep flight of steps, most of the party were exhausted. A visit was paid to Rheims Cathedral before going on to the Town Hall for the official lunch, at which Hore-Belisha had to speak. The Union Jack hung on the balcony. *God Save the Queen* and the *Marseillaise* were played.

The President of the French National Assembly, Monsieur le Trocquer, greeted the delegation, and more than two hundred distinguished guests from the town and department of the Marne sat down to lunch. Monsieur Pierre Schneiter, Deputy Mayor of Rheims and former President of the National Assembly, made a speech of welcome and was followed by Hore-Belisha, who speaking in French, expressed the pleasure it was to him to be once again in France and particularly in Rheims.

" The first speech I ever had to make in French was in Paris in July 1939, when as Secretary of State for War it fell to my lot to announce measures which ensured our definite military solidarity with France. This defensive partnership is now taken for granted and is in fact the nucleus of a wider system. To-day British Ministers are in Paris to join in another movement of solidarity between the two countries. . . ."

As he talked, he was seen to stretch out his arms towards the microphone in front of him. Suddenly, with the words " *la solidarité des deux pays* " on his lips, he fell back into the arms of the Mayor, Monsieur Schneiter, who in September 1937 had accompanied him on his first visit to the Maginot Line. Thus, with the same suddenness as his father's life had ended, his own life was over.

The President, Monsieur le Trocquer, simply and with great emotion announced later to the guests : " It is a great friend of France who has passed away." The Union Jack over the balcony was draped in black.

With a sensitivity characteristic of the French, they paid Hore-Belisha the honour due to him before he was taken back to England.

Monsieur Guy Mollet, the Premier, telegraphed to the Prime Minister, Mr. Harold Macmillan :

" J'apprends avec émotion la mort subite de Lord Hore-Belisha. La France n'a pas oublié le rôle si important qu'il a joué au début de la guerre comme Ministre de la Défense. Au nom du Gouvernement Français je prie votre Excellence d'agréer en cette triste circonstance mes sincères condoléances."

INDEX

Abyssinia (Ethiopia), 100, 103, 119

Adam, Maj.-Gen. Sir Ronald, 70, 71, 75

Alanbrooke, Field-Marshal Viscount (*formerly* Maj.-Gen. A. F. Brooke), 62, 211, 257

Albania, 24, 189

Alexander of Hillsborough, Viscount (*formerly* A. V. Alexander), 162

Alexander of Tunis, Field-Marshal Viscount (*formerly* H. R. L. G. Alexander), 65

Amery, Leopold, 20, 97

Anderson, Sir John (*later* Viscount Waverley), 151, 226, 227

Ashton-Gwatkin, F. T. A., 137

Asquith, Herbert, 54

Attlee, Lord, 33n, 195, 202

Austria, 100-5, 117-18, 135, 155, 157, 222

Baldwin, Stanley, 13, 16, 17, 20, 99, 130, 196

Balfour, Lord, 173

Beamish, Rear-Adm. T. P. H., 97

Beaumont-Nesbitt, Maj.-Gen. F. G., 225

Beaverbrook, Lord, 12, 29-30, 159, 240, 272-3, 283

Beechman, Capt. N. A., 162

B.E.F. *see* Expeditionary Force

Beharrell, Sir George, 210

Beith, Maj.-Gen. Ian Hay, 180

Belgium, 51, 58, 120, 135, 155, 169, 242, 248, 254-5, 296

Belisha beacons, 15, 19, 41, 111, 167, 257

Belisha family, 21

Belisha, Hore-, *see* Hore-Belisha

Benes, President, 119, 136, 142

Billotte, Gen., 262

Birdwood, Field-Marshal Lord, 19

Blakiston-Houston, Maj.-Gen., 61

Blondel, Mons., Chargé d'Affaires in Italy, 118

Blum, Léon, 203

Blumenfeld, R. D., 29

Blunden, Edmund, 25

Boardman, Harry, 19, 164

Bonaccorsi ("Count Rossi"), Italian filibuster, 118

Bonham-Carter, Lt.-Gen. Sir Charles, 107, 111

Bonnet, Georges, 141, 142, 145, 147-8, 169, 227

Borg, Col., 113

Bracken, Viscount (*formerly* Brendan Bracken), 272-3, 301

Bressey, Col. Sir Charles, 80

Bridges, Lord (*formerly* Sir Edward Bridges), 199

Bridges, Robert, 25

Brittain, Vera, 25

Brooke, Maj.-Gen. A. F., *see* Alanbrooke

311